MEAT

with Fergal Lynch

www.**HERO**BOOKS.digital

HEROBOOKS

PUBLISHED BY HERO BOOKS
1 WOODVILLE GREEN
LUCAN
CO. DUBLIN
IRELAND

Hero Books is an imprint of Umbrella Publishing
First Published 2021
Copyright © Fergal Lynch 2021
All rights reserved

A CIP record for this book is available from the British Library

ISBN 9781910827338

Cover design and formatting: jessica@viitaladesign.com
Ebook formatting: www.ebooklaunch.com
Photographs: Sportsfile and The Peter McDermott Collection (courtesy of Navan Library)

★ DEDICATION ★

To my wonderful mother Marie, sadly no longer with us
to spark the greatest debates about football.
Love you mam.

★ CONTENTS ★

★ ACKNOWLEDGEMENTS ★

AS A KID, getting to Meath matches wasn't as easy as it is now. I remember hearing of Meath's draw with Dublin in the 1983 Leinster SFC on the radio, but giving it little thought.

At that stage losing in the early stages of summer was the norm for a nine-year-old just discovering the fluttering of passion for football in the pit of my stomach.

Watching Dublin's 'Dirty Dozen' beat Galway in that year's All-Ireland final still regurgitates memories of a time when Meath appeared as far removed from the pinnacle of the game, as a toddler standing at the foothills of Loughcrew.

The full impact of the most important man in Meath GAA history still hadn't been felt and despite watching Meath lift the Centenary Cup in my first match ever at Croke Park, the summer of 1984 brought more heartbreak as Meath lost out to Dublin in the Leinster final despite Ben Tansey's goal.

Disappointment threatened to turn to apathy in 1985 when Laois inflicted a 10-point drubbing.

The Oracle had yet to work his magic, but while supporters started to lose faith, the players didn't.

Just over 12 months after one of the most humbling days in Meath GAA history, Seán Boylan led Meath to a first Leinster SFC title in 16 years, beating the previous year's All-Ireland finalists, the auld enemy Dublin.

Seán Boylan fanned the flames of my passion; he single-handedly reignited Meath football to a point where we exist today as one of the superpowers of the game – form is temporary, class is permanent and Seán Boylan exudes class.

Without Seán Boylan this book wouldn't happen.

Undoubtedly, Meath have had great players and many of them tell their stories within these pages, but would that potential have gone untapped without Seán's magical touch?

Those mere mortals became Gods, not just in Meath, but revered across the country, around the world, by those who heard their names.

Colm O'Rourke, Bernard Flynn, Mick Lyons, Liam Hayes, Gerry McEntee, Brian Stafford, Colm Coyle, Martin O'Connell, Joe Cassells... to name but a few, worshipped by their own, feared by everyone else.

Those men of 1986, under the guidance of Seán Boylan, brought All-Ireland titles in '87 and '88 and inspired another generation to Sam Maguire glory in '96 and '99. Those men of 1986 built Meath football on the foundation of their sturdy shoulders; to those men we salute you. To the men of 1949, '54 and '67, who lit the flame of passion in those warriors of the 80s, you were the forebearers of all that came after you and as Meath supporters we are eternally grateful.

Both my parents worked seven days a week to earn a living, so the opportunities for them to bring us to as many games as they would have liked just weren't possible. My dad always endeavoured to get to as many games as he could.

I remember parking at the church at Phibsboro and the excited walks to Croke Park and, from 1986, the pep in the step on the journey back to the car.

On days when my parents couldn't bring me, my uncle Paul, on my mother's side in Navan, took me to games. The cycle from Trim to Navan to get the lift seemed to zip by like an Olympic Time Trial; the cycle home often wasn't as sharp!

However, my uncles in Navan, Oliver, Peter and Paul helped sustain my football passion. My other uncle, Noel, in Enniscorthy was equally passionate about Meath football.

On days when none of the family could make it to the big games, a trip down Emmet Street to my uncle Michael's pub never let me down.

I was never left stranded at home. Brendan Carroll always had room in his old car. Whether the car would make it in one piece was another dilemma, but despite the holes in the floor and watching the road underneath whizz by, we always got there.

Pitstops in Clonee were the norm in those days; unfortunately not so much any more, but those were the glory days.

Thanks to Liam Hayes for allowing me the honour of compiling the stories of these great men and thanks to these great men who took time to regale me with the stories that appear in this book, and many others which don't.

Thanks to my colleagues in the *Meath Chronicle* for all their patience and support.

Without Seán Boylan and the great men of 1986, without Graham Geraghty and Trevor Giles, the two greatest players I have had the pleasure of seeing play football, without my parents, my uncles and the ever-willing drivers from Lynch's pub, I would never have had the honour of writing this book and chatting with my heroes – without Meath GAA, life just wouldn't be the same.

Finally, and most importantly.

My wife Fiona was more than patient as I embarked on this journey and my kids Sophie and Conal had to endure my retelling of some great stories over and over again. Throughout lockdown, my dad Pat and I sat for hours discussing the 'good old days'; his memory is as sharp now as it ever has been in his 81 years and his stories as witty and beguiling as they always have been – without them in my life I would be rudderless, they provide me with a purpose and a passion.

I cannot thank Meath footballers enough for all they have done in my life.

An Mhí abu

Fergal Lynch
August 2021

PETER DARBY

TRIM 3-8 BALLINLOUGH 0-7
Meath SFC Final
Páirc Tailteann
NOVEMBER 11 1962

Peter Darby sits proudly in Croke Park as Meath captain before the 1967 All-Ireland final win over Cork, but winning the 1962 Meath senior title with Trim is the day that defined his career.

★ **TRIM:** P Tully; M McGinley, **P Darby**, J O'Dare; W Rennicks, B Moynihan, S Colgan; J Ryan, J Farrell; G Kelly (1-1), MJ Greally, P Keogh (1-2); E Byrne, J Nallen (1-3), L McEvoy (0-2).

★ **BALLINLOUGH:** J Tully; S Cogan, T Ryan, M Mulvany; N Cogan, T Muldoon, H Tully; P Byrne, B Higgins; PJ Nugent, T Gibney (0-6), M Corcoran; E Gibney, J Reilly, G Baugh (0-1).

THE ACTION

BALLINLOUGH SCORED JUST once from play over the hour with Toss Gibney their scorer-in-chief and it was he who opened the scoring from a 45-metre free in the sixth minute.

A foul on John Nallen gifted Lolly McEvoy the equaliser from a free for Trim. After a spell when both sides went close to finding the net it was Paddy Keogh who edged Trim into the lead for the first time and they never looked back – a few minutes later Keogh punched Nallen's high centre to the net to make it 1-2 to 0-1.

George Kelly added a point almost immediately and moments later Nallen fired a fierce drive goalwards, which the Ballinlough goalkeeper John Tully looked to have stopped at the post, but the umpires decreed it had crossed the line.

Ballinlough responded with a pointed free from Gibney and one from play, their only one for the hour to close the gap to 0-3 to 2-3 at half-time.

After Sean Colgan's effort struck the upright, Nallen stretched Trim's lead early in the second-half before Gibney replied with two frees to make it 0-5 to 2-4.

Nallen continued his scoring form when he boxed Keogh's centre over the bar, but Gibney kept Ballinlough in contention with another free and he also forced the Trim goalkeeper Paddy Tully into a fine save.

Gibney and McEvoy exchanged a couple of frees to maintain the five-point gap, but in the closing stages Keogh kicked a superb long-range score before Nallen 'planked' a Jim Ryan free over the bar. And in the final moments George Kelly rammed home a goal to ensure no way back for Ballinlough and secure Trim's one, and only, Meath SFC title to date.

★★★★★

66

I PLAYED SENIOR hurling and football for Trim from when I was 16 years old and I first made my way onto the Meath senior football team in 1956. I played in every game from then until I retired in 1968 because of injury, and in all that time I was never taken off.

I never had my name taken by a referee either.

I enjoyed so many great days with Meath. Captaining the team to win the All-Ireland in 1967 was a momentous occasion, as was the trip to play in Australia the following year, but one of the most important games for me was with Trim when we won the Meath Senior Championship for the first, and so far only, time in 1962.

That win was very important. We had had a lot of good teams in the town that had got to finals in the years previous to 1962, but they were never successful.

I can't put my finger on why all the good teams Trim have had down through the years never managed to get over the line before 1962. There were some very good games and a lot of great teams back then, but we just couldn't do it.

Even still, I can't explain why Trim haven't won another Senior Championship – we probably should have won a couple more Keegan Cups.

Winning in 1962 was such a great feeling, especially after the disappointment of losing to Navan O'Mahonys in the 1961 county final.

I was personally very disappointed after losing that final in '61 because I was playing full-back in that game and a big high ball came in and I shouted to the boys that I'd go for it, because I knew it was mine.

I went up high and caught it well, but as I was in the air one of the O'Mahonys lads landed in on my chest and put me and the ball – the whole lot – into the back of the net.

It was a full frontal challenge in on top of me; it would be a black card if it happened now, but back then there wasn't even a free awarded. The goal stood and we lost the game.

I will always remember that incident.

I know I couldn't do a thing about it because I was off the ground when he hit me.

I wouldn't say it was a motivating factor for the following year because something like that had never happened to me before, and it never happened after that, and I also knew it was never likely to happen again because he took a run at me from about 40 yards out. He just happened to hit me when I was off the ground, there was no way I could prevent it.

We did get some consolation in 1961 when we won the Feis Cup with victory over St Vincent's. We got a few new lads then for 1962 and that certainly helped strengthen us a bit.

Jim Ryan came into the club and the Mayo player John Nallen also came in, as did Pat McManus and Mick Greally... they were all county men or ex-county men who happened to be working in Trim at the time. They were a great inspiration to bring the boys on.

After losing the final in 1961 and then winning the Feis Cup, we knew we wouldn't be too far away in '62. The championship back then was a straight knockout and we fancied ourselves against anyone. We got through to the semi-final where we played Skryne, and that was a tough game.

I had been playing centrefield for Trim and Jim Ryan, who was full-back for the county at the time, was our full-back too, but the management switched it around and he went out centrefield where he had a great game.

I fancied it in full-back too; I liked that position and I ended up playing there for ever more.

In the final against Ballinlough, from where I was positioned, I could see everything in front of me and everyone was playing really well – they were all pulling their weight. I remember Brendan Moynihan was centre-back and he had a great game. Jimmy Farrell and Jim Ryan played well in midfield. Sean Colgan also had a great game.

John Nallen was outstanding that day.

He was also a great motivator, he was an inspirational leader. He was working in the bank in Trim at the time and he'd go straight from his work up to the green for training with his boots tied to the front of his bike on the handlebars. On his way up he always stopped in Mick Leonard's pub to make sure there were none of the boys in having a drink before practice.

The odd time he would find one of the lads there, but he wouldn't go without them; he'd grab them by the lugs and drag them up to the green.

I was togging out beside John one day and he was putting these bandages on his knees and his ankles… everywhere… and I said to him he had a terrible lot of bandages. He replied that the only trouble is that he didn't put them on nearly enough; he reckoned he should have put them on when he wasn't injured and that might have helped him.

He was a great motivator. For the Feis Cup game, John was down in Mayo… it was a real winters day. But John drove up from Mayo, dying with a cold. He got an injection for the cold before he went out on the field and he played a blinder for us, that was the type of dedication he showed and that inspired others around him.

Nothing was too small or too great for John Nallen. The likes of Sean Colgan and Paddy Keogh really looked up to him.

In the final Ballinlough were a young, faster team; we were a heavier side, probably a bit stronger and that was one of the reasons for putting Jim Ryan out centrefield, because he was strong and very mobile. His brother was actually playing for Ballinlough that day too; he was their full-back so there was that rivalry between them.

He had a really good game too. He had been in Canada for a while and only came back to Ireland two or three years before that. Jim left Ballinlough and came to Trim because he was working in the D & I, managing the farm out in Carrollstown. Jim was a great addition, he was a county man at the time too.

I was marking James Reilly and they only scored once from play. We all just marked our men; I don't think we used any subs that day, everyone did their job really well.

Jimmy Reilly had been playing very well for Ballinlough and he was a dangerman, but luckily enough he didn't score. Most of our tactics that day were focused on our backs staying tight with their men and not giving them an inch, but Jimmy was roaming all over the place and he did cause us a few problems. Toss Gibney was also a very good footballer at the time too, he got most of their scores that day.

We were pretty much always in control and we managed to keep ahead of them, so when the last goal went in from George Kelly we knew that was it, we knew we had them. That was a great feeling, even though I always played to the final whistle no matter how far we were ahead because you never knew what could happen. But I knew after that third goal we had it, it was a great feeling... a very proud feeling.

Ballinlough were a very sporting team, they congratulated us on our win.

We were delighted as a team. We had put in a lot of hard work to get us there. We didn't really have a manager as such, not in the way you'd have managers now. We used to do a lot of running around the field and then play games of backs against forwards. We did train a lot and we gave it everything we had at the time; we also did a lot of press-ups and stuff like that, but it was very basic.

The players themselves would take the training and we'd have someone there with a whistle just to referee the games amongst ourselves too. We talked about tactics amongst ourselves when we'd be togging in.

Ollie Reilly would have been involved in our training, he would have been one of the selectors along with Paddy Yore and a few others, but Ollie would have been the man on the sideline making the switches.

We had plenty of celebrations after the win.

Paddy Fay – Jimmy and Mickey's father, and Darren's grandfather – owned a pub in the town at the time and he hosted a reception for the whole team and everyone involved; it was a great win and a marvellous occasion.

The normal thing in Meath was that whoever were the county champions nominated the captain for the county team, but in 1967 Gaeil Colmcille, who were the champions at the time, didn't have anyone on the team, so because I was the oldest player, at 29 years old, on the team I was given the captaincy.

My first outing with Meath was against Dublin on St Stephen's Day in 1956... a desperate foggy day, you couldn't see the other lads up the other end of the field.

I was delighted to be picked to play against some very famous names that were on the Dublin team at that time. I was thrilled to be able to say I played against them. Another really proud thing for me was to say I played with some of my greatest heroes off the Meath 1949 team that won the first ever All-Ireland title for the county. Mattie McDonnell played on that team with me in 1956 and I think Micheal Grace played that day too, so I said to myself that if I never did anything else in football at least I would be able to say I played with Mattie McDonnell... that was great.

I played all the years through from 1958, but, as I've said, I finished up playing with the county in Australia in '68.

I pulled muscles in my stomach playing in a National League match against Westmeath in Croke Park before we went to Australia. Just as I was kicking a ball a fella jumped in on my leg and across my thigh, and he stretched my muscles a bit. It wasn't too bad at the time, but when I went out to Australia... with the hard ground and all the running we did, I was nearly a cripple coming home.

I never played after that for the county.

I knew it would take at least a year for my stomach to heal up properly and I was 30, nearly 31 years old at the time. I knew I'd have to start off training again and it would take me 12 months to get back to the right level of fitness, so I gave it up at that stage. I played on a bit with the club after, but I wasn't really able.

They just put me on when they were stuck, but I was too injured... I was no good to them.

I never told anybody about the injury I got in the Westmeath game. I didn't even tell anyone when we were in Australia. On our way home from that trip we came home by Hawaii and San Francisco and Los Angeles, and we were doing a lot of touring, but I didn't go to too many of the places because I wasn't able to go.

When we came home, Peter McDermott was asking me to play in that year's championship and he kept at me, but I just kept saying I wouldn't... I never even told him that I was injured at the time. That was just the way it was back then, nobody ever really said they were injured.

The trip to Australia was a fantastic experience.

We weren't given a chance of beating them (an Australian Rules selection) when we went down there. They had beaten us when we played them here in Ireland, but we had been told to go easy on them and we did that for a little over a half hour. By that stage they were far enough ahead and they held on to win.

I knew that when we went to Australia we would be geared up for the whole thing, and so we went hell for leather at them when we went there... we played five games and won all five.

It was an unbelievable trip.

Going there, we spent two days in Rome, then we were in Singapore, then we went to Perth, Melbourne, Adelaide, Sydney... then back to Melbourne again.

We visited Hawaii, San Francisco, Los Angeles and New York on the way back, so it was well broken up and the whole three or four weeks were great fun.

We were treated like kings out there.

We were so much in demand that we could have gone to two or three outings every night if we had wanted to. We had to pick and choose.

There were people out there in Australia who had never seen a football match and they were so intrigued by us. I remember playing in Melbourne and a man came up to me... he was actually crying. He said he hadn't seen a football game in over 20 years. He had driven over 500 miles to see our match.

Every night we had banquets and presentations, it was an amazing experience.

Everybody got time off work to go and I think nearly all the boys got paid their wages too. If their companies didn't pay them the Meath County Board looked after them. A lot of those Meath lads had never even been on an airplane before, never mind getting to fly to Australia. We were really thrilled.

When I look back at my playing days I would have to say I'd be very happy with what I achieved. I played with the county from the 1958 championship game against Dublin, when they beat us by a point in Mullingar and went on to win the All-Ireland. From that day on I was never dropped, taken off... and I never had my name taken.

When I got injured I made up my mind not to even try to come back, so I finished up happy enough with all I did.

I found an old article recently from the *Gaelic Sport* magazine... it was their 35-year anniversary edition. They picked a best 15 from that spell which was from 1958 to '93 and I was the only one from Meath on it. They picked me at corner-back and not only that, they named me captain.

That was an amazing honour to find out after all these years that they had selected me on that team, alongside some great names – Johnny Geraghty and Enda Colleran from Galway, John O'Keeffe from Kerry, Gerry O'Malley from Roscommon, Jack O'Shea and Mick O'Connell from Kerry, Willie Bryan from Offaly, Larry Tompkins from Cork, James McCartan from Down, Pat Spillane from Kerry, Jimmy Barry Murphy from Cork, Matt Connor from Offaly and Kevin Heffernan from Dublin. It was a real honour to be picked alongside them lads and then to be named captain... amazing.

I had a great career, but my biggest regret with Meath came in 1964 when we lost to Galway; that was the first of their three in-a-row, but I felt we should have won the All-Ireland that year and who knows what might have happened after that.

We were four points ahead of Galway in that All-Ireland semi-final, 10 minutes into the second-half. Jack Quinn was centrefield that day and he plucked a ball from the sky and went on a solo run. With lads dragging out of him, he took a shot that flew to the net to put us seven points up. However the referee disallowed the goal because he said Jack had been fouled during his run in and that he had blown his whistle before Jack had kicked the ball.

None of us heard a whistle and Jack was fuming.

He gave a 21-yards free in instead, but we missed the free... so instead of it being 1-7 to 0-3 it stayed at 0-7 to 0-3... and Galway came back to win 1-8 to 0-9.

They were only 60 minute matches at that time and I reckon if that goal had been allowed stand, like it should have, we would have won it and I believe we would have went on to beat Kerry in the final and win who knows how many more All-Irelands.

JACK QUINN

MEATH 2-12 DUBLIN 1-7
Leinster SFC Final
Croke Park
JULY 26 1964

Beating Dublin in the 1964 Leinster final is the day that Jack Quinn feels set Meath on the road to glory. Another step was the 1966 All-Ireland final (Jack is third from left in the pre-match parade, behind captain Davy Carty and Ollie Shanley).

★ **MEATH:** P Cromwell; D Donnelly, M Quinn, P Darby; P Collier, B Cunningham, P Reynolds; **J Quinn**, P Moore; D Carty (0-2), T Brown, J Walsh (0-4); G Quinn, K McNamee (0-3), O Shanley (1-3). Sub: P Mulvany (1-0) for G Quinn.

★ **DUBLIN:** P Flynn; L Hickey, L Foley, C Kane; M Kissane, P Holden, N Fox; D Foley, S Behan; B McDonald (1-2), M Whelan, S Coen (0-3); G Davey, B Casey (0-1), D Ferguson (0-1). Subs: E Breslin for Casey, D McKane for Coen, E Fahy for Fox.

THE ACTION

A DECADE SINCE they last won an All-Ireland and a decade since they last appeared in a Leinster SFC final, Meath finally made it back to a provincial decider following a 2-12 to 0-8 quarter-final win over Kildare and a 1-12 to 2-7 victory over Louth.

After losing to Dublin the year before by a solitary point and with Dublin going on to win the All-Ireland, Meath fancied their chances of springing a surprise in the '64 final that was dubbed 'The Foleys vs The Quinns' because of the number of brothers on both sides.

The Quinn brothers formed the backbone of the Meath team, with Martin marshalling the defence from full-back, while Jack gave a solid platform in midfield, and Gerry excited up front before having to be stretched off early in the second-half following a collision with teammate Ollie Shanley and Dublin goalkeeper Paschal Flynn.

In the fourth minute, the Royals opened the scoring when Kevin McNamee shot from a difficult angle. A minute later Shanley tipped over a Jimmy Walsh free and Meath were on their way. In the 10th minute Shanley left Leo Hickey trailing in his wake before blasting a brilliant goal, and almost immediately David Carty added a point to stretch Meath's lead to four points.

Shanley made it 1-4 to 0-2, but then Dublin got back into the game when Brian McDonald punched the ball beyond Paddy Cromwell for an opportunist goal. It was 1-5 to 1-6 at the interval.

In the 10th minute of the second-half a Jack Quinn speculative shot was saved, but Paddy Mulvany snapped up the loose ball and fired to the net to put Meath in command.

Dublin were stunned and it was McNamee who stretched Meath's lead. McDonald closed Dublin's account and in the closing stages it was McNamee and Walsh who concluded the scoring to ensure Meath were celebrating a first Leinster title in 10 years.

★★★★★

66

FOR A SMALL parish like Kilbride, stuck right on the border with Dublin, it was a remarkable occasion to have three brothers, myself, Gerry and Martin, on the Meath team that started the Leinster final in 1964… Meath's first appearance in the provincial final since they went on and won the All-Ireland in 1954.

That Leinster final was being hailed, not just as a renewal of the Dublin vs Meath rivalry, but also as 'The Foleys vs The Quinns' because there were also a couple of the Foley brothers on the Dublin team at the time.

Lar and Des were the Foleys – myself, Martin and Gerry were the Quinns obviously, but the papers latched onto it and built it up.

It was also massive because it had been so long since Meath were last in a Leinster final – 10 years exactly – so to get back was a massive occasion and for me personally it was a great highlight of my career because it was my first time to play in a Leinster final.

I didn't play any underage football with Meath and even as a young lad I didn't play much football at all because Kilbride was such a small place – there weren't even enough players in the parish to have an underage team.

The only proper year that I played minor football was with Kiltale. They had Paddy Kelly in charge and he got myself, Sean Hickey and Pat Rooney to come to Kiltale to play football, which is unusual now to think that there was ever football in Kiltale, but Paddy Kelly got it going there.

We even managed to get to the county final at minor level, but we were pipped in the game after a colossal run. Kiltale is more renowned for hurling, but Paddy Kelly, and another fella with him, went around and got the three of us from Kilbride and we went on from there.

From there, Kilbride grew and we went on and won the junior, intermediate and, of course, the Senior Championship in the years to come.

Before I played minor I never really had any experience of playing matches. Myself, Gerry and Martin used to just kick the football around the field on the farm at home.

We used to play The Flathouse, which was just over the field from us; they used to come over and play us and we'd go and play them in our games in the fields around the farm. As kids we used to play those games nearly every week. They were great times and it was a bit of banter and a bit of craic… we all loved it.

All that helped when I got older; it was probably better than any training as a young lad, they were great times playing in the fields against the neighbours… great times.

Despite getting to the county final as a minor, I didn't make the county minor team… as the fella says I was one of those 'late developers'. I thought myself that I should have been on the minor team that year, but the selectors obviously didn't agree, so I wasn't selected.

Even though I didn't make the minor team, I did manage to make the Meath junior team that year, and the following year we went on and won the All-Ireland Junior Championship.

Winning that Junior All-Ireland was fantastic, it really was a great experience. I don't know what it was like for people looking at it, but for young lads coming through like I was, it was a great learning experience. There was a great mixture of lads at junior level; you had lads finishing up and others players, like myself, just starting out.

At that stage Martin was playing with the seniors and my ambition, just like everyone else who played football, was to play county senior.

I made my senior debut in the 1962/63 National League when I went straight from the junior team that had won the All-Ireland in '62 onto the senior team.

I was only 19 going into the seniors, but there were good lads who helped me settle into the team. Obviously Martin was there at the time, but there were plenty of other lads to give advice. If you weren't up to it, they'd let you know fairly quickly.

I found it a great help at the time that Kilbride were doing so well. We were getting really good matches and that helped us develop as footballers, and that stood to me when I went out to play county football.

If I didn't have those experiences with my club I wouldn't have developed the same way.

My arrival on the county team coincided with the start of some great days for Meath and that Leinster final in 1964 was certainly one of the best from my point of view.

Going into that game against Dublin no one gave us a chance at all because Dublin were the All-Ireland champions and hot favourites, but I fancied our chances because we were going quite well.

Dublin had so many great players like Lar and Des Foley, Paddy Holden and Mickey Whelan and a few more obviously… they were the big team of the day.

The rivalry with Dublin was fairly big even back then, especially for us because where I lived at the time was right on the Dublin border. Because we lived so close, our dream was always to beat Dublin, but I'm sure if you went down to Kevin McNamee he'd want to beat Offaly and if you went to someone else in south Meath it might be Kildare… but for us it was always Dublin.

Even though it was our first Leinster final in 10 years and Dublin were All-Ireland champions we knew we had a hell of a good team. We had only lost to them by a point in the Leinster quarter-final in 1963 and they went on and won the All-Ireland, so we knew we would have a chance.

Nobody else gave us a hope. I remember going to mass in Kilbride at the time and lads would be telling me that we were wasting our time even going up to Croke Park to play them, but I was very confident.

As it turned out, we were brilliant that day and won by eight points; it was a seriously good performance and the celebrations afterwards were great, particularly around our area. We lived so close that I used to ride my bike into Croke Park to watch games when I was a young lad… it was only 10 or 11 miles.

Unfortunately, the celebrations were short-lived for us because my father passed away the week after the Leinster final and we played Galway a week later. People were wondering would we even play in that game, but my mother insisted that we went out and played in the All-Ireland semi-final.

We were thinking that we wouldn't know what to do and our heads were all over the place, but my mother kept saying to us, 'If your father was alive, or if he had any say in it, he would want you all to play in it'… as would anyone's father I suppose.

We went out and played in the semi-final against Galway and it was the right thing to do for both ourselves, our family and for Meath.

That Galway side went on to win three in-a-row in 1964, '65 and '66. We had some great battles with them down through the years, but whenever I used to meet them lads in later years I used to always joke with them that if the goal I had scored in that All-Ireland semi-final in 1964 had been allowed stand they might never have won any All-Ireland.

To this day I still don't understand why the goal was disallowed because I hadn't been fouled at all, there was no one near me at all.

After winning the ball I went on a bit of a solo run and when I went to kick the ball there was no one near me, I even have an old photograph to prove it. But as I kicked the ball I lost my footing and fell over. The ball flew to the back of the net, but for some reason the referee thought I was fouled and he blew his whistle and brought play back... gave us a free in, which we ended up kicking wide.

We were beaten by two points in that semi-final while Galway went on and beat Kerry by five points to win the first of their famous three.

I suppose all these things work out for a reason and maybe if we had gone on and won a couple of All-Irelands in-a-row at that time we mightn't have won the 1967 All-Ireland and got the trip to Australia out of it.

There was some consolation for the disappointment of losing that All-Ireland semi-final in the fact that we went on and won the Meath Senior Championship with Kilbride in 1964.

For Kilbride it was a remarkable time because wins like that don't happen too often for small clubs like ours. We had won the junior in 1960 and the intermediate in 1962, and we were a tight-knit group,. There were the four of us Quinns and there were the Reillys, who were first cousins of ours and then we had Murty and Wardy Sullivan, who were cousins of the Reillys on the other side.

Between brothers and cousins we had a hell of a team; it was a kind of family affair and we played really well together so there was great consolation when we beat Gaeil Colmcille to win the senior in '64.

The following year we went through the group stages of the 1964/65 league with six wins out of six, but were beaten then by Galway in the semi-final again. However, we felt we were still in good shape going into the Leinster Championship – but then after beating Westmeath we were shocked by Longford in the semi-final.

We expected to beat Longford, but they had trained remarkably hard and they were as fit as fiddles. They were a bloody good team, but I still feel that if we had beaten them we would have gone on and won the All-Ireland that year. The only thing that beat Longford in the Leinster final against Dublin was their little bit of inexperience. They were a hell of a good team with a lot of good players and that was a big opportunity for them, but inexperience cost them against Dublin.

For us it was back to the club championship and we managed to make it back to the county final as we tried to defend our title, but then the game against Skryne was abandoned following a strange incident – we were kicked out of the championship and Martin got suspended for 12 months.

It was an absolutely ridiculous decision.

Martin caught a high ball in the square, practically on his own… there was no one within five yards of him when he caught the ball.

Next thing we knew Seamus Duff blew his whistle and he came in and awarded Skryne a free in. Martin walked towards the referee with the ball in his hand asking what was the free for, but Duff just said, 'It's a free in!' Martin put the ball down and sat on it and said, 'You'll have to tell me what the free is for because it was no free'.

The referee told Martin that if he didn't get off the ball he would send him off, but Martin said he wouldn't leave the pitch unless he was told what the free was for – and with that the referee abandoned the match, it was ridiculous.

After that incident and because he was so harshly treated, I didn't want to play football anymore and almost gave it up, but Martin insisted that I continue on playing because it wasn't something you could go back and do as you got older. So he talked me into going back.

I still believe that Martin's suspension cost us the All-Ireland in 1966 because if he had been full-back and I was midfield it might have worked out very different against Galway in the All-Ireland final that year.

I don't know what happened us that day in the final against Galway because we had played brilliantly up to that stage hammering Wexford and Westmeath, and then beating Kildare in the Leinster final, before beating Down by 10 points in the All-Ireland semi-final.

Don't get me wrong, Galway were a brilliant team, but I think if we had played up to our standard it would have been a different game, a lot tighter. I've no idea what happened that day, we didn't get going until it was too late. Martin was back by that stage and I think if the selectors had brought him on at half-time and moved me out to midfield it might have made a difference.

I preferred playing midfield when I was younger because when you were that age you liked to be in the game the whole time. Of course, I loved playing full-back, but I preferred midfield. If you were reasonably fit you could play a bigger part in the game from midfield and I loved getting stuck in.

When I got to 29 or 30 years old I preferred full-back because I didn't have to do the running that I used to be able to do.

We were so disappointed with the way we had played in that 1966 final, and we knew we were a lot better than we had shown that day, but we were absolutely terrible that day. We had a meeting after that game and made a determined pledge that we were going to give it absolutely everything we had in 1967; that was going to be our last bang at it. We felt that if we didn't do something in '67 we would give up county football altogether.

As it turned out winning in 1967 was a great one to win because we got the trip to Australia out of it.

To win an All-Ireland was fantastic and to win it with two of my brothers on the panel too made it even more special. There was a strong Kilbride contingent involved with the panel as well, with myself, Martin, Gerry, Pat Rooney, Pat Bruton, Murty Sullivan, Paddy Reilly... it was a great time for our club as well.

The trip to Australia was an unbelievable experience at the time. A lot of the lads had never been on an airplane before; you'd swear we were going to the end of the world and we might never see anyone again.

I remember people calling to the house to wish us good luck. Some people calling would have been crying because we were going; they were thinking they might never see us again.

Flying was a big deal at that time and people were afraid of it because it was so rare. If a plane was flying overhead at that time, you'd be going outside to have a look at it, so people were wary of us going on such a long flight.

I wasn't nervous. We were young and there was a good few of us all together so we loved the experience. I had been on a plane before over to America a couple of times and I had been to England on a plane, so I was used to it, but some people were so afraid of it.

The games against the Australians were tough – we quickly found out that we couldn't afford to take things easy against them. They quickly realised that we weren't going to be pushovers so they were tougher still. The football suited us more than it did them because the compromise rules suited us a bit better.

Our lads trained hard and we decided to give it everything we had and it worked out well, it was a fantastic trip. I always give great credit to my own brother Martin because he raised a serious amount of money for that trip and it was a huge success.

We also won the club championship again in 1967 against Navan O'Mahonys which was great because we had lost in '66 to Gaeil Colmcille after a couple of drawn matches.

Those matches could have gone either way, but they were a great team and deservedly won their first championship at that time. They were a great club and had Dessie Ferguson with them and even though he was past his best he was still a great footballer and a great trainer.

In 1968 we were beaten in the Leinster semi-final by a bloody good Longford side, but that was a huge shock for us because we were the All-Ireland champions. That Longford team could have won an All-Ireland; they were only beaten by two points by Kerry in the All-Ireland semi-final. It was a pity they didn't get an All-Ireland that year.

We didn't get to a Leinster final again until 1970 and we probably surprised a lot of people by getting to the All-Ireland final that year. Kerry beat us that year in the first 80-minute final. We had a very good team and with a little bit of luck we could have won that All-Ireland.

We won the league in 1975 – we had to beat Kerry, Mayo and Dublin in our last three matches so that was a great league title to win. We were given no chance against Dublin in that final, they were the All-Ireland champions and I remember the Dubs near the border where we were living in Kilbride nearly laughing at us, but they weren't laughing when the match was over.

Then we were beaten by a good Louth side in the championship – that was disappointing. I picked up an injury in a game against Ballivor; I had never had a serious injury in my life before that, but I hurt my knee and that kind of finished me. I tried to come back and play a few times after that, but I never got my knee right again for football. I was a sub for the 1976 Leinster final against Dublin, but I wasn't brought on.

I did play against Galway in the league later that year, but I hurt my knee again and that was when I decided that enough was enough and I retired.

The highlight for any footballer would have to be winning the All-Ireland and we managed to do that in 1967. That Leinster final win in '64 was also a really important one for me and the trip to Australia was another highlight of my career that I'll never forget. Winning the National League also went down very well I have to admit.

MATTIE KERRIGAN

SUMMERHILL 0-9 BOHERMEEN 0-7
Meath SFC Final
Páirc Tailteann
OCTOBER 13 1974

Mattie Kerrigan on Meath's 1968 tour of Australia. Here's Mattie (top, fourth from right) with other members of the party in Sydney. However, Summerhill's first Meath senior title is his most cherished memory.

★ **SUMMERHILL:** B White; T Flynn, A Lyons, P Lyons; PJ Gannon, D Mooney, J Colgan; M Coyne, **M Kerrigan**; P McElroy (0-2), N Byrne, P Grey (0-1); T Gibbons (0-4), P Thompson (0-1), F Fagan. Subs: B Keogh (0-1) for Grey, M Gannon for P Lyons, J Shaw for Thompson, Des McKay, Donal McKay, M Gannon, C Holmes, J Faherty, R Chandler.

★ **BOHERMEEN:** S Dunne; P Kavanagh, L Brady, S Rennicks; P Mulroe, J Kavanagh (0-1), C Burke; K Rennicks (0-1), Dermie Rennicks; B Rennicks, T Monaghan (0-1), D Murtagh (0-2); R Brady (0-1), F Coffey (0-1), L Harte. Sub: Donald Rennicks for Harte.

THE ACTION

IN JUST THEIR second year at the top table, Summerhill achieved a historic breakthrough when they won the Meath SFC for the first time with a narrow victory over a Bohermeen side that had been promoted to the senior ranks just 12 months earlier.

The *Meath Chronicle* reported that, *On the day it was also a victory for football, for the winners were the superior combination and displayed the better standard of football on view. They also won the tactical battle hands down. Certain factors may have contributed to their momentous success more than others, but overall their edge at midfield contributed immensely towards the annexing of the championship.*

With Ken Rennicks being somewhat overshadowed by Martin Coyne, the great Mattie Kerrigan really went to town, turning in a superlative display. The former countyman caught some great balls and using all of them in very intelligent fashion, he proved the launching pad for numerous successful Summerhill attacks.

Summerhill's win wasn't without some controversy when referee Brendan Gogarty disallowed a Bohermeen 'goal' in the second-half. After Richard Brady flicked on a long ball there was a scramble in the Summerhill goalmouth and one of the Summerhill defenders was deemed to have carried the ball over the goal-line. However, the referee ruled that Brady had been in the small square when he flicked on the ball and so ruled out the score.

Bohermeen's physicality counted against them as it took them 23 minutes to get their first score and by that stage Summerhill were clear. However, in the closing seven minutes of the half Bohermeen rallied and closed the gap to 0-4 to 0-5 at half-time.

After the resumption, Summerhill always managed to keep their noses in front, but there were a few nervous moments when Bohermeen claimed the goal that was eventually disallowed by the referee.

★★★★★

66

I'VE BEEN HUGELY fortunate to have played in so many big games. Winning an All-Ireland with Meath in 1967 was very special. Playing in and winning Leinster finals and National League finals are also an enormous sense of pride for me, but the one game that stands out is when my club Summerhill won the senior football championship for the first time in 1974.

Most of that team, if not all of them, started out on the journey to that senior win by playing in the Junior Championship. We came through a couple of years at junior and intermediate levels before making the breakthrough at senior.

For a club like Summerhill to win a senior championship was huge.

It is difficult to win any championship. It is as hard to win a junior B or a junior C as it is to win a senior. The Junior Championship was extremely tough. Back in those days it was a South Meath Divisional competition, so you would be playing Enfield, Clonard, Ballinabrackey, Longwood or Rathmolyon… all very strong junior teams at that time and, after playing them, there was not much left to fear!

I made the Meath junior panel in 1964 and played midfield against Kildare in the Leinster final which we won. At that stage you had to be a junior player to make the junior team, but after we won Leinster they brought in senior club players.

At those times you found out if you were on the Meath team by reading the *Drogheda Independent*, so when it came to finding out the team for the All-Ireland semi-final I was that far down the list of subs that I was almost missing off the bottom of the page. Anyhow, we went on and beat Derry in the semi-final, but lost to Cork in the All-Ireland final.

I had no county involvement at all in 1965 and it was the following year Summerhill won the junior A, in '66 with an ambitious bunch of lads. It was then that Austin Lyons and myself got called into the Meath senior panel.

In October 1966 I played my first senior game for Meath against Louth in Drogheda.

When Summerhill got out of junior, we faced a tough campaign at intermediate against strong teams… Ballivor, Dunderry, St John's, Moylagh and Martry. We eventually won the Intermediate Championship in 1972, beating Martry in the final. That was another great stepping stone.

We had two great Summerhill legends on the line, Paddy Daly and Eddie (Nedzer) Allen. Paddy held every role in the club over the years; some would say he did them all at at one stage. Eddie had a big influence on developing the underage set up in the club. Mick Gillic was our masseur and got a lot of lads back in action when required!

In 1972 Fr John Conlon, who was a curate in the area, came on board as a coach. Fr John was only in Summerhill for a year; he was a Ballinabrackey man and a brilliant athlete in his youth. He was a great operator for tactics and was ahead of his time in terms of his ideas on the field. He provided a different voice for the lads – sometimes a stern one at that. He knew what was required to get us thinking in the right direction; I learned a lot from him.

We were ready for the step up to senior. As an intermediate side we played a lot of challenge matches against senior sides from Kildare, Dublin and Offaly. We adapted well to the rigours of senior football and won the Feis Cup in 1973. That year we were beaten in the semi-final of the championship by Navan O'Mahonys after a replay in Trim.

We continued with the training and lads kept fit.

Fr Willie Behan came on board at that stage as chairman of the club and became a selector along with Paddy and Eddie. As a team we had great respect for each of these men. Whilst Fr Willie was quietly spoken, he had a great knowledge of the game and continued to contribute to the club's success for many years.

Every game we won in that 1974 Senior Championship, with the odd exception, went right down to the end of the 60 minutes. We beat Dunderry and Ballivor by a point, and Skryne by three points… all tight games. It was a long drawn-out and tough championship.

For topping our group our 'reward' was a semi-final against Kilbride; they were a great team. They maybe weren't as powerful as they had been in the years previous, but they were still a good side. That game went right down to the wire. By that stage you had to be a few points better than your opponent just to win by a point.

And that day we won by a point.

We knew we were a strong and well-prepared team; we had the self-belief that we were capable of winning the championship, but there were no guarantees, so beating a team like Kilbride certainly boosted our confidence.

On the morning of the final, we met in Summerhill for a kickaround and then travelled to Navan. We were up against a very strong Bohermeen side. It was a real battle and could have gone either way; it went right to the death. They had a goal disallowed; one of those days where luck was either with you or against you and we had it with us that day.

Ken Rennicks was the main man for them and in form at the time, but we managed to keep him a lot quieter than he had been in previous games; that was a major factor.

We hung on and won by two points and our captain Austin Lyons stepped forward to lift the Keegan Cup!

Winning that championship was a wonderful occasion. For any club to win the Senior Championship is an achievement and to win it for the first time ever was massive for us.

Summerhill were a rural club, but we didn't consider ourselves as being any different to any other club in the county. We just considered ourselves a football club, and we were either good enough or we weren't.

We were well organised and had a hard working, ambitious group of players.

To be able to go from junior to winning the senior in just eight years was great. There were a few players who missed out in 1974, but they played huge parts in getting us there. Those lads were very important to the success of Summerhill.

We went on and won four titles in-a-row and played in six consecutive finals, but that first one set the ball rolling.

We were involved in under-21 finals around that time too, so we built positively on the success of those years and the club continued to grow.

That senior championship final win for me was a huge achievement. Summerhill are still playing senior football now and that is a great legacy to have left. They are one of the most powerful clubs in the county, fielding teams in every age group, both men and ladies.

A great testament to the work put in by the volunteers of the club.

Winning the Keegan Cup in 1974 is a very, very proud day for me, and getting to that day was a very memorable journey for the club.

SEÁN BOYLAN
(& COLM COYLE)

MEATH 0-9 DUBLIN 0-7
Leinster SFC Final
Croke Park
JULY 27 1986

Seán Boylan celebrates in the rain with supporters (above) after Meath's emotional breakthrough victory over Dublin in the summer of 1986.

★ **MEATH:** M McQuillan; J Cassells, M Lyons, P Lyons; **C Coyle**, L Harnan, T Ferguson; G McEntee, L Hayes (0-1); F Murtagh (0-3), PJ Gillic, D Beggy (0-1); C O'Rourke (0-3), B Stafford, B Flynn (0-1). Sub: M O'Connell for Gillic.

★ **DUBLIN:** J O'Leary; PJ Buckley, G Hargan, M Kennedy; P Canavan, N McCaffrey, D Synnott; J Roynane, J Bissett; L Close, K Duff (0-2), C Redmond (0-2); B Rock (0-3), T Carr, J McNally. Subs: T Conroy for Rock, J Kearns for Close, P Clarke for Bissett.

THE ACTION

FREED FROM THE shackles of an extended selection committee and the memory of a humbling 12-point loss to Laois 12 months earlier, Seán Boylan finally led Meath back to provincial glory in 1986.

There was signs of hope in 1984 when Meath won the Centenary Cup with a final win over Monaghan. The following year, however, Boylan suffered a major setback when Laois humbled the Royals by 2-11 to 0-7 in the Leinster semi-final.

The day of the 1986 Leinster final may have ended in a thunderous downpour, but when the action got underway it was a dry Sunday afternoon. The sides were level three times in the opening half before Dublin pulled away to lead by 0-6 to 0-4 at the interval.

Meath started well with David Beggy opening the scoring before Barney Rock and Kieran Duff replied. Bernard Flynn ended a 23 minute barren spell for Meath with an excellent score and with Dublin managing just one further point – from a Duff free – the Royals piled on the pressure.

Murtagh snapped up the rebound after Beggy had hit the post to draw the sides level, 0-6 each, eight minutes into the second-half.

O'Rourke restored Meath's lead at the end of the third quarter before Duff brought the sides level for the fifth time with his side's only score of the half and their last of the match.

Murtagh made it 0-8 to 0-7 and when Hayes fisted a ball into O'Rourke, who extended Meath's lead to two points, it signalled the end for Dublin and sparked wild celebrations amongst the rain-soaked Meath supporters.

★★★★★

❝

TAKING OVER THE Meath footballers in 1982 it was clear it was going to be an onerous task.

I had been in the dressing-room with Mick O'Brien and Dessie Ferguson with Meath teams, so I wouldn't say it was daunting going into a room with six other selectors and a new team, but it was exciting.

It was amazing how quickly you just fit in. We were lucky we had a challenge match early on in Aghnacliffe against Longford and we won that; then we won an O'Byrne Cup in 1983 with Mickey Downes as captain that day, so we got off to a decent start.

When the National League started we tried to get as settled a team as we could, but it was amazing to think that Mick Lyons wasn't on the team; he wasn't even a sub. Then Summerhill played Walsh Island in a Leinster club match and Mick came in after that game; he was playing full-forward for Summerhill at the time.

There were lots of strange things in those early days; there was a certain wonder, but it just all came together for us.

The 1983 Leinster Championship game against Dublin was absolutely huge. I was there in 1982 when Longford beat Meath – I was there the year before when Wexford beat them in Croke Park, so to face Dublin in the first round in 1983 was massive.

We had been in Croke Park for the National League semi-final against Armagh, so that was an introduction to Croke Park for a lot of the lads. Then we drew with Dublin in the first round of Leinster in Croke Park and, by right, the replay should have been in Navan, but I spoke with Brian (Smyth) and Liam (Creavin) in the County Board and I asked them to allow the replay to be in Croke Park. I believed that once we got on a run we would be playing in Croke Park a lot of times and I wanted to get as much experience of the place into them. Unfortunately Dublin won the replay after extra-time, 0-16 to 3-9.

After Dublin won the All-Ireland in 1983 there was almost 25,000 at the first round of the league in Páirc Tailteann when we played them; the town had a bonanza.

I was marking Bernard Flynn in the curtain-raiser before the league game against

Dublin, but I went off at half-time to get the Meath lads ready. Or maybe I went off before he made a show of me.

That game against Dublin ended in a draw again. There was a guard of honour for Dublin as All-Ireland champions before the game. Dublin had three players and Kevin Heffernan suspended, but Brian Smyth insisted that those men would not be sitting up in the stand so we agreed between us to say nothing… he set up four chairs beside the first aid people and that's where they sat.

Brian Smyth was the first man to bring the Sam Maguire Cup to Meath in 1949; he was on the team again in '54 and he had won an All-Ireland junior hurling title in '48, so that was the measure of the respect he held the All-Ireland champions in. Brian would have played against Kevin Heffernan.

We won the Centenary Cup in 1984 and that was amazing for the county and amazing for the players as well to win in Croke Park – but then the Leinster final in 1984 was terribly disappointing.

For that final against Dublin there were a few particular things I wanted to do, but I wasn't allowed to. Joe McNally was only new on the scene for Dublin and he was a danger, but I wasn't allowed change Padraig (Lyons) and Bob (O'Malley). I also wanted to play JJ McCormack full-forward to allow Colm O'Rourke out, because I knew Dublin would have everything planned around Colm, which of course they did with Mick Holden in front of him and Gerry Hargan behind him.

Dublin were a man down from early on when John Caffrey got sent-off, but we saw that day the way champions played, and that was a lesson. The way they used the ball and made us chase them. It was really interesting, they were all lessons down the road for us to learn from.

I was a bit aggrieved because I felt that if I wanted to make a change or make a decision I had to almost have a board meeting with all the selectors we had, but that wasn't the way it should have been.

I had played for the Meath hurlers for a long time, but I had never experienced anything like that with them.

Everybody was entitled to their opinion and I respected their opinions, but it just wasn't the right way to do things. So I went and I spoke to Mattie Gilsenan, who had been a selector since 1939, and this was '84… 45 years on. He agreed with me that I needed to do something and that is how I ended up getting my own selectors, and I brought in Pat Reynolds and Tony Brennan.

There had to be three County Board meetings about the change. I remember Jack Devine, a great man, saying to me that his fear would be that I would end up with just my own cronies on the team; he played the Devil's Advocate and fair play to him.

Eventually Colum Cromwell proposed that I be allowed my own selectors and Jack Fitzgerald seconded it. Colm O'Rourke and Joe Cassells went to the meeting as well to say that I should be given my chance… and that was that.

Then we went and played the first round of the league against Galway in Ballinasloe and we were beaten by 11 points. We barely survived in Division 1 when we managed to get a draw up in Tyrone, but then we played Laois in the championship and they beat us by 10 points in Tullamore.

Suddenly, lads who had been great the year before when they won the Centenary Cup, were being called a crowd of old women… and I was just a hurler and what did I know!

I was opposed by Paul Kenny when they went to appoint a manager for 1986, but they decided to give me another year. I was in before the board at the end of every year and I think that was a really good idea because it allowed the delegates to have their say.

You are better off to go to the horse's mouth.

Then in 1986 we met Dublin in the semi-final of the league. Brian Mullins was managing Dublin; he had taken over from Kevin Heffernan, and at half-time he said to me, 'Listen Boylan… you can win the league and we'll win the championship!'

When I went into the dressing-room a very quiet man called Brian Stafford was standing there insisting that, 'These lads aren't worth a shite!' Brian was only coming on the scene at that stage, but he believed that.

Dublin beat us in that league semi-final, but as regards the championship that year – the rest is history.

After losing so heavily to Laois in the 1985 championship we went into '86 a bit wary. Colm O'Rourke had had an operation on his elbow, Colm Coyle had an operation on his knee… it was Mickey McQuillan's first game back. Barry Ferguson was at wing-back that first day. Bob O'Malley had been injured with the under-21s the previous year, so he wasn't back by that stage.

We tried to give everybody their chance. We are only custodians of the position and we had to do what we thought was right and that can be difficult, but it had to be done.

We had players like Liam Smith, who had been amazing for years for Meath, but then Bernie Flynn gets the nod over him. That is the way it went.

That first game against Carlow in '86 was an amazing day. I took a chance by playing Coyler and Colm O'Rourke and then Jinksy (David Beggy) was the unknown factor – he caused havoc.

Some people say that Jinksy didn't know what he was doing, but don't kid yourself about that. He had ball skills that other people didn't have and he terrorised defences.

That was an awful tough match.

People forget how good the likes of Carlow were down through the years. Fino Murtagh had an incredible game to kick five points.

After getting over Carlow we started to get our heads together; lads like Mattie McCabe came in and knew exactly what to do. The experience of the Centenary Cup was huge to us in those days.

The Centenary Cup brought a confidence to the players, as well as a certain pride. To win the first open draw competition in the history of the game gave us a real boost; just look where we went from there! It was extraordinary and it proved that anybody can do it.

That win also gave the supporters great belief. Apart from the loss against Laois in 1985 when we got a bit of slagging, the Meath supporters were very supportive. The Meath supporters know their football and they recognised back in those days that we came up against some very, very good teams. They knew that with a bit of luck that our team was capable of going somewhere.

I never worried about the supporters getting onto us because that was their right. They were entitled to go to the games, they paid their way in and if we weren't doing it right, be it me or anybody else, they were entitled to have their say. They always keep you on your toes.

After beating Wicklow in the semi-final in '86 it set up a final showdown against Dublin and after the way we had played against them in the National League I went into that game full of belief that we could do it.

They were as vulnerable as we were. Anything they earned in 1983, ' 84 and '85 was tough – they had lost the All-Irelands in '84 and '85. Some of their players had soldiered hard and long. Our older lads like Joe (Cassells), Colm (O'Rourke),Gerry (McEntee) and Mick (Lyons) had also soldiered a long time, but they didn't have the same sort of miles on them that some of the Dublin lads did at county level.

Our lads had a hunger like you could never imagine. After 1985 everything changed. The lads came up to the home place and into my mother's kitchen. There was Gerry (McEntee), Colm (O'Rourke), Liam (Harnan), Joe Cassells, Mick and Padraig (Lyons) sitting drinking tea with Mammy when I walked in.

That night the blood was on the wall.

Anything that had to be said was said and it was all so constructive and about where we come from. They knew my limitations, I knew my limitations, which was probably more important, and Padraig Lyons asked me would I put my shyness in my arse pocket! I said to Padraig, 'Do you mean that?'

At that time I was very reserved and I wouldn't have been pushing my opinion, so to hear that changed everything. That is when Meath became a unit, when Meath became a team.

We sat around in a circle and anything that needed to be said was said; in other words it wasn't said outside in the park or anywhere else, so the air was clear.

I realised after that that those lads believed I had something to contribute. I knew then that they weren't just being nice to me. I wasn't able to play like them and I mightn't have been as smart an analyst as they were, but at least they believed that along with Pat (Reynolds) and Tony (Brennan) that we would have them well prepared and that the windscreen was pretty clear.

Everything was done for Meath, it was brilliant and that meeting certainly gave me great confidence. I was immensely proud to know those men and to be working with them. From the very first night I went into a dressing-room where there were lads who were there for a long time and lads who were there for the first time – some of them didn't know me from Adam and here I was in there to coach the Meath senior football team, so why wouldn't they question me at the start.

Someone passed a remark under their breath… 'Who are these so-and-sos?'… meaning the new lads who had come in, but I just told the whole group that I didn't care if they kicked the lard out of each other on a Sunday. I didn't care whether they were from Oldcastle or Dunboyne… Ballinabrackey or Bettystown or Laytown… when they came into me on a Tuesday night they had to leave all that behind and remember they were Meath men.

In 1988, Brendan Reilly came in for a league match. He was still not 18 years of age, and he walked into a dressing-room that had lads like Mick and Padraig, and Harnan and the likes. Harnan said to him, 'Where are you going with those new fancy boots?'

And Brendan turned round and told him to, 'F**k off!'

Mick turned round to Liam and said, 'That's what we want!'

Colm Brady came in with an ear ring… some lads started to bring hair dryers for the crack. This was foreign to some of the older lads… then lads started using deodorant. David Beggy came on a motorbike with no helmet.

I remember Colm saying to me, 'Sean are you losing it?' But behind everything with David Beggy and him being a joker, there is an incredibly serious side.

When you have the ability to take on the challenge of what people might be saying about you and not allow it to get to you, and use those things to help you get to where you want to be… that says a lot about the man.

Everyone believes that Meath only won that Leinster final in 1986 because it was a wet day, but when the day started it was a fine day and we were 0-4 to 0-2 up when the heavens opened, so we were doing quite well in the dry weather too.

Back then, the frees and sidelines were all taken from the ground, so that game became very fragmented, but we did our jobs superbly and got our rewards.

Dublin did recover to go two points up at half-time, but we limited them to just one point after the break and got the job done… amazing.

For me, that day was one of the most exciting days of my life.

So many men had tried so hard to win for Meath and collectively they just didn't have the squad to get them over the line… or things like a missed penalty or a poor referee went against them.

However, we had to learn from early on to forget about excuses and that type of talk. We had to forget about the negative stuff and focus on what we could do.

In the All-Ireland semi-final against Kerry people forget that after Mickey

McQuillan, Joe Cassells and Mick Lyons crashed into each other and Ger Power scored the goal… we scored four points after that. Then Tommy Doyle got a cut over the eye and needed treatment, so that broke our concentration and momentum.

Before we got into the dressing-room Kerry scored five points on the trot.

In a way we were shell-shocked, but I knew that day leaving Croke Park that to win another Leinster in 1987 we would have to be seven or 10 points better and if we could do that then we would have to be that much better again to win an All-Ireland… and that is exactly what it was.

That was our goal and our aim. It was never talked about, we just knew that whatever it took to get the job done we would do it.

We went to Mayo for a league game and John Maughan kicked the lard out of us on his own, and the lads came back and realised that that performance was no way good enough to repeat the Leinster success of the year before. That sparked them again.

But I always go back to that night in 1985 when the lads came to see me in the house and from then on, whoever came into the panel came in with a responsibility to the Meath jersey.

I brought in Bob O'Malley and Bernie Flynn with the view to them being ready in two years, but Bob was on the team inside three months and Bernie was on it three or four months after that again, so that's an example of how quickly lads learned – they were also great footballers.

I wasn't interested in birth certificates.

If the ability was there, the attitude was right… and if they were fit and strong, that was good enough for me.

COLM COYLE

Finally defeating Dublin in the 1986 Leinster final saw Colm Coyle make the biggest step up in his career, when he immediately faced off against Kerry's Pat Spillane (above) in the All-Ireland semi-final.

"

I PLAYED MINOR with Meath in 1980 and won a Leinster title along with lads like Finian Murtagh, Liam Hayes and JJ McCormack. I was minor again in '81 along with Martin O'Connell and Robbie O'Malley, so that was my first connection with those great players who went on to carve out great careers.

I made my senior debut against Fermanagh in the National League in 1981 alongside Mattie McCabe, Finian Murtagh and Ruairi Collins, the four of us made our senior debuts together.

When we were on the minors in 1980 we were playing Dublin in Navan and the seniors were playing Dublin in Navan as well, in what was Kevin Moran's last game before he moved on to play for Manchester United. In the week before the game we had one half of the field for training and the seniors had the other half

– we had 28 training, but when we looked down at the seniors they only had 12 or 14 training, so my first impression was that there wasn't much interest in the seniors back then.

When I came into the senior panel as an 18-year-old we used to train on a Tuesday and Thursday night, and after training on the Thursday night it was a case of heading down town for a couple of pints... there was nothing unusual about that.

Being a creature of habit, I always sat in the same place in the dressing-room... my spot was the second space on the left when you went into the room. For the whole of the first year Mick O'Brien, who was the manager at the time, used to just stand there and get changed, put the whistle round his neck and walk out.

In the whole year he never spoke to me socially in the dressing-room. Obviously, he would talk to us from a coaching point of view, but there was no general conversation with him, so the contrast between that and when Seán Boylan came in was the polar opposite.

Walterstown and O'Mahonys were the dominant club sides at the time and the panel was mainly made up of players from those clubs, along with Skryne and Summerhill – that's where the core members came from, and then myself and Mattie McCabe were brought in from Seneschalstown.

In 1982 we lost a play-off against Down and missed out on promotion in the National League... but we were doing okay with minimal application.

Longford beat Meath in the championship that year – I missed the game because of pleurisy and I think Gerry McEntee was injured as well. Wexford had beaten us the year before so it was just more of the same.

There were no expectations, and the whole thing was a bit of a joke to be honest. Seán Boylan came in for the league of 1982/83 and straight away everything changed.

At that time you had Summerhill lads in one corner, Skryne lads in another corner... all the club lads grouped with their own, but in Sean's first night he brought everyone together and started introducing lads to each other; lads who obviously knew each other, but Sean wanted to break up those club groupings in the Meath dressing-room.

Up to then, club took priority over the county team, but Sean wanted to change that and one of the first things he did was drop a few players. Mick Lyons was cut from the panel because he was part of that crew that was still going for a few pints after training, but Sean moved those lads on and he changed everything.

Everyone knows how bubbly and full of enthusiasm Sean is, so straight away he brought that to the panel; and he brought in a few young lads like Martin O'Connell... John McEnroe.

One of the first plans he had was to get us fit, so he really changed the culture of the place and it kind of worked because we won promotion from Division 2 and lost out to Armagh in the league semi-final.

We also won the O'Byrne Cup that year, which was a big thing to just win something, and in the championship we lost out to Dublin after extra-time in a replay and they went on to win the All-Ireland that year. We should have beaten Dublin that day, but we made a few mistakes that cost us.

All of a sudden we went from losing to Wexford in 1981... Longford in '82 to drawing with a Dublin team that had hammered Meath in 1980 and a side that went on to win the All-Ireland, so we were thinking we were making real progress and we weren't that far away... so we started to take everything a bit more seriously.

In 1984 we got to a league semi-final again where Galway beat us by a point after a replay. We had big battles with Galway and Monaghan around that time; we were neck and neck with Monaghan... they won the league in '85 and the Ulster title that year as well, but they didn't really kick on and our paths parted.

Winning the Centenary Cup was huge and getting to the Leinster final that summer in '84 where we lost out by four points to Dublin was still progress for us. Again, we probably could have beaten them because they had 14 men for a while in that game, but we played poorly and were very naïve. But we were showing progress, and we were looking at Offaly's progression around that time as our yardstick.

To lift the Centenary Cup in the stand in Croke Park was a massive occasion; it mightn't have meant much to other counties, but for us it was huge because it proved we could win big games in Croke Park and that drove us to want that more. By that stage Bernard Flynn and Bob O'Malley had come onto the panel, so you could see the evolution of the team.

1985 was a strange one for me personally.

Myself and Liam Smith went to Chicago early in the year for work, but I came home for the Leinster Championship game against Kildare in Navan and ended up getting a bang on the head. I had to come off at the start of the second-half and the comment at the time was, 'That was a waste of money bringing him home'.

I had booked my return ticket to go back to Chicago after the game and Larry Tompkins, who was playing for Kildare, had also flown in from America for that game. I believe the Kildare County Board had rung the Meath Board to see how much my ticket was – it turned out that Larry's ticket was dearer because he hadn't booked his return flight and it was dearer to book the return closer to the time; so they ended up disagreeing about the cost of his flight and because of that he left Kildare and went to Cork. Little did we know we'd cross paths again later.

Before I headed back to Chicago after the Kildare game I told Sean I wouldn't be back for the Laois game, but that I would be home for the Leinster final; that's how sure I was that we would beat Laois, but of course Laois went on and beat us.

Sean didn't have a problem with me coming over and back from America; there were a lot of lads doing that at the time – Johnny Mooney did it for Offaly in '82 and Gerry McInerney did it for Galway. I was playing football out there and I was training hard, but not to the standard of Sean's training and I could see when I came home in 1987 and '88 that the lads were way fitter than I was.

In 1985 I was fit. I had been working on the buildings so I was physically very fit, but nobody saw that Laois game coming. From my point of view it was an arrogance that we would beat Laois and that I would be home for the Leinster final. I even had my flights booked.

I had to go to Chicago at that time for work, the money was good and there just weren't those opportunities for me in Ireland at that time. Ireland is probably more advanced now, but at that time Ireland was a dire place. Unemployment was high, wages were low and being young and looking for some excitement, well… there were more opportunities out there in the U.S…. those were the things you did when you were young.

I don't regret doing it.

After losing to Laois the knives were out for Sean and his newly appointed selection team and he was under a bit of pressure, but thankfully they stuck with him.

I came home as planned even though Meath were out and I wasn't home long when Seneschalstown were playing Castletown in Navan and I made bits of my knee – I ended up with a pin in my knee from that injury.

Keyhole surgery was only in its infancy at that time, so I was in Navan A & E where they had a primitive way of doing operations back then. I have a 14-inch scar on my knee and was in a cast for three months.

When the cast came off my leg muscle had all withered away.

Because of the nature of the injury, the doctors had told me that I would be lucky if I was ever able to run again, never mind play football. I was only 22 at that stage; I had come home from America to play football, but all of a sudden I was in bits.

I suppose some lads were annoyed that I had gone to America, but I was annoyed at the time that I hadn't had any contact from the Meath management when I was in hospital. In hindsight, they might have been mad at me and they were also under a bit of pressure because there was uncertainty over their positions.

That game against Castletown was in late-August and I was in Navan hospital for a week before they operated. Then I was in a cast for three months and after November I spent a month trying to straighten my knee... then I spent another month trying to bend it, so I was well into January 1986 by this stage.

Francis Lee and Miriam Creavin were the physios in the rehab in Navan and I remember talking to them years later – they used to feel sorry for me coming into them because I was thinking I was going to be playing football again and they were sure that I wouldn't.

I had snapped my knee completely, it was a fairly bad injury, but I was determined and it still swelled up any time I trained after that. Sometimes when the pain would be bad, I would go for treatment and one of the treatments was a deep heat treatment directly onto the knee. Ann Burton, the Meath physio, used to ask me about pins or bolts in my knee, but I didn't even realise I had a pin in it at the time, so she used to put this deep heat stuff on it and my knee would kill me after each of those physio sessions.

It was only in 1996, 11 years after I did my knee, after the Leinster final... my knee was sore again and Sean arranged an x-ray and the doctors then revealed that I had a pin in it.

All those times I was getting that deep heat treatment it was heating up the pin and causing me pain – I never even knew I had the pin, I don't remember being told I had a pin.

I was meant to get the pin taken out then, but we said we'd wait until after the Tyrone game and then we said we'd wait until after the Mayo game, but then I was suspended!

That winter of 1985 and early '86 was fairy dark for me.

I had been working in Chicago, earning decent money and here I was back in depressing Ireland, in a cast for three months and not working at all – it was all doom and gloom for the Meath team and for me personally.

At that stage I thought that was it for me, I was being told I'd never run again.

I had to build the muscle back up in my leg and did that mainly by cycling and that helped get the flexibility back, but I never got to get my leg fully straightened again.

Seneschalstown asked me to play in a league game against Skryne; it was probably around February or March, and I said I would. I actually wore tracksuit bottoms in the game because my leg was so skinny and I said to the fella that was marking me that I was just going to stand in corner-forward. I told him I wasn't even going to go for the ball so please don't tackle me and, in fairness to him, he said he'd leave me alone.

It was madness what I did, but I just wanted to prove that I would get back playing football again, so I just stood in the corner.

It ended up that the three lads from the Meath management team, Sean, Pat (Reynolds) and Tony (Brennan) were onto me that evening to go back into the Meath set-up. Obviously I wasn't ready and I had given a commitment to train Donaghmore/Ashbourne at the time, so I told them I wouldn't go back in.

There was no point, I wasn't strong enough. I shouldn't even have been on the Seneschalstown team, but it just showed to me that they were going to leave no stone unturned.

After a while, as I got stronger, Sean rang me again and asked me to come in again and it is very hard to say no to Seán Boylan. I spent my whole life going against the grain, but when Seán Boylan asks you for something it is very hard to say no to him.

That was the type of faith Sean had in a lot of us. I was just coming back from that awful injury, but he wanted to do what he could to get me back and in the first round of the championship against Carlow in 1986 he picked me. Colm O'Rourke was also just coming back from injury and they were playing us in that game to get us back to match fitness; it was a bit of a risk, but Sean had faith in us and felt it was a risk worth taking.

At that time Bob O'Malley wasn't on the team, Martin O'Connell wasn't really getting a look in and it is only when you look back at these things that you realise Sean and his team put a lot of faith in me.

When I was in hospital I was feeling sorry for myself. I was in a ward with a bunch of old fellas and when I came out of the anaesthetic I was moaning and groaning and in pain, but there was a young fella about 10 years old in the bed beside mine… his name was Damien McAdam from Belturbet and he had brittle bones. He was like a breath of fresh air, and when I looked at him I realised I was just feeling sorry for myself.

Then when I got back to training I used to say to myself that I was lucky that I could play and that I could train and get fitter, so I quickly realised there were other people far worse than me and that put my injury into perspective and inspired me to go back training. I didn't give a shite if the knee went again.

Before the injury, football was the be-all and end-all for me. While I was injured I was out and it was a case of when you're out, you're out… and so after that I decided to adopt an attitude that I would play football to suit myself.

We only managed to scrape past Carlow in the first round in '86. The scars from the Laois game the year before were still there, even though I wasn't there it was clear that we were obsessed with Laois and getting our revenge on them. They were a good side and they won the league that year.

The planned path was that we would face them after the game against Carlow, but then Wicklow beat Laois.

We beat Wicklow by nine points in the end, but there was only four points in it until PJ Gillic got a goal – then we put on a couple of more points to pull away in the end. There was no expectation going into the Leinster final and the management were under serious pressure because no one really gave us a hope; the knives were out for them again because we appeared to have struggled in our games.

Starting the year we were of the opinion that if we wanted to win the Leinster Championship we would have to beat the league champions and the All-Ireland finalists from the previous three years. Then when Laois got knocked out it gave us a bit of a lift and we went into the Leinster final with a bit of hope.

We had a few players back and a few new lads in. Liam Harnan was back… Jinksy, Terry Ferguson, PJ Gillic all came into the team. Dublin were red-hot favourites and there were a lot of question marks about Meath still.

I know we went on and won All-Irelands afterwards, but that Leinster final win is the game that stands out in my mind because we never dreamed of winning All-Irelands, our dream was to win a Leinster title. I was at games in 1976 and '77, and in '80 in Navan where Dublin just bullied us and beat us. It was 16 years since we had won Leinster, so everyone was obsessed with winning Leinster and as players, we were focused.

We set attainable goals, and winning Leinster was the Holy Grail for us; so we celebrated that one probably even more than when we won the All-Ireland the following year.

The weather wasn't really a factor that day.

Dublin had beaten us on a scorching hot day in 1984, but they could play it any way. On a wet slippy day teams can get bullied and Dublin traditionally would have bullied Meath teams, so that could have been an issue, but the weather wasn't really a problem – as it turned out we were the new bullies on the block without realising it.

Myself, Liam Harnan and Terry Ferguson were the half-back line and at the time people were saying that was a weak half-back line. Joe Cassells was picked at right corner-back to pick up Tommy Carr, so it was a strange team selection and at half-time we were 0-4 to 0-6 down. Then Liam Harnan hit Barney Rock a shoulder and dislocated Barney's shoulder.

That was a big lift to us because Barney was a huge player for Dublin at the time. We outscored them 0-5 to 0-1 in the second-half, so defensively it was a great performance.

Harnan was outstanding that day. We didn't have Mick (Lyons) on that day in 1984, but he was there in '86. We lost again to them in 1989 and Mick wasn't around that day either, so it shows how good he was for us.

Outside of the camp nothing was expected of us, but within the group we were confident and Sean's confidence grew as well despite the pressure that was on them. To win that Leinster title was amazing.

Sean was brilliant. When we came in at half-time in that game the jerseys were soaked on us, so Sean told us to get them off us and he produced a completely different set of jerseys for us to wear; it was those small things that Sean had in hand, you could always trust Sean to have everything organised.

I was marking Charlie Redmond, but I don't remember much about the game other than Rourkey getting the point that sealed the thing. It was a massive, massive relief, especially from what had happened the year before against Laois and from a personal point of view after being told I would never play football again. This was my Holy Grail... the All-Ireland never even came into it for me.

Even at club level, Navan O'Mahonys had been dumped out of the championship, so ourselves and Summerhill were in the county final – it turned out to be quite a good year for me after the disaster of the year before.

After we won the Leinster final I went on two weeks holidays to Bulgaria... that was how confident I was we would win Leinster! So between the Dublin game and the Kerry game I headed off on holidays.

In fairness to Sean, there would have been a chance of cancelling the holiday and getting reimbursed, but he told me to go and get the rest – that was my recollection of the conversation anyway... maybe Sean's is different!

After what had happened the previous year I had a different approach to football; it might have seemed selfish or whatever, but I was determined to do things my way and enjoy myself. So I went to Bulgaria for the two weeks and relaxed on the beach. There were lifeguards on the beach, about 14 of them, who used to go for a run every morning so I asked them could I join in with them and they welcomed me.

I trained every day over there and I was looking forward to the game.

I had grown up in the 70s looking at Pat Spillane, Jack O'Shea and the Kerry legends and I knew we would be playing against the very best, so I was looking forward to it and knew that if I was selected I was going to be marking Spillane – I knew I had to do training while I was on holidays.

The feeling was that the Leinster title was the ultimate thing and we were delighted with that. We weren't ready at that stage of our development to beat

Kerry and even if we had beaten them, the way Tyrone started and played in the final I don't think we would have beaten them. I honestly don't think we were ready at that time.

Martin O'Connell was full-forward, Stafford was on the '40', O'Malley still wasn't on the team, so we weren't ready. Look what happened the following year – Martin and Bob won All Stars and Stafford was Footballer of the Year.

At the start of 1987 when we looked back we had regrets that we didn't go further in '86… the next plan was to go a step further.

The team changed again and there was an overhaul of the 1986 side to make it better for '87 and one of those changes was that I went off to America again.

We played Mayo in a league match in Charlestown and we lost 0-6 to 0-3. I felt we were going nowhere and it was playing on my mind that I wanted to go back to America. In my head I had won the Holy Grail and being 24 years old there were various things going on and I wanted to go back… so I went back to Chicago in March.

Sean wasn't happy with my decision, but he said we'd stay in touch and I remember watching the Leinster final over in Chicago and I was delighted to see them winning again. I was even more delighted for Mattie McCabe because Mattie got a raw deal in '86, and he banged in a goal in that Leinster final. The two of us would have grown up together, so I was delighted for him.

It killed him that he had stepped away and I had won a Leinster even though we had both been on the same journey, so I was delighted to see him get his Leinster medal.

After that game Sean started ringing me to come home, but I didn't feel a part of the set-up and I didn't really want to. However Sean was persistent; he was of the attitude that he wanted to win the All-Ireland that year and he made it clear that I wouldn't be starting, but that I would strengthen the panel.

It was great to hear how much I was being valued by Sean, but I said no to him a few times. However, it's hard to say no to him forever, so I said I would come home.

I didn't get home until the Saturday before the All-Ireland semi-final against Derry, and as you can imagine I wasn't exactly flavour of the month with a lot of the lads on the panel. It came across as if I was just coming back for the end of the campaign, but the truth was I didn't want to come back... but I did because of Sean.

I only did it for him because he was putting his neck on the line.

A lot of the players weren't happy and they tried to kill me in training, but they were wasting their time because I was never as fit and as strong in all my life. In fairness, I would have been the same. If I had been a player on the panel all year and I saw the management bringing someone in just before an All-Ireland semi-final I'd have been questioning it too.

Anyway I was home for three weeks; we won the semi-final, I got thrown on for 15 or 16 minutes in the All-Ireland final... we won the All-Ireland and the following Friday I was back in Chicago.

I didn't really feel part of that victory.

The following year, Meath were part of the All Star trip to Boston and San Francisco and Gerry McEntee, who didn't go on that trip, rang me and told me to go to Boston and meet up with the team. I went to Boston and met up with the lads, but I said I was staying for another while. Meath went on and won the league when they came back, so this was a side that had won an All-Ireland, won the league... they were flying.

Sean was on to me about coming home again, but this time he said I had to come home earlier than I did in 1987, so I agreed to come back in July – I actually played in the Leinster final. That was it, I never went back to Chicago again.

I still didn't feel part of the group in 1988; it took me a long time to win them over. The players were right. They do all the hard running and work on the Hill of Tara and I didn't do that. The glory comes in September, but all the hard work is done in January, February, March, April... but I didn't do any of that.

That is why I was delighted to win in 1996 because I had done all the hard work, but unfortunately I didn't get a full game in the All-Ireland final that year.

I was disappointed to be sent-off in that final, but I was more disappointed that there was no consistency in the decision making. There were at least 20 lads that merited a sending off, but on the word of an umpire saying to Pat McEnaney, 'Oh Coyler is after hitting five or six of them!'... I got picked out. It sounds good for the 'legend' that I hit five or six lads, but the truth of it is that I didn't. So on the basis of something that the referee didn't see and I didn't do… it was only half that amount… I was sent-off.

What did McHale do that was any worse than anybody else? David Brady had come in like a bull in a china shop.

In the Wexford vs Limerick hurling final there was a bit of a row early on and the referee came in and told everyone to calm down and warned them that the next lad that stepped out of line was gone… and one of the Wexford lads then got gate. That is what McEnaney should have done.

There is always going to be a bit of tension in a replay; it happened against Cork in 1988, there is always going to be an explosion. The annoying thing for me was the huge effort we had all put in. I had had a bad game the first day in the drawn game, apart from the last 20 minutes. I was surprised Sean didn't take me off in that first game and, as it turned out, thankfully he didn't because I came into it in the last 10 or 15 minutes and ended up scoring the equaliser.

For the replay I was determined to play better, but I only got six minutes. I'm not feeling sorry for myself. If it happened again, I'd do the exact same thing again.

In the first game, Brendan Reilly and Tommy Dowd were bullied by about six Mayo lads. Mayo had a lad in from New Zealand who was coaching them to bring an attitude of 'one-in, all-in'. Stuff had been bubbling after the drawn match when a couple of Mayo lads made comments in the hotel, so there was stuff there.

I know Meath supporters aren't his biggest fans, but I do feel sorry for McHale out of that whole thing. He has said to me, 'Well at least you won an All-Ireland', which is fair enough I suppose.

I put serious, *serious* effort in, in 1996, but then I only got to play six minutes in the All-Ireland final win, whereas in the other finals I put in hardly any effort and got to play in them – so I suppose it kind of balances out.

Looking back after 1988, I was around for the whole of '89 and was wing forward on the team. I was playing well and then got sent-off in the Leinster final when we were going for three in-a-row and we lost. I was thinking the lads were going to kill me.

The one thing that kept me going was that sense of guilt of being brought back in 1987 and '88 and winning an All-Ireland. I wanted to stick around then and prove that I wasn't in it for the bit of glory.

I had an injury in 1998 so I didn't really get any game time and at the end of the year Eamonn O'Brien, who was a selector at the time, said they wanted me to stay because of what I could give the young fellas in the dressing-room, but he made it clear I wouldn't be getting any game time.

There was no point in putting in that effort knowing I wasn't going to get any game time, so basically 1997 was my last year. At that stage I was 35, almost 36, so I just stepped away and they went on and won the All-Ireland in 1999 and, hand on heart, I was delighted for them and I didn't regret not staying on.

I didn't want to hang on and maybe steal a couple of minutes in an All-Ireland final from some young lad who deserved it.

LIAM HAYES

MEATH 1-11 LAOIS 2-5
Leinster SFC Quarter-Final
O'Moore Park Portlaoise
JUNE 14 1987

Liam Hayes wins the ball against David Foran in the famous four-game series against Dublin in 1991 (above), but the years of glory for Meath were built on a tense three-year fight with Laois.

★ **MEATH:** M McQuillan; B O'Malley, M Lyons, D Lane; B Ferguson, L Harnan, T Ferguson; **L Hayes**, G McEntee; D Beggy (0-1), J Cassells (0-1), PJ Gillic; C O'Rourke (1-0), B Stafford (0-7), B Flynn (0-2). Subs: K Foley for B Ferguson, F Foley for K Foley, L Smith for O'Rourke.

★ **LAOIS:** M Conroy; E Kelly, Martin Dempsey, P Dunne; M Ahearne, P Brophy, C Browne; Michael Dempsey, P Roe; G Browne, T Prendergast, L Irwin; L Turley, G Lawlor, N Roe. Sub: J Costello for Turley.

THE ACTION

IT WAS TWO years in the waiting, but Meath eventually exacted some measure of revenge on Laois for the 10-point drubbing they suffered in 1985 when they held on to book a Leinster SFC semi-final spot against Kildare with just three points to spare.

Meath had dominated the opening half, but shot 10 wides with Colm O'Rourke accounting for four of them.

Meath gave their hosts every chance with the concession of a soft goal that drew the sides level, but that calamitous goal sparked the Royals into life and they played their best football subsequently to get over the line. Laois were left to rue a missed goal opportunity in the first minute when Tom Prendergast blazed over the bar with just Michael McQuillan to beat. Meath responded with Brian Stafford in fine form to edge them into a 0-3 to 0-1 lead after 11 minutes.

Four minutes later Laois were two points clear after Liam Irwin converted a penalty and a free, and by the 22nd minute a Prendergast point pushed Laois three clear before Meath rallied in the run-in to half-time to restore parity 0-6 to 1-3 at the break.

Seven minutes after the restart O'Rourke converted a penalty to put Meath back in the ascendancy and when Stafford added a point three minutes later it put a comfortable margin between the sides for the first time.

However, Irwin kept Laois in touch from a 40-metre free and eight minutes later Colm Browne's fortunate goal, which skidded off the greasy surface and beyond McQuillan, restored parity again. Meath dug deep and in the closing 12 minutes they outscored Laois by 0-4 to 0-1 with Stafford, Bernard Flynn, Joe Cassells and David Beggy firing over in response to a Gerry Lawlor effort that proved to be a mere consolation score.

★★★★★

66

THERE WERE BIGGER games.

And games that I casually remember more often, like the rainy day in Croker in the summer of 1986 when we finally beat Dublin and were crowned Leinster champions. That would be the easiest game to select as the defining game of my life, and the defining game for the whole Meath team of the 80s.

We could not believe we had done it.

We had beaten them! That was something we wanted more than anything else in our football careers, but it was never something we dreamed of – honestly, I could never imagine the day when we would, at last, beat them! Have Dublin in a loser's dressing-room! Have the magnificent Brian Mullins and his selectors coming into our room to congratulate us.

That day, as far as we were concerned, we had achieved everything we had ever wanted to achieve. No one thought of doing more. *Winning an All-Ireland?*

Not even the tiniest of thoughts!

That day in Croker, when we took off our second set of jerseys (we took the first set off at half-time because we were drenched through), we would not have asked for more. It would never have dawned on us to ask for more. At that point in our lives, it was all about Dublin... only Dublin.

We would beat them five more times in the next six years in Leinster – counting drawn games, we met them nine times. Five wins, three draws and one loss.

Nah... nobody in the Meath dressing-room, back on that wet, wet day in the summer of 1986, imagined anything like that.

It was far beyond the powers of our collective imagination!

But, the day that defined us as a football team, and formally allowed me to have the career I eventually had, came almost 12 months after 1986. It wasn't Dublin... and it wasn't our first All-Ireland final. It was the first round of the Leinster championship.

It was Laois in the opposite corner.

In O'Moore Park, Portlaoise, of all the unremarkable, dull football grounds.

That afternoon we faced a game of football that was going to be the making of us, or the breaking of us possibly.

We had two games in Portlaoise that year, two competitive games back-to-back, and after we lost the first one (when we were fairly hopeless against Galway in the National League quarter-final), we had one more game in O'Moore Park.

I was thinking for those weeks – between losing to Galway and waiting for the first round of the championship – that two games in Portlaoise could be the start and end of our whole year. Losing to Laois would leave the whole of 1987 on the scrap heap.

It would also wipe out our momentum.

It would riddle our newly minted self-belief. The Leinster win in 1986 might suddenly appear a one-off. Worse than that, if we lost to Laois, then where would that leave us the next time we had to face Dublin… in 1988 or whenever?

Dublin had always, before 1986, felt an entitlement when they played us. We knew that, and they knew that, like someone had done a deal with the devil on the side that Dublin would always beat us. They had absorbed that entitlement.

Winning in 1986 would make them think twice, and if we made it through to the Leinster final in 1987 to face them again, we knew that it would probably be the first time in our lives that we would run onto a level playing field (mentally!!) against Dublin.

Beat Laois in O'Moore Park and march back into Croke Park a month or so later, and Dublin would be the team thinking – and second-guessing themselves!

It was all that simple.

Laois!

O'Moore Park!

It was a game which held a barrel of fears for us, for all sorts of reasons that I will come to in a minute!

Beat Laois and we would have Dublin, suddenly, desperate to beat us and avenge 1986, Dublin wanting revenge, Dublin feeling the pressure of knowing they would have to dig into their own reserves of self-belief … and dig deep, perhaps deeper than they ever thought they would have to dig in order to beat us!

It didn't matter about the semi-final that summer in 1987. History tells us all that we beat Laois by three points, and we beat Dublin by four in the Leinster final – but I actually had to google to find out that we beat Kildare by six points in Tullamore in the Leinster semi-final. Kildare didn't matter.

Kildare were never going to beat us. We knew that, and they knew that.

Another secret side deal!

For me, personally, my Meath career had also hit its first bump on the road, after beating Dublin in the 1986 Leinster final and before the start of the 1987 Leinster Championship.

I lost my place in middle of the field.

Not only that, I didn't get my No 8 shirt (at that stage I considered myself the custodian of that shirt), but was instead handed No 12.

And worse still, I was taken off midway through the game!

It was one of those many occasions when Seanie (Boylan) and I had one of our giant tiffs! We had so many of those little stand-offs.

I owe Seán Boylan everything for what I experienced and gained in my football life. I mean EVERYTHING!

Sean and myself were so close. We had a friendship that, I felt, was closer and tighter than any other friendship between Sean and any other player in the room. Maybe that was just in my head, but we were incredibly close, maybe too close for a manager and a footballer.

And, we'd have all those tiffs, and then become even closer after them, I felt that too.

He dropped me from the middle in the autumn of 1986.

It was unfair of him. I thought that then, and I think that now!

Worse, he never talked to me about why I was moved. He never sat me down, and laid it out on the table for me to see.

Sean never did that with players.

I think it was something he was not good at, to be honest. He loved his men. And he was not good at sitting down, face-to-face, and hurting us with the brutal truth.

Sean always tried (with me at least) to get his message across without words.

So, when I told him at the end of the summer that I was going off for a two-weeks holiday with Anne (my future wife; we were having our first holiday together) and that I would miss the first round of the league against Dublin in

Croke Park, he did not appear vexed. He said nothing.

One game is all I was going to miss.

I felt it was no big deal – and if it was a big deal in Sean's head, then he should tell me. And he didn't! I felt I deserved a holiday.

One game!

The first and last time in my whole 12 years playing senior for Meath that I would ever decide to miss a game.

Anne and I went to Gran Canaria for our fortnight. Meath, meanwhile, played Dublin and the game became a dogfight and in the middle of it Rourkey got ganged up on by several Dublin lads at the far end of the field, and I was informed that our lads were too slow in getting to him.

I believed Rourkey wasn't happy with either Meath or Dublin lads after that game. Mattie McCabe had played in my place, in the middle for the game, which we won. Mattie was the most naturally talented ball-player on that Meath team. He got some brilliant goals for us, but he never got the credit he fully deserved. He was double blessed with the smoothest, effortless talent.

Actually, Mattie scored goals in the 1987, '88 and '89 Leinster finals, and on each occasion I made the pass that resulted in him majestically scoring. Nobody remembers that, only me and Mattie – and he knows, because I kept reminding him!

But Mattie was no midfielder.

Sean knew that too, but he didn't pick me in the middle on the team for our second game in the league that season, when we played Down in Newry... in The Marshes, as they call it.

I hated that football ground. Newry and Hyde Park in Roscommon, both of them were bogs. Anyhow, as I travelled up to Newry on the team bus that morning, I was thick as a ditch with Seán Boylan.

If he had turned his back on me, I might have aimed a kick up his backside. I was THICK! I miss one game and I get chucked into the half-forward line and I get taken off, even though I was playing damn well in that 'foreign position'.

I was even thicker with Sean as we travelled home from Newry.

And I stayed thick with him for weeks, and months!

That's probably another reason why I choose the first round of the Leinster

Championship in 1987 as the defining game of my football life.

I was back in the middle with Gerry Mc, but Sean and I were still edgy with one another. Everyone was edgy.

If the team ever felt under serious pressure, it was in the weeks and days leading into that game. We had almost everything to lose.

Laois, you see, were our equals.

That's something that history does not tell, but they were. They were our equals for three or four years. In Leinster, it was us and them... and Dublin!

Both of us thought we might have half a chance of one day beating Dublin. Every time we played Laois, it was a bruising battle. Every time I played against Laois, I was never as sore for days.

A little bit of history for you.

Laois had won the National League in 1986. They had beaten Dublin in the semi-final, and got over Monaghan in the final. Also, they had beaten us by 10 points in the Leinster semi-final in 1985. That defeat almost had Seán Boylan out on his ear as manager.

In 1986, Laois had been ambushed in Aughrim (and had two men sent off in the same ambush) by Wicklow, so when we journeyed to our first Leinster title in '86 we beat Wicklow in the semi-final, not Laois. It should have been Laois.

Laois and Meath were due, overdue, our OK Corral afternoon!

We knew they fancied taking us out.

We had a genuine fear of losing to them and, on top of that, Sean did not have his best week as manager when it came to his team selection.

Sean, now and again, would get it wrong. Very wrong!

He'd see something in somebody that nobody else saw – and certainly, we all knew that he got it wrong in his selection for Laois.

Of all teams.

That added to the pressure we all felt.

We all knew we had no room for error. The game would be a tightrope. Always was against Laois. Always would be!

We all felt that Sean had made our day that little bit harder still.

Laois had serious players.

For me and Gerry Mc, there was a queue of tough opponents we faced every time we were playing Laois. After their league title win, some of them were now All Stars, which is more than I could say for myself at that time.

Liam Irwin was one, and they chose him on the wing that afternoon. He was a flyer, a magnificent athlete. John Costelloe was a huge, powerful fetcher and carrier of the ball (they had him in the subs, and brought him on!).

That afternoon, Laois started Michael Dempsey and Pat Roe in the middle. Roe was a battler and someone who would never say die. Dempsey was all knees and elbows, and he threw himself into games with abandon.

Nobody ever expected games between the two of us to be pretty – we were one another's alter ego, I guess.

This game was one long afternoon of attrition. We didn't play brilliantly.

We just went out and we sought to win as many five-minute spells as we could, and that's what we did. Every one of us was all-business. Me?

This was one game, luckily, when I was focused from the first minute to the last. I don't remember doing anything brilliant. I didn't get a score. But I worked and worked, and I made sure that if I did not win the ball in the middle, then my man was not going to win it either.

We felt that if every one of us won our individual battle by inches, we would be okay! And that's how it was. Except, we were winning those battles by slightly more than inches. We were mentally as tough as we had ever been – and that game, I believe, instilled in the team the 'toughness' for which we would become known.

We were the better team, by some, but we kicked 10 wides in the first-half. Rourkey was kicking wides for fun! Four or five or six of those were his… that big left foot of his whacking them wide from 40 yards out.

They should have had a goal early on, but Tom Prendergast tore through our defence and blazed over the bar. We were 0-3 to 0-1 ahead midway through the first-half. Liam Irwin then scored from a penalty. He then kicked a point. We scrambled.

It was level at half-time.

Thirty-five minutes in Portlaoise, and the Meath team might have been buried in 1987, and never won the All-Ireland that September, and never really have taken a firm grip of the collar of Dublin's famous blue shirt.

Rourkey scored from the penalty spot early in the second-half.

Why was Rourkey taking a penalty? I have no idea. I was the penalty taker for the first half of the 80s, and Staff took over from me.

What was Rourkey doing taking a penalty? I imagine, he grabbed the ball and wouldn't give it to either of us?

We were controlling the game. We were owning the ball.

Then, about 10 minutes from the end, Colm Browne kicked in a high centre and the ball bounced in the small square, and the ball was in the net.

We were level.

Ten minutes left in Portlaoise, with everything to win or lose… football careers to be won or perhaps lost! When the ball hit the net, I was in the large square. I clearly remember us all looking at one another. But no one said a word.

No one f****d anyone out of it.

We all just STARED!

I think we knew what we had to do in the 10 minutes.

We won the game by three points.

Each point was hard earned, each was deserved.

That last 10 minutes was like a whole new 70 minutes, and whichever team wanted it most was going to win.

In our hotel, in Portlaoise, after the game we were eating and drinking.

The Laois lads were there too. We had a few words and, I'll never forget thinking, as I shook their hands… *They are not devastated.* They did not look like men who had their world destroyed an hour or two earlier.

I remember thinking… *They didn't expect to win.*

They didn't think they deserved it. They didn't even imagine they might have a destiny.

We did.

That was the difference.

That was the single difference that day, perhaps!

99

BOB O'MALLEY

MEATH 1-13 DUBLIN 0-12
Leinster SFC Final
Croke Park
JULY 26 1987

Beating Dublin in 1986 was only a breakthrough, and for Bob O'Malley the victory over the old enemy the following year actually defined Meath as Leinster's new No.1 and future All-Ireland champions.

★ **MEATH:** M McQuillan; **B O'Malley**, M Lyons, T Ferguson; K Foley, L Harnan, M O'Connell; L Hayes, G McEntee; D Beggy (0-1), M McCabe (1-2), PJ Gillic; C O'Rourke (0-2), B Stafford (0-6), B Flynn. Sub: F Murtagh (0-2) for Beggy.

★ **DUBLIN:** J O'Leary; D Carroll, G Hargan, M Kennedy; D Synnott, E Heary, N McCaffrey (0-2); J McNally (0-2), D Bolger (0-1); D de Lappe, C Redmond (0-1), K Duff; B Rock (0-4), M Galvin (0-1), A McCaul (0-1). Subs: J Roynane for Bolger, T Carr for de Lappe.

THE ACTION

LIKE A SHEEP entangled in briars, Meath struggled to break clear of Dublin's clutches for half an hour of this tense, dramatic, exciting, nail-biting and pulsating but fiercely rugged Leinster SFC final, wrote Tom Mooney of the *Meath Chronicle* as he reported on the Royals second Delaney Cup success in as many years.

It was only the fourth time in their history that Meath had managed to retain their Leinster title. After a blistering start Meath looked unstoppable as they raced into a 1-5 to 0-2 lead after 15 minutes, but as they *struggled in the briars*, Dublin took advantage and established a 0-9 to 1-5 interval lead. Meath's goal came when Flynn broke Liam Hayes' sideline ball to Mattie McCabe, who kept his cool to side-foot to the net.

Also in that half, as referee Aldridge was about to book Mick Lyons for a heavy challenge on Kieran Duff a brawl broke out off the ball and after the dust settled the Kildare official dismissed Kevin Foley and Charlie Redmond for their part in the melee.

Meath did manage a brace of pointed frees from Brian Stafford when play resumed to retake the lead, but they still looked shaky as McCaffrey drew the sides level for the third time.

Another Stafford free edged Meath ahead again and O'Rourke followed with a fine score to make it 1-9 to 0-10 13 minutes into the second period.

With Dublin out on their feet, Meath delivered the knockout blows.

Finian Murtagh and Colm O'Rourke made it 1-11 to 0-11 with 10 minutes left, and then Murtagh and McCabe completed the Royals' tally as they eased over the finish line to retain the Leinster crown for the first time since 1967, and cap a memorable victory on the day Stephen Roche won the Tour de France.

★ ★ ★ ★ ★

66

I DON'T RECALL much about the nuts and bolts of that Leinster final in 1987, but I do recall at the time, and retrospectively, the importance of it.

The history of our trajectory and the development of our team is well documented, and Seán Boylan's reign is well known – coming in in 1982, all of a sudden within a matter of months Sean had Meath back in Croke Park in a National League semi-final against Armagh. That was no small deal to get Meath back into a competitive clash in Croke Park on the national stage.

Then in his first championship campaign to bring the eventual All-Ireland champions of 1983 to a replay in the preliminary round of the Leinster… that was huge. When Dublin went on to win the All-Ireland that year, things started to sit up in Meath because we had drawn with them and then brought them to extra-time in the replay; we started to believe that maybe we had something going on and maybe we could compete again with the best.

Fast forward to 1984 when we won the Centenary Cup, which was a novelty, but it was still a national competition. Then we got back into a Leinster final in 1984 for the first time since '77. Granted we were beaten, but we were beaten by the All-Ireland champions so it was no disgrace. For those first two years of Sean's tenure things were going north, generally speaking.

Then in 1985 the backside fell out of it all in the first round of the championship against Laois in Tullamore when we were beaten by 10 points; we were humbled, absolutely humbled and more pertinently we were back to the drawing board, back at square one where we started to think had the previous two and half years been a complete illusion, a false dawn. We started to wonder if we were as good as we thought we were… we needed to have a serious look at ourselves again.

Then we went on and won the Leinster title in 1986 and all hell breaks loose in the four corners of the county. We were back in the big time, we were back in business and we finally buried the Dublin ghost for the first time in a long, *long* time; we were back on that northward track again and we had to be serious contenders.

The greatest team of all time, Kerry, beat us by only a few points in an All-Ireland semi-final, but we were on the rise.

My thinking at the time was that if we didn't at least win Leinster again in 1987 the show was all over. I understand that in most people's book winning the Leinster final in 1986 was the cornerstone of it all and there is a legitimate argument for that, but if we didn't win the first round of the Leinster Championship against Laois in Portlaoise in the following early summer, and we didn't go on to beat Dublin in that Leinster final in 1987, then we would have disappeared, in all probability, without trace – 1986 would have been a flash in the pan.

You have seen down through the years countless counties winning a provincial championship and then giving a good show of themselves in an All-Ireland semi-final or an All-Ireland final... then they would disappear into oblivion. So if we didn't manage to put back-to-back Leinster titles together, given what had happened over the previous two and half or three years, we might never have appeared on the record as All-Ireland champions in 1987 and '88.

Talk about being nervous going into that Leinster Championship in 1987 against Laois! Only two years previous the same opponents had completely derailed us, so we knew what they were capable of doing to us; our wounds from 1985 were still raw and open and that defeat was still very much in our memories.

Absolutely we were on edge going down there that day because of what happened in 1985, but there was also the extra belief and incentive that we needed to win that championship again or it would all go south again and we would never recover.

If we had been beaten that day in early summer 1987 Sean probably would have had to walk or would have been frog-marched out of the place. I dare say I wasn't the only one who went down to Portlaoise that day believing that it was such a crucial game.

From when Sean took over in October 1982 to that day in June '87 we had done a huge amount of work and we felt that if we didn't win every match from then on, until we reached the top of Everest, then it all would have been a waste of time and a series of false dawns.

Out of the trauma of the 10-point loss to Laois in 1985 came a savage dose of reality and also a complete wakening up to the realisation that we had to approach everything as being one game at a time.

Dublin were the kingpins in Leinster having reached six consecutive All-Ireland finals from 1974 to '79… Offaly came for a period of time, but then Dublin took over Leinster again for a few years. The Metropolitan domination of Leinster was back on track, we were the only ones with a chance of up scuttling all that, but in that period it was very much the heavyweights against the young up and coming contenders – and the heavyweights felt at the time they had to put us back in our box after we had upset them in 1986.

In our minds we were serious that we needed to win again in 1987 otherwise it would have been back to the status quo.

There was always that ferocious edge with Meath and Dublin and the 1987 meeting was no different. There was a dirty row early in that final in the shadow of the Hogan Stand, around the 50-yard line, after about 15 minutes. It certainly wasn't just a stand-off, it was a serious row and we had to send out a signal that we were not there to be bullied.

We were serious about our business; we understood Dublin were serious about their business too, but if it was coming down to two stags going head-to-head then we weren't going to back down.

That is the way gaelic football was for a century before that; a lot of it has changed since, but on that day it was naked aggression against naked aggression and whoever was left standing at the end of it would come out on top.

I wouldn't have been as comfortable with that physical element because I didn't have the physique or the mindset naturally, but I was long enough around county football at that stage, having been in there as a minor in 1983 and had played three years minor before that, so it had dawned on me that senior county stuff can boil down to fairly Neanderthal action – and if it came to that and you were not prepared to meet whatever you were being met with, with at least as much ferocity, if not a degree or two more, then you had no business being out there and you'd know what the end result would be.

I think I got a booking as a result of that row. I did things that day in that row that I wouldn't normally be associated with, let's put it that way.

I'm not sure how much the row affected the game; it was just something that needed to be sorted out. We had started well and were in a good position, but then maybe we became too satisfied that we had 'won' the row – and we had to win it – and eased up a bit and they went in ahead at the break.

There was no panicking in our dressing-room.

Sean wasn't a panicker and he would have fed that into us as well. The only thing that mattered was who would hit the finishing line first... who would be ahead at the final whistle? There were times when Sean might have had to say to us, 'Lads, start concentrating on the ball again', but having played senior hurling for Meath for many, *many* years he was long enough around the county scene. He was an extraordinary little man; he knew that if things had to be sorted out on the pitch between players or teams, then he wouldn't interfere too much in that. Then when it was sorted, he got us refocused on the ball.

In the last 15 minutes of that game, I dare say, and I'm only hypothesising, that unconsciously the likes of the Laois game from 1985 was in our minds and we were probably driven by a sense of desperation.

There was so much pain between 1970 and '86 that we were being driven by desperation in that last 15 minutes because we couldn't afford, for the sake of our own mental health, to repeat the pain that visited Meath teams and the Meath people too often between 1971 and '86.

We also had to dig deep for our own older lads, the likes of Gerry McEntee, Mickey Lyons, Colm O'Rourke, Joe Cassells, Liam Hayes... for all their years on the team they hadn't much to show for all their hard work. They had been in Siberia for a long time, so we just couldn't go there again... that would have driven things a lot in those last 15 minutes.

There was a huge sense of relief at the final whistle, more so than anything else. If you are a seriously ambitious individual or a team you won't lie happy in your bed or your grave unless you get to the top of Everest, so we had still only won a Leinster title and were relieved to do that, but we wanted more.

The unspoken goal was an All-Ireland title, but if we were serious about our business that was what we had to aim for. To use an analogy, if you are going to be a serious mountaineer then there is only one mountain in the world you want to climb and get to the top of.

Seán Boylan had gathered around him a cohort of similarly driven, ambitious, desperate souls, they were all driven to success and to climb that mountain.

The little man on the line used to say we have five forwards over six foot and one that thinks seven foot, but I'll add to that statement – we had five forwards over six foot, one that talked seven foot and the little man on the line who was thinking 10 foot; he was hugely ambitious.

Sean also demanded the best and he did so out of necessity and he also led by example. He often trotted out the phrase in the early days that he wouldn't ask the team to do anything that he wouldn't do himself, and he backed that up.

He was an incredibly fit man, he was so strong and flexible. We used to stretch for 20 minutes to half an hour before training even started – that was unheard off before he came along, the man was ahead of the game.

The All-Ireland semi-final against Derry was once again purely driven by desperation. Whether we knew it at the time or not, but we were desperate to win. There would have been no point in getting this far and losing to Derry.

To the collective group's credit, there was probably an unspoken view that if we didn't achieve an All-Ireland win then we were probably wasting our time and lives, and each other's time and lives.

That was driven by what Sean was putting us through at training at well.

Training was utterly, utterly gruelling and painful.

I would hate to do it all again because it was pure hell he put us through, but that drove something in us to say… *Well if we are after putting ourselves through all this, then we had to get our reward.* We didn't half test ourselves in those sessions by necessity, that delivered a subliminal message… *Are you going to make this count, or is this a waste of time?*

There was no point in not going to the Nth degree in terms of what we could win, we had to win to justify the work we did.

Winning the All-Ireland fills all the clichés… *You've dreamt about this since you were a child… It was what you worked toward.*

For me there was a sense of surrealness around it… *Can this be really happening?* I was only 22 years of age, so it was a great feeling to have at such a young age.

The following year we put ourselves back in a position again where we won the first round of the Leinster Championship, reached the Leinster final and the All-Ireland final again; but again we were saying to ourselves that if we didn't win again that year would 1987 then be seen as a flash in the pan?

So for me, 1988 was more real, more satisfying because now no one could ever point the finger at us and accuse us of just being a flash in the pan and winning just one All-Ireland and then not winning again.

We got back to within sight of the summit again in both 1990 and '91, but there's an old saying that a club man of mine used to say many years ago and it struck me in its simplicity, profundity and accuracy… 'Championships are hard won at any level'.

At All-Ireland level you are coming up against the best in the country, teams that are exceptionally well prepared, exceptionally hungry, maybe hurting from previous disappointments, equally ambitious, equally talented, equally strong, so you are not going to have it all your own way all the time.

I do feel sorry for teams whose efforts over a long period of time can go south on a day because of an official's ineptitude.

Weren't we blessed to win two All-Irelands?

We worked damn hard for them, we could have won four or five, but we got there twice, we reached that summit twice.

DAVID BEGGY

MEATH 1-14 CORK 0-11
All-Ireland SFC Final
Croke Park
SEPTEMBER 20 1987

David Beggy's arrival on the Meath team in 1986 was dramatic and within two years he was celebrating as an All-Ireland winner after defeatng Cork (above) in the '87 final.

★ **MEATH:** B O'Malley, M Lyons, T Ferguson; K Foley, L Harnan, M O'Connell; L Hayes, G McEntee (0-1); **D Beggy (0-3)**, J Cassells, PJ Gillic (0-1); C O'Rourke (1-1), B Stafford (0-7), B Flynn (0-1). Subs: C Coyle for Cassells, P Lyons for O'Connell.

★ **CORK:** J Kerins; A Davis, C Corrigan, D Walsh; N Cahalane (0-1), C Counihane, T Nation; S Fahy, T McCarthy; J O'Driscoll (0-1), L Tompkins (0-6), J Kerrigan; C O'Neill (0-1), C Ryan (0-1), J Cleary (0-1). Subs: J Evans for Corrigan, T Leahy for Fahy, P Hayes for Ryan.

THE ACTION

RTE's *SUNDAY GAME* 'expert' Enda Colleran selected Liam Hayes as Man of the Match after the 1987 All-Ireland final, but in truth anyone of at least eight Meath players would have been worthy of the accolade and flying forward David Beggy was certainly in the running following his personal haul of three points in a game where only two other players, Brian Stafford and Larry Tompkins, managed to point more than once.

A Colm O'Rourke goal was crucial as a first All-Ireland title in 20 years looked to be slipping from Meath's grasp with Cork opening up a four-point lead.

Colm O'Neill, three Larry Tompkins frees and scores from Christy Ryan, Niall Cahalane and John Cleary boosted Cork to that early advantage with Meath's replies coming from PJ Gillic, O'Rourke and Gerry McEntee. Indeed Cork could, and probably would, have been much further clear had it not been for a heroic flying block by Mick Lyons that stopped a certain Jimmy Kerrigan goal. However, then came the crucial score and it was Beggy who played a hugely influential role in O'Rourke's goal.

Moments later Beggy produced a sublime moment of skill when he linked up with O'Rourke and gave evidence as to why he is called Jinksy as he left the Cork defence trailing before rifling over the equalising point. Stafford added a point from play and, in the space on nine minutes, Meath went from being four points down to being one up.

Tompkins restored parity with his fourth free, but Stafford closed the opening half scoring with a fine point from play to secure a 1-6 to 0-8 interval lead for Seán Boylan's side.

Cork managed just one point in the first 31 minutes of the second-half (a Tompkins free) as Meath assumed complete control. Beggy added his second from an acute angle, Stafford converted a free after Flynn was fouled and before Cork managed to score again Stafford (three), Flynn and Beggy were all on target again as Meath opened up a 1-14 to 0-9 lead.

★★★★★

66

THERE HAVE BEEN so many games down through my career I could choose, but as an individual the 1987 All-Ireland final stands out personally for me simply because I had a hell of a day.

I was very young, I had no baggage… it was one of my best performances and a game I look back on with immense pleasure. The feeling out on the pitch at the final whistle was amazing; everything came together that day.

People often say that I was new to the GAA and that I didn't play the game much when I was young, but that is blown out of all proportion.

Sure, rugby was my first love because I had been playing rugby since I was six or seven years old, but I was also playing gaelic in Scoil Mhuire and I won championships at under-14 and under-16 for Navan O'Mahonys against Trim, so I had played plenty of football at underage.

However, I had never really trained at gaelic football.

Paddy O'Brien was the man who looked after us in O'Mahonys and certainly gave us a grá for the game, but while I was raw at gaelic I wasn't as raw as some people made out.

Paddy O'Brien was a brilliant man. He put sport first; he gave us the love for the game. There was no such thing as win, lose or draw with Paddy, it was always… 'Do your best and enjoy yourself'. He never cursed at us, he never gave out. If someone had a bad day he wouldn't say a word, he just wanted everybody playing football.

He knew that it was when you are young that you develop a love for something and was aware that later on in life it becomes harder, so he didn't want to make it hard on anybody.

Everybody got their chance and everybody was great, no matter what you did… you were great. That is all a young lad needs to hear.

These days as a 12-year-old, you are being coached to make sure you are better at this and better at that, but that wasn't Paddy's style at all.

His style obviously worked because he brought through such a huge amount of players that stayed with the game and who absolutely loved it both at club and county level. He was an amazing man, there is no doubt about it. You will meet one or two lads like that and he was one of them, a very special man.

So while rugby was my first love, I did keep going back to gaelic football and to O'Mahonys during the summer to keep fit and I was very much encouraged by Jackie Farrelly, who would often pick me up on the side of the road and bring me home to get my gear and bring me to matches.

Jackie chased me an awful lot. I would literally be coming in the door from rugby training and Jackie would be at my door waiting to bring me to a match with O'Mahonys, so he really kept me interested in GAA.

When I did get going with gaelic I was picked for the O'Mahonys seniors as an 18-year-old in 1985 and we went on to win the county final that year.

I was picked at midfield on that team – Joe Cassells was the midfielder and I was the runner, that is basically how we worked and I was called into the Meath set-up after that.

The reason I keep going back to 1987 is because I decided to give up rugby to concentrate on playing for Meath, but I didn't just want to play for Meath, I wanted to win something.

I had never seen Meath play football before so I had no ambition to play for Meath, so when I decided to play football for Meath I decided to do it for one reason and one reason only and that was to win an All-Ireland. I wasn't doing it to just wear a Meath jersey, although I did grow to love that over time.

Two weeks before Meath played Carlow in the first round of the 1986 Leinster Championship I was called in to play in a challenge match against Monaghan at the opening of the Walterstown pitch and two weeks later I played my first championship match against Carlow where I scored 1-2.

Within six weeks I had a Leinster medal, it was a remarkable start to my Meath career.

I had never played at any level with Meath before that. I was called into a trial with Meath under-14s and I think I made the team to play Dublin, but there was an athletics event on at the same time and both coaches were on to me to show for them and not the other, so in the end I went away for the weekend with my folks to Roscommon rather than showing up for either the football or the running.

That was the last phone call I got about football with Meath until 1986.

Winning the Leinster in 1986 was great and the enormity of it was evident to me because of the size of the crowd at the game and the outburst of emotion after the game. I also remember having no money to go out drinking that night, not a penny, but somebody gave me £20 to go out for that night… that was quite funny.

It was a great feeling to win that Leinster final, I certainly didn't take it lightly or too casually. I might have taken myself very casually, but I was very serious about the event itself.

The devastation when losing to Kerry was huge. When I gave up rugby I did so to win with Meath and that is why 1987 is so important to me.

It was a huge sacrifice for me to give up rugby. My dream was to wear the green jersey for Ireland, end of story… nothing else mattered, so it was a huge turn for me to give all that up and concentrate on playing with Meath.

Looking back now, it is easy to say that I might have made it with Ireland. At that time I was from Navan, so I would have had to move to play in Dublin and go through those steps. Playing for Ireland would have been the dream and I did end up training with Ireland when I went back to rugby in the mid-90s, but it was too late in my playing days and I just didn't get there.

I did play for Irish Wolfhounds and stuff like that, but I never got that Ireland jersey. Maybe if I had kept at it from an early age I might have made it, but that's easy to say now looking back. However in 1987 I made the decision that it was going to be all out football for me with the view to winning.

Training was quite demanding and was very heavy work with Meath, but it was fun. I was very young coming into the panel; a lot of the team were middle aged, whereas I was new and because I had no bond with other lads who would have played underage with Meath before, I didn't really know anyone.

I was a little bit strange and a bit different to the other lads.

I was a lad on a motorbike arriving at training, and it took some of them a long time to build trust in me to be honest; they would have been a bit wary of me coming from a rugby background.

I think Liam Hayes even wrote in his autobiography that I had come from *The wrong side of the tracks*… as he put it. They would have been very suspicious of me and it would have been uncomfortable for some of them to see that I got onto the team straight away and managed to stay there, because I hadn't done the hard yards like they had.

Winning the Leinster in 1986 wasn't enough for me or for the rest of the team. I remember the devastation after the Kerry match, that really affected us and there was a lot of learning done out of that game… we had to get harder and had to get stronger and had to get fitter and had to be more ruthless and cuter, Kerry certainly taught us a lot.

Winning a Leinster wasn't enough for that group of players and I felt the same, so getting through Leinster again in 1987 was great, but we wanted more.

In the semi-final against Derry I started very slowly and wasn't playing well. Sean was warming up Fino Murtagh to come on in my place after about 15 minutes, but then I got a point and he left me on – and I went on to get the RTE Man of the Match award from that game.

I was two seconds away from being taken off in that game and if I was, I might not have won my place back for the All-Ireland final or indeed ever, so it is amazing to think that I got that point at just the right time that saved me in that game.

That is luck and fate and everything else.

I enjoyed the build-up to the All-Ireland final. I'm not a shy person, so it was very enjoyable for me; it was a novelty and the build up didn't distract me, if anything it enhanced the importance of it and put the right type of pressure on me.

For me the build-up was great motivation and it was good fun as well. I always loved being in Croke Park on the big day in front of the big crowd, that is when you can show off… and that whole build up was very intense, but really enjoyable.

The fact that there was over 68,000 people at the game fed me more so than frightened me. The more the merrier and the more intense the better, it was something that I absolutely loved… out in Croke Park when the place was packed was my best place to be, it's the only place I wanted to be.

I had loads of off days too, but I never reflected on them. The key for me was to always stay in the moment.

During a game I never looked back, I never looked back at the first five minutes and thought that was crap. I always looked to see what I could do in the next one or two minutes, or what was happening in front on me.

I never dwelled on anything in a game or wanted the ground to open up and swallow me. I have had some horrendous moments on the football pitch and after a match I might have looked back on them, but during games wasn't the time for reflection. It was always focused on getting the next thing right.

The early stages of the All-Ireland final in 1987 against Cork were horrendous, but there was never panic. Our team never ever panicked. It was going shit early on alright, but there was never a time where we felt we were in trouble. We were determined to keep going and keep doing the right things. When Mick Lyons made his massive block on Jimmy Kerrigan that sparked everything off for us.

I was involved in the lead up to Colm O'Rourke's goal and that got us right back into the game. Martin O'Connell did a great job on John O'Driscoll; that was a perfect example of how to tackle and not foul.

O'Driscoll ended up nearly throwing the ball away in the end because he was that pissed off with the intensity of Martin's tackling. I intercepted his attempted pass and flicked onto Rourkey and he put it into Flynn, who took a shot which was saved... but O'Rourke followed up and put it into the net.

I remember that game really well. I kicked three points that day and one of the points I scored was probably the best point I ever scored. O'Rourke passed me the ball, but I dropped it first, then when I recovered it I took off and weaved in and out of a few players and put it over the bar with the outside of my foot.

To score three points in an All-Ireland final at a time when points weren't scored too often from play was a fair return. I felt so good in that whole game.

I was marking Tony Nation; he is a lovely guy, but I felt no pressure at all. Honest to God, I felt like it was a walk in the park. Maybe my scores did help my confidence, but it was just one of those perfect days in sport that don't happen too often. Being so young and naive and then experiencing all that was phenomenal.

The last couple of minutes were amazing. It was like being at a concert at that stage because we knew the game was done and dusted, so we were able to enjoy it. That didn't happen after that, that's probably the only match where I can honestly say we could feel like that in the closing stages. It was pure enjoyment.

The sheer joy at the final whistle was enormous. After going 20 years without an All-Ireland it was amazing to win it and I remember my dad running onto the pitch and giving me a big hug. In those days you didn't hug your auld fella that much or he didn't hug you, but I remember that hug well that day.

It was very special.

Waking up the next morning was even more amazing. I went for a walk on Malahide beach and taking it all in, it hit me a lot more then. After the final whistle was brilliant and that night was mayhem, but that moment by myself the next morning on the beach was lovely.

Liam Hayes picked up the Man of the Match award for that game; he was superb that day, unbelievable. For me, winning those type of awards wasn't really in my head, they're not important at all. I don't really agree with Man of the Match awards because for me to score a point, somebody had to give me the ball… and someone else had to win it before that.

Everyone has to do their work for another player to do well. A Man of the Match performance in gaelic football is a bit redundant really because you are only as good as the people around you. Same as the All Stars… they are nice to have, but they are just an opinion; I'd rather have the players appreciate me rather than a journalist or a pundit.

The journey home the next day after winning the All-Ireland was amazing. I remember stopping in Clonee and seeing lads from Navan there and then going on to Skryne and all the other places with huge big bonfires before getting back into Navan, where we were met by Paddy Fitzsimons and having a chat up on the stage.

After that I just wanted to get into Bermingham's, which was my watering hole, for a few pints. The whole occasion was great. One day ran into another – it was a long time ago now, so I can't remember a whole lot of individual stuff, but we had a great time.

I had to finish up the celebrations on the Wednesday because we played Slane in the county semi-final the following Sunday. That game finished a draw, so we had the replay the following week, the county final the week after, and the first round of the Leinster club the week after that – it was all football and very hectic.

In 1988 we were almost in cruise control. We learned a secret and we held on to it and got a good measure of success, but then we lost that secret because I think we got too cocky.

I don't think we were beaten in 1988; we were in an invincible position and won another All-Ireland. In 1989 I think we took our eye off the ball – the same effort wasn't put in and that caught up with us. We did get our act together again in 1990, but took our eye off the ball in the All-Ireland final and underestimated Cork.

Then in 1991 it was the last hurrah. Lads were getting old and many were in bits and very sore. 1991 was the ultimate effort by the lads.

I don't believe the stories that we probably left a couple of All-Irelands behind us. We won the All-Ireland in 1988 and I don't think we should have because on the day Cork were in the driving seat and I won a free in the last minute to equalise the match. Cork were very unlucky that day because they hammered us.

We deserved to win the replay, but we were lucky to get that second chance.

Against Cork in 1990, I don't think we deserved to win that match. I remember before the match one of the selectors did an article in the paper where he said Cork would never beat us. That type of an attitude was there and if you under-estimate a team you will get your ass kicked.

Maybe I'm reading that all wrong. I was living in Scotland at the time, so I wasn't around for a lot of the build-up to the 1990 final, so maybe I've got that all wrong, but I do think that whoever wins an All-Ireland deserves to win it, end of story.

You can never be bitter about not winning one.

You can say what you want about the 1991 final, but Down hammered us. We were missing Colm O'Rourke and Bob O'Malley and you can point to huge errors, but the facts are that Down were immense for 40 minutes that day. When you win an All-Ireland you deserve it, I don't believe that any get away from you.

I suppose you have to be remembered for something, so scoring the winning point in the four in-a-row against Dublin in 1991 isn't a bad thing to be remembered for, particularly as it was probably the worst game I ever played against Dublin.

There was never any doubt in my mind about taking on that shot.

Nothing I did that day went right. I had a terrible day, but I still kept in my mind that if I got a chance I was going to take it. If I reflected on the match at the time I would have wanted to have been taken off because I was that bad, but I stayed with it and I kept my head in the moment and got my chance in the last minute of the match.

That is what I was always like.

No matter how bad or good it was going I was always thinking it was the next thing I do that counts.

99

COLM O'ROURKE

MEATH 2-13 DUBLIN 0-11
NFL Final Replay
Croke Park
MAY 21 1988

Defeating Cork in the 1987 All-Ireland final (above) was the realisation of all of Colm O'Rourke's dreams, but the following year's National League final win over Dublin after a replay was possibly his greatest performance in green and gold.

★ **MEATH:** M McQuillan; B O'Malley, M Lyons, P Lyons; K Foley, L Harnan, M O'Connell; L Hayes (1-0), G McEntee; B Reilly (1-0), PJ Gillic, M McCabe (0-1); **C O'Rourke (0-2)**, B Stafford (0-5), B Flynn (0-5).

★ **DUBLIN:** J O'Leary; D Carroll, G Hargan, M Kennedy; D Synnott, N McCaffrey, P Clarke; J Bissett, D Bolger; V Murphy (0-2), C Redmond, K Duff (0-1); D de Lappe, J McNally (0-1), B Rock (0-7). Subs: T O'Driscoll for Synnott, B O'Hagan for Carroll, J Prendergast for O'Driscoll.

THE ACTION

THE HEADLINE IN the *Meath Chronicle* roared... FLYNN AND O'ROURKE OUTSTANDING. Beneath it, the local paper declared *Meath do double as they drub the Dubs* and off the back of their sensational eight-point victory it is hard to describe the Royals' NFL final replay victory over the 'auld enemy' as anything other than emphatic and Colm O'Rourke's performance as sensational.

In the first encounter on April 17, Joe McNally had rescued parity for Dublin with his late, *late* point ensuring a 1-8 to 0-11 draw, to set up a replay. There were certainly days when Skryne man O'Rourke contributed more to the scoreboard, but rarely, if ever, was he as instrumental in ensuring a Meath victory than he was in the stunning replay win.

Bernard Flynn and Brian Stafford took the scoring plaudits with 10 points shared evenly between them, while Brendan Reilly and Liam Hayes added goals – Hayes' in particular was one of the finest ever witnessed at GAA HQ, but it was O'Rourke who was at the epicentre as Meath survived the 11th minute sending off of Kevin Foley to crush Dublin. With Dublin opting to deploy their extra man as a third midfielder, Colm O'Rourke moved out the field. Bernard Flynn won the official Man of the Match award, but O'Rourke was the name on everyone's lips after the final whistle.

Dublin opened the scoring in the third minute with a point from Vinny Murphy, but that didn't last long as O'Rourke's fierce shot was only parried by goalkeeper John O'Leary into the path of Brendan Reilly, who coolly slotted it to the net.

The returning Barney Rock, who was making his first appearance of the league, scored seven points from frees, with four of them in succession – and one from Kieran Duff boosted Dublin to the lead, 0-6 to 1-2, for the final time by the 27th minute. Meath finished the half on the front foot with two frees from Stafford and two from Flynn, the second after quick thinking by O'Rourke from a sideline, ensuring a 1-6 to 0-6 interval lead.

When play resumed Stafford added another point from a free within 60 seconds, but it was Hayes' goal that stunned the Dubs and the 33,260 in the crowd, as he finished off a rampaging 40-metre run with a piledriver from 25 yards that gave O'Leary no chance and put the issue beyond doubt, 2-7 to 0-6.

★★★★★

66

PURELY FROM AN individual performance point of view, the National League final replay in 1988 is one game that stands out for me.

In many respects, the most important game for us as a team and as a group would be the Leinster final in 1986 because that was the breakthrough game, but I'd look on the 1988 league final replay as probably my best performance – probably the team's best performance over that period of years. That was probably the best Meath display of that whole era.

I don't think there was any hint that we had left the win behind us after the first game. The general feeling from us all, and from me in particular, was that we would win the replay. I hadn't played well at all in the drawn game and a lot of the other players were also disappointed with their own individual performances, so we were all determined to do a lot better in the replay.

There was almost a month between the drawn match and the replay because Meath went on a trip to America to play in the All Star games, but I didn't go because my son Shane was born while they were on that trip.

There was a lot of supposed aggro between Kieran Duff and some of the Meath players on that trip, but all the Meath lads who were in America will tell you that that was a figment of the imagination; the incident where Kieran Duff was supposed to be set upon by Meath lads never happened… it was all baloney.

There was a game over there in San Francisco where Kevin Foley and Duff were stuck into each other and I think that formed the basis of some of the stories that came out of that trip.

There was a very hostile build up to the replay by the media towards Meath on the basis of the supposed incidents that happened in America, but again our lads will still say to this day that those alleged incidents never took place.

There was a serious rivalry between Meath and Dublin at that time because we had beaten them in the Leinster finals in 1986 and in '87, then we were meeting them in the league final in '88. Dublin had the same problem with us back then that we have with them now, so that fuelled the rivalry and we went on to win the league final – then we beat them again in the Leinster final that year too.

All the big games against Dublin at that time fell our way and even though they beat us in the Leinster final in 1989 we came back again and beat them in '90 and '91. For a six-year period things very much went in our favour... the Dubs were riled up by that fact.

We had a good team back then, a very good team.

We had everything going for us. We had the physique, athleticism, the ability and a wonderful camaraderie and attitude among the players. In the opposite corner, Dublin weren't nearly as talented then as they are now.

Dublin were probably the second best team in the country at the time. It was between themselves and Cork and we felt at times that Dublin were even better than Cork at that time, even though Cork did go on to win two All-Irelands in that spell as well, whereas Dublin didn't win any until 1995.

Over a 10-year period Dublin had a very good team, but won nothing because we were so strong and kept knocking them out.

During the group stages of the league in 1988 we met Dublin in Croke Park and it was a very dirty game that finished as a draw. A lot of the Meath players felt at the time that Dublin had tried to rough us up – I think there were a few incidents in that game that the Meath lads weren't happy with.

The drawn final wasn't a dirty game, it was actually a pretty tame game.

It was a poor game of football; we went a point up near the end without playing anywhere near our best at all, so I don't think we left it behind us. We knew we would be better the next day – a lot of the players were unhappy with their individual performances, so they had a good look at themselves and were determined to improve.

Those Meath players very much took responsibility for their own individual performances, they never blamed anybody else and nobody had to tell anybody else that they didn't perform; we all knew it ourselves when we weren't up to scratch.

We always went away and analysed it ourselves, and normally came back better for it. We always felt that there was a case of, 'Give a dog a bad name' about our team. No matter how good our football was, we were still going to retain the image of being a fairly hard outfit.

There *was* a hard edge to us.

The two Lyons, Foley and Harnan... they were really tough, hard men, so maybe some of the reputations were deserved, but it came at a price where our good football was often forgotten. To some extent, that perception worked in our favour because some teams approached us and didn't seem to understand that we could also play football too and they ended up taking their eye off the ball.

The final replay had been built up beforehand that it was going to be a big shoot-out between Foley and Duff.... everybody else seemed to want to get in on the act too. There was definitely a mood in the Dublin team early on that they wanted to sort out the Meath lads, and Foley in particular.

They tried to do it in the wrong part of the field.

I didn't see the incident which led to Kevin Foley's sending off. I had the ball and was running towards the Hill 16 end; the referee blew the whistle while we were on the attack and everyone was looking around to see what was going on.

I looked back up the field and there were a few Dublin players on the ground, I don't know what happened to them. The whole incident wasn't mentioned at half-time, it was only when we got together for a drink after the game that we got round to asking some of the lads what had happened.

Most of the Meath forwards were focused on the ball and saw nothing.

The fact that Foley was the only one to be picked out by the referee really annoyed the Meath lads that had seen what happened because they said that Foley had only stood up for himself after Duff had started on him.

The general feeling was that we had been badly wronged.

The media build up to the game, and Foley being bandied about as being some sort of thug, had actually played a huge role in the referee's decision and Kevin paid a price for his reputation rather than actually doing anything wrong.

The referee was Pat Lane from Limerick, and there is no doubt he had been influenced by some of the build-up to the game too. Pat passed away recently.

We felt he had treated Foley badly, but we always liked him as a referee. We never had any complaints about him really; we thought he was wrong that day, but in general we felt he was quite a good referee who never came down too heavy on us. We always thought he was very fair.

Dublin tried to play their extra man as a third midfielder, so I came out from the full-forward line to add more numbers to that area. At that time, Seán Boylan didn't have to tell us that much what to do, we always tried to work it out on the field.

Sometimes Staff or Flynn would tell me to drift out or else stay in, and that was the way it worked out that day. I went out to midfield because we were outnumbered in that area.

Liam Hayes and Gerry McEntee were in midfield and PJ Gillic was centre-forward, so we had a lot of big men around the middle who were well able to look after each other.

Our first goal came when my shot was parried by John O'Leary and Brendan Reilly followed in to put it in the net. Once Foley was sent-off Sean moved Brendan Reilly back onto Duff, but he then basically left it to ourselves to work it out on the field where we needed to place ourselves without making any formal switches.

At that time I'd have drifted out towards the middle anyway, so it wasn't a particularly new tactic for us.

We defended very well and kept most of their scoring to frees, and I don't think they had any really good chances either; they didn't open up our backline at all, our defence was very tight.

The last 10 minutes of the first-half is what really stands out for me.

We really got on top in that spell and played a lot of good football. After about 20 or 25 minutes we got into a rhythm and nearly devastated them as we got on top in every sector of the game and played lovely, flowing football.

I did a lot of tackling in that game.

Most of my good work that day was destruction rather than construction; I felt I broke up a lot of ball. Staff and Flynn were better scorers than me, so the idea was to win the ball back and get it to them – Flynn had an absolute bonanza that day, he scored points from all angles.

We really turned it on. Liam Hayes got that wonder goal early in the second-half and that was that. We always slagged Liam that he was going for a point with his shot… we would never let him think that he was after doing something great.

It was such a fantastic goal and typical of the type of runs that he was capable of making. He had a massive long stride; he was a great solo runner on the ball and was always very much in control. Then he buried it in the top corner.

The way we were at the time, we didn't give each other much credit for anything. Everybody's feet were kept very firmly on the ground and we always had a good laugh at everybody's expense, but that was the secret of our relationship.

We treated each other harshly at times, but we were entirely supportive of each other all the time.

That approach was a factor in our success in that period. If you stepped out of line or weren't up to scratch, we were our own harshest critics, but we accepted that from each other, we accepted it in the spirit it was intended.

It was never personal, it was never looked at as someone having a go at someone else for the sake of it; it was always for the benefit of the team.

Sometimes some of the criticism could have been fairly hurtful, but it kept everybody on their toes and when it was all over we all sat down and had great fun – that is the secret of our relationship for the last 30 years. We still enjoy that very close bond.

While it mightn't have looked like it on the pitch, we actually liked the Dubs, and we got on very well with them. We battered them and they battered us as much as they possibly could, but when the games were over we would have been on friendly terms with them. There would have been no animosity at all.

Even though we thought Duff was out of order in that game, he would still have been very popular with the Meath lads. He was the sort of lad that, when the game was over, he'd be the first to congratulate you, there wasn't a bad bone in his body.

The importance of that league win was crucial in ensuring we beat them again in the Leinster final that year. A lot of us on the team at that time were fairly old and we realised that our opportunity to win trophies was closing, so we were determined to win as much as we could.

None of us had won a league title. We hadn't won a Leinster before 1986 or an All-Ireland before '87, so we felt we had a limited amount of time left and we had to cash in on anything that was going… that was our attitude.

As soon as the league was over, we had a few drinks that night and that was the end of it. We were playing Louth in Drogheda in the Leinster Championship a couple of weeks later, so our attention shifted straight away to wanting to win the All-Ireland again.

We played Dublin in the Leinster final again and Charlie Redmond missed a late penalty which would have drawn the game, so it was always nip and tuck between us. We played poorly in that game, but we managed to get over it.

We struggled in some of those games because we were after going constantly since 1986. We won the All-Ireland in 1987 and we kept training on after that win because the league started again before the new year, so we had to be right for that.

By the late spring of 1988 – when we played Dublin in the League final – and the early summer we had been on the road non-stop for 18 months and the lads were getting tired and mentally fatigued more than anything else.

We struggled on and got to another All-Ireland final, which went to a replay and that carried the season on way into October again, so we were really flat by the time all that was done.

At the end of 1988 and into '89 we had a poor league and we were only starting to get warmed up by the Leinster final in '89. Mick Lyons was injured after breaking his leg, but he was coming back and he would have been ready if we had got over Dublin. However, we didn't play well and even though we got in front with a few minutes to go, Dublin got a deflected goal to beat us.

I look back on that one as the one that got away – we could easily have won three All-Irelands in-a-row.

There is a special significance about teams that win three in-a-row, so that is a regret that we didn't manage it. We could also have won the two after that in 1990 and '91 as well, but then again there were also big games in that period that we could have lost, so you win some, you lose some… but there was one more All-Ireland in that team, at least one more.

The fact that we were greedy to win leagues might have affected that.

We won the league again in 1990, but if we had approached the league like Kerry used to do and not pass any remarks on it, we might have peaked for the championship and we might have been better off.

However, we were winning games and we wanted to keep that going and get as much out of it as we could in the few years we had left.

In 1990 and '91 we left them behind us.

Everyone will remember 1991 as the one that really got away. Football players tend to remember defeats more than victories and there will always be regrets about big games that got away… the '91 final was the ultimate. A win that year would have finished the team nicely.

If we had won in 1991, I might have chosen that as the game of my life. If everybody on our team was to be honest I'd say they will admit that that game grates heavily on them even still.

I got pneumonia about a week before the All-Ireland final against Down... Bob O'Malley had broken his leg and was missing.

Because of the way the year went with the four in-a-row against Dublin, we didn't actually train that much because the games came thick and fast.

In the second-half of the semi-final win over Roscommon we were playing as good as ever. Then there was about a month before the All-Ireland final and we had to start training again; we would have been better off if the game had been a week later, that would have suited us better.

A lot of our problems started between the semi-final and the final, but that's life. In reality that team was more or less finishing its natural life-span and the likelihood is that if we had won in 1991 four or five of the team would have finished up on a high, but the disappointment of losing left us wanting to come back and win one more.

One of the great regrets I have for present players is that none of them are getting to experience the great times and the great fun that we had as a group together. The lads now will probably go through their whole football career with Meath not knowing what it was like.

Take the likes of Donal Keogan, who has spent 10 years playing with Meath – if he was around in our day he would have been a great corner-back for us. He would have had a stack of medals to his name and he would have seen the craic, the fun, the enjoyment and the great bond that existed between us.

MARTIN O'CONNELL

MEATH 0-13 CORK 0-12
All-Ireland SFC Final Replay
OCTOBER 9 1988

Martin O'Connell was awarded the Man of the Match after his magnificent display against Cork in the 1988 All-Ireland final replay (above).

★ **MEATH:** M McQuillan; B O'Malley, M Lyons, T Ferguson; C Coyle, L Harnan, **M O'Connell**; L Hayes, G McEntee; D Beggy (0-1), J Cassells (0-1), PJ Gillic; C O'Rourke (0-3), B Stafford (0-7), B Flynn (0-1). Sub: M McCabe for Gillic.

★ **CORK:** J Kerins; N Cahalane, C Corrigan, S O'Brien; T Davis, C Counihan, T Nation; S Fahy, T McCarthy; P McGrath, L Tompkins (0-8), B Coffey (0-2); D Allen (0-1), D Barry (0-1), M McCarthy. Subs:| C O'Neill for M McCarthy, O'Driscoll for McGrath.

THE ACTION

AFTER BEATING CORK to win their first All-Ireland SFC crown since 1967 just a year earlier, the Royals' rivalry with The Rebels continued in 1988 with both sides advancing to the All-Ireland final once again.

After conceding an early goal in the final on September 18 Meath battled back brilliantly with a late Brian Stafford free securing a 0-12 to 1-9 draw.

However, Meath suffered a major setback after just six minutes in the replay when Gerry McEntee was sent-off for striking Niall Cahalane, but boosted by a heroic display from Man of the Match Martin O'Connell, Meath dominated and raced into a 0-13 to 0-9 lead which, despite Cork's late rally, proved insurmountable.

It was 0-5 to 0-6 at the break, but within two minutes of the restart Brian Stafford restored parity with his only score from play. Again Cork managed to edge two points clear with Tompkins converting frees after both he and Paul McGrath had been fouled.

O'Rourke make it 0-7 to 0-8 in the 43rd minute and that sparked a Meath purple patch which saw Stafford equalise from a free before both Bernard Flynn and David Beggy were on target to make it 0-10 to 0-8. Tompkins closed the deficit to the minimum with another pointed free, but again Meath took control with Joe Cassells on the mark after Stafford's effort came off the upright. Stafford put three between the sides for the first time from a free after Beggy was fouled and when O'Rourke made it 0-13 to 0-9 with seven minutes remaining Meath looked comfortable.

Denis Allen ended Cork's 11-minute drought with a point, but as they went in search of a goal all they could manage were late points from a Tompkins free and Barry Coffey as Meath held on to make it two All-Ireland SFC titles in succession.

★★★★★

66

AFTER THE FINAL whistle of the All-Ireland final replay in 1988 it was the most amazing feeling ever; of all the All-Irelands I played in and won, it was probably the best feeling.

I remember my father was out on the field looking for me.

I could hear him shouting, 'Martin... WHERE ARE YOU?'

The crowds on the field made it difficult for us to find each other, but he did find me and it was probably the first time he had hugged me after a match since I was a child.

It was great for us and for our families, so to see my father on the field shouting for me was amazing. It was a huge thing to win an All-Ireland the way we did... with just 14 men. It was probably the best feeling ever in my career.

There are a few other games that spring to mind when I look back, but the All-Ireland final replay in 1988 is the one that sticks out in my head.

In the Leinster final against Laois in 1991 I had a good enough game and got Man of the Match, and in the National League final in 1994 against Armagh I played full-back and that game also stands out for me.

In 1994 Ger Houlihan had been doing divil and all in the league and was in top form for Armagh leading up to that final. He was after scoring a pile of goals... he was their main threat, but thankfully I managed to hold him to just a point that day, so that game sticks out a little bit.

However, to get Man of the Match in an All-Ireland final after being down to 14 men after just six minutes, that was a day I'll never forget and is certainly the game that sticks out above all others for me.

That year the league final had also gone to a replay so that proved to be invaluable experience for us ahead of what was to come later.

That league final win over Dublin in 1988 was an outstanding team performance. After the drawn game in the league final we went to San Francisco, Boston and New York on the All Star trip, but we trained for the replay over there because the replay was just a week after we came home, so we had to be ready.

The replay of the league was a good game. We had a lot of good performances by a lot of different lads that day.

At that time we had a big rivalry with Dublin, but Cork to me were our biggest rivals and I suppose it just came about because we met so often in so many big games in that period. We had met in the All-Ireland final in 1987 and then again in '88 and over the years we got to know each other very well, but it is hard to understand why the hatred became so strong in that period between us.

I don't really know where that hatred stemmed from, but there really was a hatred of each other at the time for some reason. Thankfully, all that is in the past now, we can all meet each other now and ring each other and we all get on well.

The relationship with Dublin was different.

The row that started in the 1988 league final between Kevin Foley and Kieran Duff was blown out of all proportion, but when the final whistle went that was the end of it; you shook hands and moved on.

However, the Cork rivalry just seemed to carry over. In 1988 the two teams went on their holidays at the end of the season and we ended up in the same complex in Gran Canaria and the Cork team were on one side of the pool... we were on the other side of the pool, but no one moved at all to speak to each other.

It was horrible when you look back on it now. The carry-on of two groups of grown men was terrible. We never spoke to each other... ignored each other the whole holiday, we were kind of like two rams just butting heads off each other.

Unfortunately it took the death of John Kerins to bring us together. When John got sick with cancer, I think it was Gerry McEntee who was looking after him at the time and that kind of broke the ice. When John did pass away we all went down to his funeral where we were treated like Lords and from that we have never looked back.

Unfortunately it took a death to unite the two teams.

In the drawn All-Ireland final in 1988 a couple of our big names had been hurt badly by the Cork lads. Mick Lyons got a bad elbow into the face, Brian Stafford had to get a few stitches into his lip and Colm O'Rourke had shipped a fairly heavy belt as well.

We kind of stood off them a bit that day and probably let them bully us a little bit, but in the replay it was the other way around and we weren't prepared to take any of that type of stuff again and that probably resulted in Gerry McEntee getting sent off very early on in the replay.

Between the drawn game and the replay it was very much on our minds that we wouldn't let ourselves be bullied again. We didn't decide to go out and take the heads off lads or be dirty or start fighting. Seán Boylan never sent us out to do things like that, but we were determined not to be pushed around again like we were in the drawn game.

It was in every individual's head at the time to stand up stronger. After watching the video of the drawn game we were determined it wouldn't happen again and we didn't let it happen.

In between the two games we worked on not standing off them and we were determined to be in their face from the word go.

We had a meeting on the Monday after the drawn match in the hotel in Dublin and from then on we decided that we couldn't let what had happened the previous day happen again. So we went back to training and we trained harder and got stuck into each other in training – we never gave anybody an inch. We then brought all that out onto the field a few weeks later in the replay.

The training between the two games was very intense.

We went up to Cooley in Louth for a training camp – we trained on the Saturday and played a training match amongst ourselves on the Sunday morning, but Seán Boylan had to call the game off after about 10 minutes because the lads were just going hammer and tongs at each other and he had seen enough.

There was no team talk needed after that game in Cooley. That was exactly a week before the replay and Sean had seen enough in the 10 minutes of the training game that he knew our tempers were up and we were ready to take on Cork.

It didn't take that game in Cooley to ignite our tempers. We were building for the game for the two or three weeks between the two games with our own training in Dalgan Park or in Páirc Tailteann, there was more of a bite to us in those few weeks and that was probably because the way the lads had been injured in the drawn game. Every individual knew themselves what they had to do – Seán Boylan didn't have to say a whole lot.

I remember looking back on my own performance and thinking I had been giving lads too much room, and the forwards were letting their backs out with the ball. Everybody knew deep down that we had to up our game big time or we were going to be beaten. Everybody did that without Sean or his selectors having to say anything to us.

There was a huge drive amongst the group and we weren't shy about saying things to each other. I'd say my performance in the drawn game was probably better than the one I had in the replay, but the few mistakes I did make in that game were pointed out to me by the older lads like Gerry McEntee, Colm O'Rourke and Mick Lyons.

I was only 23 or 24 at that time and I'd listen to those lads, but if those older lads made mistakes they would be told about it too. Everybody said their bit about what we should have done, what we could have done and what we had to do the next time... that is what gelled us and got us going.

The training sessions after the weekend in Cooley were tame enough. It was a fair battle down in Cooley and a lot of heavy tackling went on, so we couldn't really bring that to Dalgan Park on the Tuesday and Thursday when the supporters would be there watching. We had enough done in Cooley to get us right for the game, the rest of the week was just kicking the ball around and signing autographs for the supporters.

On the morning of the replay everybody had their own plan for what to do in the game. Sean was a great motivator and a great talker in the dressing-room, so he told us to find a balance, not to be over-aggressive... and not to stand back either.

I was always good at getting myself psyched up for a game and every man had to look after his own direct opponent and get the better of him and that is all we were focused on in the dressing-room before the game.

Gerry McEntee's sending off came from a sideline ball that I took under the Cusack Stand. That time sidelines were taken off the ground, so they were slow and lethargic and nine times out of 10 they were just kicked as high and as far as you could. PJ Gillic went up for my sideline, but he lost the ball and as it hopped, Niall Cahalane came in for the breaking ball.

PJ made a wild pull on the ball, but missed it and got Cahalane. And as he was falling Gerry gave him a little bit of a clip. I wouldn't say it was much of a box, it was more of a slap than anything else, and then all hell broke loose.

It was right under the referee's nose so he probably had no other choice only to send Gerry off. Having gone down to 14 men just a few months earlier when Kevin Foley was sent off against Dublin in the league final we knew what we had to do, and we knew there was no need to panic.

Everybody upped their game, including me, when Gerry was sent off. I was pleading with the referee not to send Gerry off, but he did and when you see a man like Gerry McEntee just turning his head and walking off it was not a nice sight – I'm sure Gerry never thought he'd experience something like that, but from then on the lads really knuckled down and upped the ante big time.

With 10 minutes to go in that game, my tongue was hanging out, but we all knew we just had to keep going and thankfully it turned out okay.

When Gerry went off we did look to Tony (Brennan), Pat (Reynolds) and Sean for some words from the sideline, but at the end of the day it was down to ourselves to react. I think Tony Davis might have been their spare man, but Colm O'Rourke came out to around the half-forward line, PJ Gillic also drifted back a bit more and we ended up with three or four midfielders... and there seemed to be loads of room inside for our forwards to utilise.

I wouldn't have been the greatest passer of the ball, but I had loads of space to aim for in our forwards and I just kicked it as hard as I could. Thankfully, Bernard Flynn started to get into the game and Brian Stafford managed to pick up a few passes and it was just one of those things where everyone put their shoulder to the wheel and upped their game. I know Sean is a great communicator and motivator, but when you are out there in the heat of battle you do things yourself and things start to fall into place; you adapt and survive and hope things go your way.

I often look back at the DVD of that game and Colm O'Rourke got away with murder that day. He was involved in everything and was almost even refereeing the game. We just took the bull by the horns and got over the line.

Mick Lyons was constantly shouting at lads to track back and if we happened to get a break we had space up front. We crowded midfield and if we were fouled our drill was to put the ball down quickly and Liam Harnan would come up from behind and drive the ball in quick to stop Cork from getting their extra man back into defence.

Nowadays, teams often plan for scenarios where they might go down to 14 men, but that possibility never came into our heads; thankfully we figured it out on the field. Whether it was luck or experience some might debate it, but I'd put it down to experience because we had gone through the same type of scenario in the league final just a few months earlier.

It helped having men like Flynn and Stafford inside to capitalise on our quick ball. Bernard hadn't had a particularly good year up to that point, he had been taken off a few times, but thankfully that day he came into himself and he was involved in many of the scoring situations, either by scoring himself or being fouled for frees which Brian Stafford converted.

I didn't have to change my game much after Gerry was sent off. I was marking Paul McGrath, he was the new kid on the block, but I just stuck with him. I had been moved onto Barry Coffey in the first game and I got the better of him that day, which was huge.

Then for the replay Sean made a few changes and he named Colm Coyle at left half-back and put me at right half-back, that's why I was wearing No 5 that day. Myself and Colm went to Sean after he named the team and we both said we'd prefer to play on the opposite sides to where we had been selected, so we changed sides… and I ended up on Paul McGrath, Colm marked Barry Coffey and we managed to stop those threats.

I didn't change my approach much after the sending off. I might have gambled a little bit more by leaving McGrath in behind me once or twice or letting him out in front of me a couple of times, but overall I just played my normal game.

There was nothing really said about the sending off in the dressing-room at half-time. It was all encouragement and Gerry was there telling everyone to keep it going. There were no sad faces, we just got on with it. No one was feeling sorry for themselves, especially Gerry McEntee or Seán Boylan; they were just encouraging everyone to give their all.

Of course, after the game we all had sympathy for Gerry, but we won it for him, so it didn't matter

I was always comfortable in the game and I was always confident we would win it. In the last 10 minutes and the last three or four balls were hopping in and around the edge of the square with Mick Lyons shouting at us to get them out. I kicked two or three balls out the field straight to Cork men and the pressure came straight back on us again, but Mick kept at us and we weathered the storm.

Nowadays you would keep control of the ball and hold onto it, but back in 1988 it was just all about getting rid of it, so Mick was a huge plus in behind us urging us to do just that.

I was surprised to be named Man of the Match.

I thought I had played better in the first game, but I knew I had a fairly good enough game… however I was still surprised to be named. To get it was fantastic, but as I said to RTE after the game, I think there should have been an award for all of the players. To win with 14 men and with the performance all of us put in, including the lads who came on, it was a great team performance.

To win back-to-back All-Irelands was an acknowledgement of just how good a team we were, but we probably should have got another two or three All-Irelands.

We were probably a bit lucky to win the two we won, but to lose the two we lost in 1990 and '91 that was cruel. That team deserved to win both those All-Irelands.

We had a bit of a blip in the 1989 Leinster final against Dublin when Mick Lyons was injured and a few little things didn't go our way. Vinny Murphy scored a goal that went in off the top of my shoulder and we never recovered from that, but we came back in 1990 and '91 and just missed out. I think that team definitely deserved four All-Irelands.

To win two in-a-row is a sign of a really good team, but I believe we could have got another little bit more out of that great team.

While winning in 1988 was the greatest feeling ever, winning another one in 1996 was huge too. It was a different set-up and a different team. I was 33 or 34 at that time, so to win one at that age was great. I knew my time was coming to an end. I had been there from when Seán Boylan took over in 1982, so to be still winning an All-Ireland 14 years later was amazing.

I was very lucky to win three All-Irelands, but to lose two was heart breaking. However, to win again after losing in 1990 and '91 was another great part of my career.

Myself and Colm Coyle were still part of it in 1996… Brendan Reilly had been there for a while and John McDermott was another of the leaders, but to win it with the young lads who had produced the goods at minor level was amazing.

Most of our team of the 80s and early-90s never had much underage success, but lads like Graham Geraghty, Mark O'Reilly, Darren Fay, Paddy Reynolds and Trevor Giles were after winning underage All-Irelands… getting to play with those lads who were so confident was simply amazing.

BERNARD FLYNN

ST COLMCILLE'S 1-11 DUNDERRY 2-7
Meath IFC Final Replay
Páirc Tailteann
NOVEMBER 27 1988

There were so many amazing days in Croke Park for Bernard Flynn, including the historic summer of 1991 (above), but leading St Colmcille's to senior ranks in 1988 is a day he remembers more than any other.

★ **ST COLMCILLE'S:** R Carr; B Beakey, B O'Malley, M Brodigan; P Beakey, J Stafford, G Berrill; C Hilliard (0-1), M O'Neill; **B Flynn (1-10)**, J Carr, D Black; B Watters, G Campbell, D Brodigan. Subs: N Cooney for Campbell, Campbell for Cooney, J O'Boyle for Campbell.

★ **DUNDERRY:** M Kelly; P Leavy, O Callaghan, P Gibbons; M Newman, P Cahill, R Rennicks; P Fay (1-2), N Rennicks (0-1); D McGurty, T Dowd, B Rennicks; B Fulham, D Hickey (1-0), J Brady (0-4). Sub: P Gough for Newman.

THE ACTION

PLAYED ON NOVEMBER 27 in 1988 the IFC decider replay between St Colmcille's and Dunderry became known as the 'Bernard Flynn final' after the Meath star had scored 1-10 of his side's winning tally in their 1-11 to 2-7 victory.

It was Flynn and Bob O'Malley's third medal won following replays that year, having already claimed the All-Ireland SFC crown and the NFL title, but this was probably one of Flynn's greatest performances.

Just as was the case in the replay, St Colmcille's only had two scorers in the drab drawn encounter as Flynn clipped over three points while Brian Watters grabbed the only goal in the 1-3 to 0-6 stalemate. John Brady accounted for three of Dunderry's points, with Niall Rennicks kicking the other three in a dire game.

The replay wasn't played until two weeks later because of Dunderry's involvement in the IHC latter stages, but that game was far from a bore as St Colmcille's recovered from the concession of two 'soft' goals to claim the title – with Flynn the hero, grabbing a late point to seal the win.

Having lost the final the previous year, Dunderry were keen not to slip up again and looked in a strong position as a couple of goalkeeping errors gifted goals to Phil Fay from long range after just four minutes and to Derek Hickey a few minutes later after Ruairc Carr had dropped Brendan Fulham's cross.

Those goals boosted Dunderry to a 2-3 to 0-4 lead, but then Flynn started to find his groove that won him an All Star that year. He kicked two points in succession to close the gap to 0-6 to 2-3 by half-time. Flynn bagged a brilliant goal with 12 minutes remaining after great work by Neil Cooney and O'Malley to boost St Colmcille's chances. Fay responded with a point on the counter-attack for Dunderry, but in the dying moments, just when another draw seemed likely, Joe Carr picked out Flynn from a free and the Meath star kicked the winning point to spark wild celebrations in the St Colmcille's camp.

Dunderry went on to win the IFC in 1990.

★★★★★

❝

IN 1983 WE won the junior championship and won promotion to the intermediate grade which was massive for the club. The game that stood out the most for me in that campaign was the semi-final against Dunboyne, as I ended up marking Seán Boylan.

Sean was manager of the Meath team at the time having just taken over the role at the end of 1982 and he was getting the Meath team ready to play Dublin in the first round of the NFL later that afternoon, after our game, so there were 20,000 jammed into Navan that day.

I had never met Sean before and here he was at left half-back marking me.

At half-time in the game he rubbed me on top of the head and said, 'Bernard, you've a great future ahead of you. I'm going in to get the Meath team ready here… so best of luck to you'.

We went on to win the junior that year, but then we lost the intermediate final against Slane in 1984. We were the favourites to win that day, but we didn't perform well, so that was a big blow to us… it was a huge setback.

Then we came again in 1988.

In the semi-final against St Michael's I scored eight points to get us over the line, but the battles we had with St Michael's back then were unbelievable.

The craic my father and Martin O'Connell's father used to have running up and down the line… the battles they used to have were ferocious. We played them a lot over those few years, we had some great games. They were a massive obstacle for us to get over.

We went into the final in 1988 as slight favourites, I'd say, but in fairness to Dunderry they had a good bit of homework done on us. They had lost the 1987 final, but with myself and Bob O'Malley coming off the back of the All-Ireland replay win over Cork we were probably just slight favourites for that final.

Dunderry had a very well balanced side at the time, well-drilled and physically very strong. The first game ended 1-3 to 0-6, but there was a lot of pulling and dragging in the first game and a huge amount of stuff went on off the ball.

The same happened in the replay, but there was more intent in playing football the second day out.

In the drawn game I was being double marked and they targeted Bob as well. To be honest, we didn't play as well as we should have done and I know myself I got involved in a lot of off the ball stuff. Every few minutes I was involved in something with somebody – but they had their homework done and they did well, and hats off to them.

I got the three points of our tally, but I probably missed a couple of chances that I wouldn't normally miss as well. At the end of the game I wasn't happy, O'Malley wasn't happy; it was just one of those games that left me frustrated.

The emphasis on defensive play at the time caught both teams off guard; we were both very defensive in the game and at that time we had a brilliant young attacking team, but we didn't play like that. We got sucked into a dogfight.

In the drawn game I came in for a lot of focused attention and rightly so, I suppose. That was just the way it was, it was no problem because I was coming off the Meath team so I'd come to expect that.

However, an incident happened towards the end of the match. I was being tightly marked by Ray Rennicks and fair play he got stuck into me, but I waited until the end to get my own back.

As the game wore down I was more intent on watching the referee because I was determined to do him right as the referee blew the final whistle, so I couldn't get the line. And I did.

I hit him right as the referee was blowing the final whistle.

To be honest, as he hit the ground I think I might have walked on him as well – but then as I moved towards the stand I could see my now wife, Madeline, calling me up because my father was fighting in the stand.

I stormed straight up the stand to get stuck in and help my father, still in my jersey... and into the middle of the crowd where I ended up in the row too.

I know the Rennicks' well. I played with Bill at underage, they are a wonderful family. I remember Brian well, they really are a great family, but that day I got involved in the row in the middle of the stand with a few of them.

It took me about 10 minutes to get back into the dressing-room after that game and my blood was boiling. I have a good temper, but I can honestly say that I never focused more between a drawn match and a replay than I did between those two games. I was a man possessed... so was O'Malley.

We had two weeks to recover and prepare for the replay.

We had a four or five man leadership team including myself, Bob, and the likes of Jackser Kavanagh, Brendan Beakey and Colm Hilliard... wonderful, wonderful guys, and we knew that if we did not win that replay we would never get up to senior.

After winning the junior final in 1983 and then losing the intermediate final in '84 we thought we'd get there, but after four years without winning it with a really good young team, I genuinely felt that the '88 final was last chance saloon for a lot of our older, good players.

After the drawn game we made a pact not to leave it behind us and Jackser Kavanagh, who I would rate as one of the most influential people in my career, pointed out a few things we needed to get right for the replay. Along with Mattie Kerrigan and Seán Boylan... those men had a massive impact on my career,

Jackser was a wily old fox. We didn't use O'Malley in the drawn match the way we should have done. O'Malley was also in the backs, but in games we needed to win and drive on O'Malley would come to midfield. He was so influential with the ball in his hands. Me and him had telepathy... when I'd move he'd automatically know where I was.

He came to midfield in the replay and he gave me the brilliant final pass for the goal that I scored in the top corner, but it was all about the wonderfully timed pass from O'Malley.

We had a very good way of playing football, it didn't look that way in the drawn match, so we promised ourselves we would implement that in the replay.

Dunderry bullied us in the drawn match and we said we wouldn't let that happen again. It was a bit like what happened us in the drawn match of the All-Ireland final against Cork that year too.

In the replay we were hit by a couple of sucker punches when Ruairc Carr made a couple of mistakes and if that had happened in the drawn match we would have been gone. If it had happened in the year or two before we would have been gone too, but as a group we were so mentally tuned in and those mistakes didn't faze us.

We had a young enough back-line and those mistakes were a blow and right sucker punches, but we came back up the field each time with a crucial score which kept us in it.

At half-time we were happy with what had happened. We were still in touch despite what had happened.

They led from the fourth minute to the 52nd minute. They were well ahead, I don't think they could actually believe what was happening, but we genuinely didn't panic.

I went a bit deeper and I wasn't as static as I was in the drawn match. I kept moving and the boys played a lot more through me early on, so it kept Dunderry on the back foot. They changed their marker on me fairly early on.

We had Colm Hilliard at midfield and he was hitting hard and dispossessing people; we were much more physical than we had been, and we played to our strengths much more.

We talked about different scenarios happening in the game. I was prepared for a lot of treatment in that final, but I knew after a couple of minutes that Dunderry weren't interested in that.

The slickness of our movement blew them away.

We were hit with sucker punches, but some of our play back then was like something you'd see from Dublin now. I was a yard quicker in my mind and in my brain, but we moved the ball so fast and so slick.

None of us allowed them time to stand in positions to be able to hit or nail us, particularly myself. All credit to Dunderry that day, I got no 'special' treatment, which might have been a bit naïve, they probably should have tried to put us off a bit more.

When they were ahead by so much and got the goals at the right times they really should have closed us out, but they didn't; our movement from start to finish kept us in the game.

Dunderry were brilliant after the game.

They came over and had a few drinks with us and even the fellas over their club were great men, there was always great respect there.

The replay was as good a final as we've seen, it was a great game of football. I remember getting the goal and a few super points, but I can't put into words the satisfaction I felt after that win.

After the game I looked at Jackser, Colm Hilliard, Gerry Berrill, Brendan Beakey, Gunner Brady… stalwarts of our club who had tried so hard for years, and the sense of relief was immense.

The joy I felt that day was very similar to the year before in 1987 when Colm O'Rourke, Gerry McEntee, Joe Cassells, Mick Lyons... all those lads finally won the All-Ireland their years of service and hard work deserved. To see the outpouring of emotion was brilliant.

When I was thinking about what game to pick I was thinking about the National League final against Dublin or the All-Ireland against Down in 1991 or the under-21 game against Offaly when I scored plenty, but winning this championship meant so much to my family, to Jackser Kavanagh, to Paddy Brannigan, to Pat O'Neill, to Tommy Weir, to Brendan Beakey, to Gerry Berrill – the fellas that drove me and coached me and looked after me.

To see what it meant to them is why it matters most to me and I was able to deliver one of my best games when it mattered most to them.

I picked the 1988 Intermediate Championship replay out of respect to the people of St Colmcille's. What Pat O'Neill, Paddy Brannigan, Jacker Kavanagh and my own father did for me and the likes of Bob O'Malley can't be recognised enough. Those men minded us better than they minded their own kids.

One night before a big game with St Colmcille's I couldn't sleep at night with a bad toothache. Pat O'Neill came and collected me at my house at 1am, brought me into his dentist practise at that hour of the night and told me to sit in the chair and not ask any questions. Whatever he gave me certainly did the trick; he killed the pain completely and I was able to play the next day.

We also had our altercations, but Pat never held a grudge – a great man.

Nowadays, if a county player is after winning an All-Ireland final and then goes back to his club to play in an intermediate final they wouldn't be too bothered. They'd go about their appearance and whatever, but I vowed to get back and help my club as much as I could.

We had a good time for a week after the All-Ireland win, but myself and O'Malley got back to our club as quick as we could after the All-Ireland win because we were so determined... that had a big impact on the club and particularly for the younger players.

We won the NFL that year after a replay too, so I think our experience with replays in 1988 certainly stood to myself and Bob when we went training.

Myself and O'Malley can always hold our head high. I left to set up home, family and business in Mullingar – that was the hardest and toughest decision that I ever made, but I still hold St Colmcille's so dear.

To this day, I still struggle with that decision to move to Mullingar, I still don't know if it was the right one, but I had eight or nine great years with Mullingar Shamrocks. I won four in-a-row with them and was involved in training and coaching, but always in the back of mind was St Colmcille's.

I made the decision to change and to this day I still struggle with whether it was the right one or not. I'm 29 years in Mullingar now, it has been a huge part of my life and I might never have the kids I have now without moving here.

I can honestly say that I gave every ounce I had in every game I ever played for St Colmcille's. I never shirked and I always tried my best – county players don't always do that. I think that was the difference for me and O'Malley after the All-Ireland final.

O'Malley was a brilliant, brilliant club man.

KEVIN FOLEY
(& FINIAN MURTAGH)

MEATH 2-10 DUBLIN 0-15
Leinster SFC First Round Third Replay
Croke Park
JULY 6 1991

Kevin Foley scored the greatest goal in Meath football history when he shot to the Dublin net in the closing minutes of the 1991 four-game saga, though Meath's summer would end in heartbreak after losing to Down in the All-Ireand final (above).

★ **MEATH**: M McQuillan; B O'Malley, M Lyons, P Lyons; **K Foley (1-0)**, L Harnan, M O'Connell; L Hayes, PJ Gillic; D Beggy (0-1), C O'Rourke, T Dowd; C Coyle, B Stafford (1-6), B Flynn (0-2). Subs: **F Murtagh** for P Lyons, G McEntee for Murtagh, M McCabe (0-1) for Flynn.

★ **DUBLIN**: J O'Leary; M Deegan, G Hargan, M Kennedy; T Carr, K Barr, E Heery; J Sheedy, P Bealin; C Redmond (0-5), P Curran (0-2), N Guiden (0-4); D Sheehan (0-2), P Clarke, M Galvin (0-2). Subs: R Holland, for Carr, J McNally for Clarke, V Murphy for Redmond.

THE ACTION

THERE HAVE BEEN many iconic goals scored in GAA but none compare to Kevin Foley's wonder goal that helped to finally bring the curtain down on the greatest saga in GAA history... the Meath vs Dublin four in-a-row in 1991.

Martin O'Connell won possession close to the end-line in the corner, between the Canal End and the Cusack Stand, and despite heavy pressure from Declan Sheehan he managed to get the ball to Mick Lyons... Lyons delivered a short foot pass to Mattie McCabe down along the Cusack Stand sideline.

McCabe managed to execute a quick release under pressure to Liam Harnan, who punted over halfway towards Tommy Dowd, who held off Ray Holland and managed to knock the ball into Colm O'Rourke's path where he was fouled by Mick Kennedy.

O'Rourke's quick free from the middle of the 65-metre line was played behind David Beggy into the shadow of the Hogan Stand. Beggy had one hop and one solo before off-loading to Kevin Foley, who in turn quickly gave it off to PJ Gillic inside the '45'. Without hesitation Gillic played it to the in-rushing Dowd, who then linked up for a penetrating one-two with O'Rourke and, from the edge of the small square, Dowd handpassed to Foley, who finished from close range to draw the game... the greatest goal ever scored.

The rest, as they say, is history. Mattie McCabe won the next kickout for Meath before Liam Hayes and Gillic combined to pick out Beggy, who fired over what proved to be the winning point.

★★★★★

66

ON MY WAY up the field as I was following the play I passed Mattie McCabe around the middle and he told me to keep going forward. His thinking was that he would bring one of the defenders away from the goal area, and that no one would be bothered to pick me up as I went upfield.

That was Mattie being clever.

He was a very, *very* good player, a very clever player and he knew exactly what he was doing by creating a bit of space for me… and I certainly needed lots of space.

When we were three points down and the ball was on our end-line my idea was just to try to get forward and get numbers up there and, hopefully, something would fall to one of us.

We played lots of games like that in training.

We would play 10- or 11-a-side games trying to move the ball quickly or keep possession, so that was something we had practiced a lot.

Time was running out quickly at that stage, so you'd be inclined to drift forward anyway and if you happened to arrive in a place where you got the ball that was well and good… if you didn't get it you just dropped back.

Play developed as it happened. It wasn't a pre-arranged move or anything like that, but players knew what to be doing, where to be moving and to be looking for the ball.

In training we often played games where it would be 'no solo and no hop' or 'one solo and one hop' with the idea to move the ball as fast as we could and get into space where the player with the ball would never run out of options.

The idea was to get the ball up the field as quickly as we could before Dublin could get back into a defensive position.

We won that ball on the end-line, so they had clearly pushed up and left space somewhere out the field – it was up to us at that stage to go and find that space.

I was wing half-back at that stage of the game and was on the opposite side of the field when the move started. As the play moved on I was just inclined to drift forward. Sometimes you'd be an option to take a pass, and other times you'd be just making space for someone else by being there.

I just kept drifting forward and when I met Mattie in the middle of the field

I was thinking that he should be the one to move forward, and that I'd head back to defence, but Mattie was taking one of their defenders away from their defence and he told me to keep going.

I'm not sure who I was marking at that stage; it could have been Vinny Murphy, but he obviously didn't track me as I moved forward. Mattie's man followed him out the field so that left space for me to wander into.

I was involved in the middle of the move and then kept going and I had to be conscious that I didn't end up in the square.

The play kept moving down the far side, the Cusack Stand side… where Tommy Dowd gave it to Colm O'Rourke and he gave it back to him all very quickly.

Not that I was famous for scoring goals, but I was still conscious of not ending up inside the square and I tried to make sure I was just arriving running onto the ball rather than getting it standing still.

I'm sure Tommy got a surprise when he got through and saw me at the edge of the square, but he passed it to me anyway because there wasn't anybody else he could give to and that is basically how it happened.

I never saw John O'Leary in my vision at all as I kicked the ball.

Liam Hayes gave me a couple of photos about a year after the game and in those John O'Leary is diving on my right foot, but to me I was kicking into an empty net as far as I could see.

The photos made it look like he got nearer to me than he actually did, but I don't think I could miss from there. When Tommy gave me the ball I had an open net, or at least three-quarters of the goals, to kick it into… so no way I was missing that. As I turned to head back to my position Brian Stafford hit me with a left hook for some reason; maybe he was jealous, I certainly remember that.

That goal still only made it a draw, so it was my job to get back into defence as quickly as I could and hope they didn't get up the field to score a winner after all that.

As I mentioned Vinny Murphy was left up the field, so with me up one end he was all on his own down the other end – I had to get back as quick as I could. That was all I was thinking, I had to get back to where I should be.

It wouldn't have surprised me if the final whistle had gone immediately after

I had scored the goal. Tommy Howard made lots of draws out of those game; he always seemed to blow them up when the scores were level, but maybe he was under instructions to keep going for that one. I was surprised when the whistle didn't go with the next kickout.

I had just about made it back into my position by the time the next ball was kicked out, so I was just a spectator for that. We won possession straight away and got it in fairly quickly.

A bit like myself, you probably wouldn't have been betting on it being David Beggy as the one who would come up with what proved to be the winning point, but he did the job… he was well able to do that.

Jinxy was a very important player for us. He had his own way of doing things, but he was always impossible to mark. A lot of the time we didn't know what he was going to do and he didn't know what he was going to do, but the Dubs certainly didn't know what he was going to do. He created havoc when he got the ball.

Before the fourth game against Dublin, Sean had brought us to Scotland. It was all arranged pretty quickly and we ended up near Lough Lomond, I think. We arrived on the Friday night and had a rough session in the bar and had an even rougher training session the next morning where a lot of lads were running around with sore heads and puking. The drinking or training probably didn't make much difference, but it was good to get a break and freshen up things and have a bit of craic.

That was Sean's idea when he took us away. It took us away from all the hype for a while. Sean was good on the psychology of the game and keeping lads fresh and keeping them interested and sweet… that was his strength.

I had a good relationship with Sean; he was the boss. He never did me any harm. I was dropped a couple of times, but if you are dropped there is usually a reason for it, so I had the height of respect for Sean and all he did for me and for the team.

You would always be disappointed when you were dropped, but if you are dropped it is generally because your form has dipped, or you weren't playing well or you were lacking in confidence a bit. You'd be just hoping that you'd get your chance again and get back in to do your stuff.

The overwhelming feeling at the final whistle was mostly relief.

Any time you beat Dublin is a great day, but at that stage Dublin were thinking they couldn't get past us... we had the upper-hand on them. A lot of that was in the head, but we were able to pull it out of the bag in that last game and get ahead of them.

We didn't get beaten by them too many times. I think I only lost once to Dublin in the championship.

Looking back, that was a great time, but it would have been a whole lot more special for us and for the Meath people if we had gone on to win the All-Ireland. We went out the following week after beating Dublin and got it hard to draw with Wicklow, so that brought us down to earth fairly quick.

It would have been a great finish to a lot of our careers if we had won the All-Ireland that year. A lot of us were pushing on at that stage. In truth, as a team we were probably past our best, but it would have been a nice way to finish. Unfortunately we didn't manage to get there.

For the final in 1991, Colm O'Rourke was sick and Mick Lyons was injured during the game; we just ran out of numbers and ran out of luck at the very end. Pity.

Looking back at that time, our never-say-die attitude was so important to us. Knowing we were always capable of getting back in a game was a great thing to have and Dublin also knew that we were never beaten – that also gave us an edge.

Knowing they were never going to put us away certainly played on their minds. We had the players to give us that belief. We had very good scoring forwards and players like PJ Gillic, who was a fabulous player and probably underrated a little bit.

He was a savage man to win ball; he was as strong as an ox and could kick his scores too. None of us ever gave up, there was no point in giving up until the final whistle. If you are beaten at the final whistle then you are beaten, but never before that; while the game is still going on you always had a chance.

The rivalry with Dublin was a special rivalry.

At that time, we were the best team in Leinster and they were the second best; that is where the rivalry comes from... if you were no good you wouldn't have a rivalry with anybody.

Every team likes to beat Dublin... wouldn't every team like to beat them now?

It is great to beat them any day, whether it is a challenge match or a league game… it was great to beat them, but especially in the championship. Back then if you beat Dublin they were gone, there were no second chances; they couldn't come back and have another go at you.

I enjoyed some decent games against Dublin in my career. I got sent-off in plenty of them too, but those things can happen. I really enjoyed the games against Dublin, I always did.

A lot of the stories that surrounded the All Star trip to America in 1988 and the so-called troubles between the Meath lads and the Dublin lads was bullshit to be honest.

There was nothing out of the ordinary from that trip, as I remember. There was the odd row in the game, but there are rows in every game. I think Kieran Duff made a bit more of it for his TV programme than there was, and one of the newspaper journalists was talking like he was in the Meath camp and knew what was going on – but he was never near it.

I did get sent-off a few times, that was probably down to my temperament more than anything else. Sometimes it just got the better of me, and I can't have a lot of complaints.

Any time I was sent-off I probably deserved it, but I did learn to be cleverer, more disciplined, because there is not a lot you can do for your team when you are sitting on the sideline. You have to temper that a bit and try to stay on the pitch. I probably figured that out a bit better as my career went along.

I can't say that any one game against Dublin sticks out in my mind as been more enjoyable than another one. I remember one game in the league where we hammered them; I'd say it was the only time we actually hammered them. We were totally dominant that day.

Any day we played Dublin was a special occasion and any day we beat them made it even better. I remember the games against Dublin with plenty of joy because we won most of them, but those games were always tough and always in front of a big crowd.

You'd be conscious of the crowd in those games because you could always hear them when you did something good or something went wrong, they were great occasions. Croke Park can be intimidating, but it is a great place to play and there is nothing like going out in front of a full house in Croke Park and playing your heart out.

Every time we played Dublin we learned. That is how you gain experience and how you learn how to win games by playing against the best. We learned how to stay in games when we were not playing well… and we learned how to figure out how to win.

I remember Colm O'Rourke saying that in his early days there was always a thought that there was no way Meath could beat Dublin, but as the years went on that changed because it got to the stage where we believed there was no way Dublin could beat us. That mentality was important.

In terms of regrets, I think a lot of us would have been happy if we had won three All-Irelands, but it wasn't to be. When you were a kid the dream was always to win one All-Ireland, but as a group we certainly had another All-Ireland in us.

A few teams have won two All-Irelands, but if we had won three it would have moved us into a different league. However, we didn't get there and nobody counts the losers medals. We certainly had the talent to win three, but unfortunately it wasn't to be.

The first All-Ireland would have to be the highlight of my career.

I had only started to play with Meath the year before, so for someone who was only into their Meath career I had an All-Ireland medal after playing maybe just six championship games. I got my All-Ireland very quickly, whereas a lot of players had played minor through to senior and never got that All-Ireland medal.

A lot of the lads that played with me had been playing a long time before they won their first All-Ireland. You can't pass your first All-Ireland as a highlight of a career.

FINIAN MURTAGH

Blitzing past Mick Holden in 1983 (above), Finian Murtagh was an electrifying presence in the Meath attack, but the Navan O'Mahonys star remembers the 1991 saga against Dublin because it was his final appearance in green and gold.

"

MY VIEW OF the fourth game against Dublin in 1991 is probably completely different to what anybody else's will be, because it ended up being the last time I ever played for Meath… and it turned out to be a very short appearance.

That win over Dublin, to eventually get over the line, was a fantastic achievement, but without a shadow of a doubt that performance in that fourth game was the worst display of the four games. We didn't play well that day at all, but we hung in there and we got our reward for that and our persistence and never-say-die attitude was a big thing for us in those days. But for me personally, it was a tough day.

I had been a sub for the first game of that series against Dublin, but I never got a run. The Tuesday night after that first game I picked up a bad injury in training when I damaged muscle and bones in my back, so I wasn't fit for the second game... or the third game either.

I eventually got back training for the week after the third game and ahead of the, by now famous, trip to Scotland.

That trip to Scotland was a brilliant weekend.

It was one of my greatest memories in my time as a Meath player; if you ask any of the boys that were on that trip they will tell you it was one of the best memories they have of that time... a fantastic weekend.

As well as being a great weekend, it was also so important for the team. Mentally the trip away was brilliant; physically I don't think it did us any good at all because when you see the way we played in that fourth game we were flat... but mentally it brought what was already a close group even closer together.

We had great craic that weekend, absolutely fantastic craic and when you look back on your career it is not only the games you reflect on, it is about the enjoyment of your career and the craic you had with the other players.

The greatest memories are the times we spent as a group together, rather than the actual games we played. The games, at times, were so tough and so hard that they were quickly forgotten about and often went by in a flash, but those trips away... the training weekends, the training sessions... the nights out... that's where some of the best memories are.

On that trip to Scotland we had a great night out together on the Friday night. I've no idea what time we went to bed. Then we trained on Saturday and Sunday. The Saturday morning was hell... Oh Lord Jaysus Christ, most fellas were just falling around the place, but we got through it.

I trained that weekend.

I hadn't trained at all for four weeks, so I was mad to get back at it and make a bit of an impression and hope to get a chance of a game.

I was included on the panel for the fourth game – I was mad to play. They brought me on early when Padraig Lyons picked up an injury and around about that time Colm O'Rourke also picked up a really heavy bang to the head, so he ended up going off too.

That injury that O'Rourke got left him out cold. When the doctor, Jack Finn, was treating him on the sideline, Sean asked Jack how he was because he had wanted to make a change, but Jack just shouted back up the sideline… 'Hold on there Sean… I think he's starting to come to!'

Can you imagine that happening now with all the HIA regulations and safety precautions that are in place? No chance… that would be a mortal sin now.

When he did eventually get back to his feet he was still clearly shook and, to be honest, he probably shouldn't have come back on.

Jack Finn was a real football doctor and he wanted players on the field at all cost and as a player, that's what you wanted. Jack would never tell you there was no hope or that you might be out for six months. Your leg could be in your hand, but Jack would do his best to have you right for a game.

I'd say I was only on for 10 or 15 minutes, and then I was taken off again.

I wasn't fit to play, it was as simple as that. I thought, and everyone else thought, I was fit enough to play, but I wasn't half fit enough… I wasn't at the right level at all.

That lack of fitness showed immediately as I wasn't at the races for the first couple of balls at all. To be honest the management were right to take me off because I was playing terrible.

I was delighted to get on, but I remember going for a ball and Mick Kennedy beat me to it. I had two or three yards on him, but he still got there before me and I remember thinking… *Jaysus… if Mick Kennedy is beating me to a ball, I'm in trouble here!*

I was thick as an ass when I was taken off, but when I was thinking about it afterwards, they were dead right. I wasn't next to near fit enough to be playing and sadly that was my last game… I never got another chance after that.

That's probably why it's my greatest memory… not my happiest memory.

You can imagine what it was like in the dressing-room after the game, it was euphoric, but I was sat there with a big thick head on me, feeling sorry for myself.

Jack Finn, who was my doctor since I was a kid and someone I always got on well with, came over to me and put his arm around me and said, 'You know what Fino, it's better to have one fella envying you… than 10,000 feeling sorry for you'.

I'll never forget that. I told him he was dead right, but it didn't make it any easier. I was annoyed at the time, but it was more because I didn't do well enough when I had come on. In hindsight they were right to take me off, when I watched the game again I was useless, they shouldn't have put me on at all really because I wasn't fit enough. In that type of situation all I wanted to do was play so I wasn't going to say no when the call came to go on. I wasn't going to tell Seán Boylan that I didn't think I was ready. I thought I was going to play well, but quickly realised I wasn't right at all.

I only really remember Kevin Foley's goal from watching it back on TV. I can't really remember it happening at the time. No matter how well Dublin were playing at the time, they probably always had that doubt in their minds when they played us.

I don't know if there was the belief in us that we could win the game, but we never gave up, whereas Dublin always doubted themselves when they played us.

We wore teams down.

They were always wary of the fact that no matter how hard they worked, or how far ahead they were, we were never beaten and that played on their minds until the final whistle.

In the closing stages of that game it was caution to the wind and we just bombed forward. Kevin Foley played off the cuff anyway. You wouldn't be telling Kevin how to play the game, he just played the way he played.

He followed the attack that time. Most other times he felt he didn't have to do that and he just stayed where he was, but for some reason he kept following the attack in that moment and as lads threw caution to the wind it was one last hurrah – and he ended up in the right place at the right time.

We used to do a simple drill from one end of the field to the other in training. That drill could go on for 10 or 15 minutes and you'd be whacked after it. The idea was to stay with the play, not fall behind and eventually the ball would come back to you. That is exactly what happened that day, lads just followed the ball and made sure they stayed in the play and it worked out brilliantly.

I didn't get a run for the rest of the year after that day. Sean was picking the team and they were winning games, so there was no place for me to get on.

The only reason I got a run, an opportunity, in that fourth game was because the team hadn't been playing that well up to that point and Sean wanted to do something different. I remember at a training session in Gormanston after the second game, Pat Reynolds saying to me, 'If only you were fit!' He was implying that if I had been fit then I might have been picked. O'Rourke was there when he said that and he replied to him that I had been fit for the first game… but they wouldn't put me on!

Looking back at those games, I don't know how we always managed to stay in games that looked to be getting away from us. I have often thought about that so-called 'never-say-die' spirit… I think a lot of it had to do with Sean's attitude of… *We never give up!*

Lads like Mick Lyons, Gerry McEntee, Colm O'Rourke, Joe Cassells… they were hugely influential and really set the tone. We used to question what drove Gerry McEntee to keep playing. Every time he went out onto the field he put his professional career as a surgeon on the line, but he didn't see it like that at all and when you saw his commitment you would follow him.

He was regarded as the top surgeon in the country and he still wanted to play with us, so we certainly didn't want to let him down.

We made sure that whatever he asked us to do we would do, simply because he was doing it even though he had so much to lose. Mick and Joe were the same.

That never-say-die spirit and will to win came from a determination not to let those lads down and the last man you wanted to let down was Seán Boylan… he had your corner no matter what. Numerous times when you were feeling down Sean would put his arm around you and have a chat; he was a great man for that.

Winning that series against Dublin meant nothing at the time because we didn't go on and win the All-Ireland. That was the way that team was at the time; nothing less than an All-Ireland was the target. I guarantee that most of the lads from that time will agree that while we did win two All-Irelands, we definitely left two others behind us.

To be fair to Cork in 1990, they showed great courage to come back and beat us after being beaten twice in 1987 and '88. That was a measure of that Cork side that they bounced back and won in 1989 and then beat us in '90.

I watched an interview with AP McCoy recently. He was the greatest jockey of all time, but he didn't really speak about his victories, he spoke more about the couple of big races he lost and I think most sports people at that level reflect on the defeats more than the victories.

For six or seven years we were the top team in the country and while winning two All-Irelands was great, we could have won a lot more.

When I finished up playing, I looked back on the fact that I was involved in five All-Ireland finals, including the replay in 1988, and we also won two National Leagues, so that was seven big national finals that I was involved in but I didn't get a minute in any of them... and that bugged me for a long while.

It is only really since I started getting involved with teams as a coach and a selector myself that I accepted my role on the panel in those years.

I had to make a decision to be part of a panel and never getting to play in the big games, but I made that decision.

I wasn't alone in that position, there were a lot of lads who could have got games, but who didn't. It is only when you are on the other side, the management side, that you realise decisions aren't made to get at a player. They are honest decisions and some lads gain from it and others lose out; that is just the way of sport, I suppose.

Apart from those disappointments I wouldn't change a thing.

I would have loved to have played in some of those finals. It might sound silly, but I have a grandchild now and I'd love to be able to say to my grandchild, 'Look... there's me playing in an All-Ireland final!'

Just to be able to say that would be nice.

I envy the lads that have that opportunity to be able to do that.

I first broke onto the Meath team in 1981 and I played in the Centenary Cup final in '84. People tended to dismiss that tournament that year, but given the year that was in it that probably should have been the All-Ireland championship for that year... the centenary of the GAA.

When you look back at the Centenary Cup final, the best player we had that day was Liam Smith. He arrived on the Meath scene maybe two or three years too early. I remember when I came onto the team first, Liam was an absolutely fantastic player. He was small, not particularly quick, but he was absolutely class.

That win in 1984 was great and gave us great belief, but I think the belief that we could do something special started to rise in '83 when we played Dublin in the Leinster Championship we drew with them.

They went on and beat us after extra-time in the replay and then went on to win the All-Ireland, so that definitely gave us the inner belief that we could play and compete against the top teams.

Then the Centenary Cup, which was an open draw, was brilliant. There was the sense that the top teams like Dublin and Kerry didn't really take it that seriously, maybe that is why that tournament wasn't as highly regarded as it probably should have been. That win in '84 really gave us more belief. The thing with the championship back then was, one defeat, one mistake… and you were gone, so in 1985 we lost out to Laois, but then the breakthrough came in 1986.

We drew with Dublin in the league in Croke Park that year and that added to our belief that we could kick on and win Leinster, and it moved on from there.

It was only from 1985 that Seán Boylan started to have more of a say on the picking of the team. Before that he might have picked two or three lads and someone else picked two or three others and so on; so it was only in '85 that he started to get control.

There were wholesale changes and while he got rid of a few selectors, I'd say there were a few lads he would have liked to have kept.

Tony Craven was one of those lads, I'd say. Tony was well liked by the players, and he had a great way about him. He was a lovely man.

I remember we went up play Down in a challenge match in Newcastle. Myself, Joe Cassells and Gerry Reynolds were subs and as the game wasn't going well, one of the selectors turned to Joe and shouted at him, 'Mick Ryan… warm up there!'

That pretty much summed it up at the time.

That was back around 1982; there were six or seven selectors at that time. Sean didn't have as much say as he needed to have in those early days to make teams his own, but eventually that changed and he was able to pick his own selectors… the rest is history.

For me, the highlight of my Meath career was the 1986 Leinster final, I'll never forget it… it was a wet, dreadful day. I had been there five years by that stage, so to get to a Leinster final and win it was really, *really* special and a fantastic achievement.

That set up the team for the rest of their achievements in 1987 and '88.

I also had great days with Navan O'Mahonys, and they were everything to me. Whenever you felt bad about not playing in the championship or if things weren't going great, you would go back to the club and they would take you back in and look after you with open arms.

99

TOMMY DOWD

MEATH 0-15 ROSCOMMON 1-11
All-Ireland SFC Semi-Final
Cork Park
AUGUST 18 1991

Future Meath All-Ireland winning captain Tommy Dowd made his mark as a legend of the future with powerful displays (above) in his breakthrough summer in 1991.

★ **MEATH:** M McQuillan; B Reilly, M Lyons, T Ferguson; K Foley, L Harnan, M O'Connell (0-1); L Hayes, PJ Gillic (0-1); D Beggy (0-1), T Dowd (0-2), C Coyle; C O'Rourke, B Stafford (0-9), B Flynn (0-1). Sub: G McEntee for Ferguson.

★ **ROSCOMMON:** G Sheerin; D Newton, P Doorey, E Gavin; J Connaughton, P Hickey, M Reilly; S Killoran, J Newton; V Glennon, T McManus, T Grehan; E McManus (0-3), P Earley, D Duggan (1-8). Subs: M Donlon for Glennon, D O'Connor for Reilly.

THE ACTION

AFTER SURVIVING THE four in-a-row against Dublin and a serious wobble that needed two attempts to shoot down Wicklow before eventually seeing off Offaly and Laois to claim the Leinster crown, Meath advanced to the Sam Maguire showpiece, but not before another almighty scare.

Roscommon could, and really probably should, have been 2-5 to 0-0 clear inside just eight minutes. Paul Earley blasted a goal chance wide after just two minutes... moments later he was also denied by a superb Michael McQuillan save, and Eugene McManus blasted another opportunity over the bar. In that spell Roscommon also squandered four very scoreable point chances.

However they depended too much on the scoring exploits of Derek Duggan, who converted eight frees and capped a wonderful display with a magnificent goal just before half-time that secured a 1-7 to 0-7 lead for Roscommon. With the Roscommon full-back line tenacious and Meath struggling to create opportunities they needed a revamp for the second-half.

Martin O'Connell went right corner-back, Liam Harnan to right half-back, Kevin Foley to centre-back, Colm Coyle to left-half and PJ Gillic to centre-forward to make room for Gerry McEntee at midfield.

Meath still trailed by five points with 17 minutes left. They cut the deficit with Bernard Flynn and Stafford on target, while Liam Hayes was denied by a great Gay Sheerin save.

Meath had their tails up. Stafford scored five points in the last three minutes – three from play – while all Roscommon could muster was a pointed free from Duggan from virtually the last kick of the ball as they learned the lesson first hand that you never write off Meath.

★★★★★

66

I HAD BEEN taken off at half-time in the Leinster final against Laois in 1991 and I wasn't happy, but who is happy when they are taken off? On reflection I wasn't playing well enough, so I probably deserved to be called ashore.

At that time Gerry McEntee was in and out of the team because he was based in America, I think. What used to normally happen in those games was, I would be taken off and Gerry would be brought on, but to be taken off at half-time left me a bit annoyed and I suppose it made me more determined to make a point the next chance I got.

I wasn't sure whether I would get my game in the All-Ireland semi-final against Roscommon, so obviously I had to try twice as hard in training to try to impress Sean and the selectors. At that time, there was nothing ever said about why you might have been taken off, you just had to accept the decision.

Sean was a good communicator, but it wouldn't be like today when lads get taken off and they have shrinks and all sorts to help them get over it.

In those times you had to grin and bear it, and you had to be man enough to just get on with it and work harder to get on the team for the next day.

That was the way we were brought up too; we took the knocks, took the rough with the smooth and did the best we could with the next chance we got.

I certainly didn't hold it against anyone for being *taken off*, I was just a bit annoyed with it, but there were no grudges. I just got back into my routine and got as much training in as I could.

I was in and out of the team in 1990 as well. I made my inter-county debut against Longford in the first round of the championship, and I played in the Leinster final against Dublin and we beat them. Then I started the semi-final when we beat Donegal, but I was taken off, and for the final against Cork I was dropped.

Colm Brady was playing very well at midfield at that time. He was moved to half-forward and I was dropped, with Gerry McEntee picked at midfield. I wasn't too annoyed about that because I knew that with the talent that was there it was always going to be two or three years before you could be considered a regular on the team.

You really had to prove yourself because we had so many good players at that time, so I certainly didn't take it to heart, but it did make me work harder to become a regular on the starting team.

When I came onto the panel first, I was in awe of the whole lot. Seeing the likes of Gerry McEntee, O'Rourke, Flynn, Stafford, Harnan, Lyons… lads like that, they were all household names and had won a couple of All-Irelands and three or four Leinsters, so they were like superstars.

It was always my aim to get onto the Meath team and to wear the green jersey and represent my county. As a young lad that was all I ever dreamed about. I never thought it would happen, but it was a huge dream of mine, so to be actually there and among men like that… it was really special.

Then to have a manager like Seán Boylan to cap it all off, it was a huge honour. The training was fierce hard, it was incredibly tough, but looking back now you would love to be able to go back and do it all again. You tend to take it all for granted when you are there at the time, and it's only when you look back at it, 20 or 30 years later, when you are finished playing that you really appreciate it.

When you look back at the old clips on the TV it makes you appreciate just how lucky we were to be involved at that time. The crowds going to the games those days too were amazing.

I remember meeting people from Wexford and Waterford coming up to watch Meath against Dublin in Leinster finals, and people coming down from Monaghan just to watch the physicality of those games and the hard hitting involved… people loved those games.

I used to love the physical element of the game. You gave as good as you got in those games and I used to relish those tough, hard games. Once those games were over that was it, end of story; there was never any jawing afterwards or hard feelings.

If Dublin beat us there would be no bitterness; we would wish them the best of luck and then focus all our attention on getting a rattle at them the following year again, and they did the same to us. Those games were tough and physical, but there was no animosity or grudges held.

There were a lot of tough tackles and stuff went on in those games, but that was what people paid their hard earned money to go in to see.

The four games against Dublin in 1991 were very special – I think we nearly broke the county with the amount of games people had to pay into. Every weekend people had to find more money to buy tickets to bring their kids to games and feed them on the way home.

I'd say between the four games both sides used about 25 different lads each. There was nothing between Meath and Dublin at the time and all those games were nail-biters. It was only by the grace of God and the ability to keep playing to the very end that got us over the line. That determination to keep going and never give up was something that was instilled into us from very early on by Sean.

The week before that fourth game against Dublin, he brought us over to Scotland to a place called Drymen, the home village of Billy Connolly. Jinksy (David Beggy) was working over there at the time and he found this place. It had a lovely hotel and a soccer pitch about half a mile outside the village, so Boylan brought us there and it was a fairly gutsy thing to do because if we had been beaten the following week the county would have went mad.

We had two great nights out… great drinking sessions.

On the Saturday he brought us out to do a training session and for a solid hour he had us up and down the field, three in-a-row interchanging passes… up and down, up and down… and I think that had a huge bearing on that goal against Dublin.

We needed a goal at that stage in the final game against Dublin; nothing else would do and that's what we got, that's what we had worked on for an hour solid in Scotland. We had the mentality to work the ball into position for a goal, so I firmly believe that training session in Scotland had a lot to do with that.

When I looked up to pass that last ball into Foley for the goal in the fourth game, I hadn't a clue who I was passing to… I just saw the green jersey and sent it on.

The biggest shock for me was the fact that O'Rourke had played the ball back to me after I had played it into him. It's a wonder he didn't try to blast it to the net himself, but I suppose because my momentum was carrying me towards the goals he had to pass it back to me.

If you look back at any of my games against John O'Leary, you will see that I never took a shot at him because he was such a great goalkeeper, a great shot stopper. I always tried to get around him or else flick it on to an in-rushing player because nine times out of 10, he would stop a shot from any distance.

So in that instance, when I saw the green jersey out of the corner of my eye, I was always going to pass it. I thought Foley would have just flicked it to the net, but he ended up with enough time to grab it and put his boot through it. In fairness to O'Leary, he nearly got his hand to the ball, he had great reflexes, but Foley got his shot away in a split second and stuck it into the net.

In the Leinster final against Laois I was marking Pat Roe. Pat was a very sticky player and he didn't allow me make much room for myself, so obviously the selectors wanted to use the experience of Gerry McEntee coming on. Someone had to make way, so unfortunately it was me. McEntee didn't like sitting on the line. He would eat the bench while he'd be there, so he would have been eager to get on and start grabbing the ball around midfield and I was the one who had to make way for him.

I worked hard at training to try to show the lads that they were wrong to take me off. Bob O'Malley broke his leg in that Leinster final against Laois, so that opened up a space on the team.

They moved Brendan Reilly into corner-back and that freed up a space out the field for Gerry McEntee to come in; so luckily enough I got the chance to impress again against Roscommon in the All-Ireland semi-final and I certainly took it.

That was our ninth game in about 12 weeks, so you'd imagine we should have been getting tired at that stage, but we all felt good enough – we were flying fit at the time.

Sean had us training in the swimming pool at Gormanston at the time, so we weren't flying around fields killing ourselves. Sean had us very fresh at the time.

He was after buying buoyancy suits in America, so he had us treading the water for an hour or an hour and 15 minutes. It was horrid hard training. We were running on the spot in the water, moving our hands and legs the whole time; it was very tough. Then he would blow the whistle and we'd have to go fast for 20 or 30 seconds… it was exhausting. None of us were used to this type of training at all, but yet when we got out of the pool our limbs and joints were grand because we hadn't been putting any pressure on them.

Similar suits had been used by a woman called Joan Benoit, who won a gold medal in the women's marathon at the Los Angeles Olympics. She had injured herself six weeks before those Games and needed an operation on her knee, so she did all her training in the water wearing one of those buoyancy suits.

Sean heard this story. We had been in Florida the January before that, so he bought 27 of the suits at the cost of £3,500 and brought them home. Sean was always thinking one or two steps ahead of other managers all the time. There was always a method to his madness.

Roscommon started well and had us under pressure.

Paul Earley was giving Mick Lyons a fairly hard time of it and he missed a sitter of a chance. Junior McManus also went flying through at one stage, but he blasted over the crossbar. They had some great chances early on.

Tony McManus was a great player and the type of player I would have looked up to over the years, and gave a great pass into Derek Duggan, who was completely on his own. When the ball was passed to Duggan, Terry (Ferguson) raced back to try to get a challenge in on him, but Duggan sold him an unmerciful dummy, and took a drop-shot that was like a missile hitting the net. Mickey McQuillan hadn't a chance of saving it.

I managed to get a couple of points in the first-half and they came at crucial times of the game, when we badly needed them.

For a lot of the game Roscommon were three or four points ahead, so my points happened to keep us in the game at crucial times when it could have gotten away from us.

After they got their goal, and just before half-time, PJ Gillic kicked a huge point from way out the field that gave us great hope. For all the chances Roscommon had, we were still only three points down at the break without playing well at all.

There was never any panic in the Meath dressing-room. The more senior players would always say a few words while Sean was out talking to Pat Reynolds and Tony Brennan, but it was always constructive criticism. There was never anyone at anyone's throat.

You would always have had Mick Lyons or Harnan... or McEntee or O'Rourke, and maybe Kevin Foley, offering plenty of advice and encouragement; they were the ones who would say a few words. All you needed were a few words from those boys to get your act together.

I never saw any panic from Sean or any of the players in the Meath dressing-room… ever. We always felt we had a chance and a lot of the games we won were won in the last 10 or 15 minutes, so we knew there was a long way to go no matter how far we were behind.

We had that resilience to keep going until the end. PJ Gillic was another great man to talk in the dressing-room too. They were lads you looked up to and would always listen to. You would never go out for the second-half of any game with a hump on you.

I was marking a lad called Paul Hickey that day against Roscommon; he was a very good footballer, but he just held the centre and never really moved from his position, so I used to go to midfield and to the other side of midfield to get breaking ball and he didn't come with me, so I ended up on a lot of ball that day.

It was one of those days for me, whether the ball broke left or right or centre, I caught it. I had drifted into the full-forward line at one stage and Jinksy kicked in a ball from the sideline and I jumped between two or three Roscommon lads, and caught it. On another day that ball would have broken and might have been cleared, but I managed to catch that one and lay it off to Stafford, and he got a very important point off it.

We all know the days when things go very wrong, but that was just a day when everything went right for me and nothing did go wrong. For every good day you have, you could probably recall 10 bad ones I suppose, that's the way sport is.

I won the Man of the Match award that day against Roscommon, so my feelings were in stark contrast to the Leinster final where I had been taken off against Laois. I wasn't too worried about losing my place for the final, so that was a huge weight off my shoulders.

Jack O'Shea picked the 'Man' for that game and he was such an iconic player at the time, a real legend, so for him to praise me and to say that I had kept Meath in the game was a huge compliment. To hear a statement like that from a legend like him was a huge confidence boost, and certainly helped me believe that I might start the next day.

Going into the All-Ireland final the county had gone mad. The green and gold was everywhere and it was an amazing experience.

I thought those things would happen every year. In my first year on the panel we

GAME OF MY LIFE

reached the All-Ireland final too, but unfortunately lost and here we were back in another final. I was sure this was just the norm. Of course, that's not how it turned out, but at the time it was a great feeling to be back in another All-Ireland final.

Unfortunately, nothing went right for us on the day against Down. They just got too far ahead of us for us to be able to pull it back.

They had lads like Mickey Linden, James McCarten, Peter Whitnell, Paddy O'Rourke and Conor Deegan… that was an incredible Down team and they even came back to win another All-Ireland in 1994, so their win in '91 was no fluke.

They got so far ahead of us it left us with a huge mountain to climb. Colm O'Rourke, who had pneumonia in the week leading up to the game, came on and he helped drag us back into the game. Bernard Flynn missed a sitter of a chance that he would normally have scored, but the goalie saved it.

Even though we were so far behind, we had chances to win it, but we fell just short.

Even in defeat we still showed great character and a huge mentality to claw our way back into the game… to be 11 points down and only lose by two, we were so close! A fella called Seamus Prior from Leitrim was refereeing the game and he couldn't wait to blow the final whistle when time was up. I'm convinced if that game had gone on for another minute or two, we would have got a draw and earned another replay.

In saying that, that was an incredible Down team. They had Pete McGrath training them too and he was a great coach. McGrath was cute enough too. I was supposed to marking Paddy O'Rourke, but they moved him out to wing back and put a lad called John Kelly on me. Kelly would have been faster than O'Rourke and he absolutely dogged me for the day.

When you look back on that All-Ireland, any opportunity Kelly had he came in with the two knees on top of me when I went down on the ball.

McGrath was cute enough; he sent him out to do a man-marking job on me and he did it well. I haven't any regrets. I always trained hard and did my best.

I can't say I should have trained harder or I should have done this or done that, I always tried my best and once you can say that, then you can't have any regrets.

99

132

TREVOR GILES

MEATH 0-10 DUBLIN 0-8
Leinster SFC Final
JULY 28 1996

Trevor Giles won his first Leinster title on a wet summer's day in 1996 when his four points made all the difference against reigning All-Ireland champions Dublin.

★ **MEATH:** C Martin; M O'Reilly, D Fay, M O'Connell; C Coyle, E McManus, P Reynolds; J McGuinness, J McDermott; **T Giles (0-4)**, T Dowd (0-2), G Geraghty; E Kelly (0-1), B Reilly (0-2), B Callaghan (0-1).

★ **DUBLIN:** J O'Leary; P Moran, D Deasy, M Deegan; P Curran, K Barr, E Heery (0-1); B Stynes (0-1), P Bealin; C Whelan (0-2), P Gilroy, J Gavin; D Farrell, J Sherlock, C Redmond (0-4). Subs: D O'Brien for Gilroy, D Harrington for Bealin, S Keogh for O'Brien.

THE ACTION

LESS THAN 12 months earlier, Dublin had inflicted one of Meath's heaviest defeats when they trounced the Royals by 1-8 to 1-18 in the Leinster SFC final. For many that was expected to be the end of the line for Seán Boylan and his legion of heroes that had brought glory to the county in 1987 and '88. However, Boylan held on and a few of his old stalwarts stayed with him as he attempted to rebuild from the foundation stones of All-Ireland minor winning teams in 1990 and '92 and an All-Ireland under-21 success in '93. There was plenty to enthuse about, but no-one saw coming what happened next.

After a tight first-half in tough and slippery conditions, Dublin took a 0-4 to 0-3 half-time lead to the dressing room in the 1996 Leinster final. Trevor Giles opened his account nine minutes after the restart with a converted free after Brendan Reilly was fouled, and a minute later the Skryne man found his range from play with a brilliant score to make it 0-5 each. Redmond edged Dublin ahead again after a fine break by Paul Curran, but again it was Giles with his third of the afternoon to level it up after Tommy Dowd had been fouled.

A converted '45' from Redmond and a super score from Eamonn Heery looked to have put Dublin in the driving seat as they led 0-8 to 0-6 with 10 minutes remaining. However, that proved to be the All-Ireland champions last score as Meath took over.

Brendan Reilly halved the deficit with an excellent point and with seven minutes remaining Giles tied the game again with another free after Graham Geraghty was fouled.

Operating from centre-forward, Barry Callaghan gave Meath the lead for the first time since the 23rd minute and with two minutes remaining Callaghan's clubmate Tommy Dowd concludes the scoring with a fine effort as Meath held on to claim a first Leinster crown in five years that also put them on the path to All-Ireland glory.

★★★★★

66

WHEN 1996 CAME around it was my third year on the Meath senior panel and by that stage we had already lost two Leinster finals, and we had lost the second one by 10 points. The contrast between those disappointments and my first few years as a minor couldn't have been any more stark.

I had played two years with the minors.

The first year we won the All-Ireland and the second year we lost the All-Ireland final, so over my two years with the minors I had played about 10 county matches for Meath and a lot of them were in Croke Park, some of them in front of Dublin matches; so there was almost always a big crowd in for our games.

So when I look back on my years as a minor that was great preparation for playing in Croke Park as a senior because I got used to playing there and in front of a big crowd. Apart from losing the final to Cork in 1993, we won all our games as minors, so I had a good experience of winning there too.

We were lucky to get to play there as young footballers and that put us in the shop window for Seán Boylan to have a look at what was coming through.

I was just about to turn 19 when I was brought into the senior panel in February 1994. I didn't think I was ready to play senior for Meath because I was slight and that Meath team was such a strong physical side, so I just thought I wasn't ready for it at that stage. However, Joe Cassells, who was a selector at the time, rang me and he told me I was ready and asked me in. Going in at that time of the year we were training in Páirc Tailteann and it wasn't very glamourous.

Sean used to have us doing some exercises under the stand and then we might be out on the back pitch where the lights weren't great, so it was a sharp introduction to senior football with Meath.

Fermanagh was my first league game when I came on as a sub with 10 minutes to go – after that I started every game. Brian Stafford broke a thumb in the next league game against Galway and I was next in line to be the free-taker, so I kicked the frees for the rest of the league and thankfully it went quite well.

I was always conscious that I didn't want to be on the team just to be the free-taker. I wanted to be on the team first of all because of my ability, and then because I was also able to take frees. To be fair to Brian Stafford, he came down to

Skryne when I was on the minor team in 1992 and he spent an hour with myself and Peter Sullivan talking about the practice that we needed to put in and what he had put in to make him such an outstanding free-taker. That was the only coaching I ever got on free-taking, but I did put in the work after that. It takes about two years of hard work to become a good, reliable free-taker.

When you got picked on the Meath team the ethos at that time was that you worked very hard, you tackled, you supported players… worked even harder and never gave up. If you got a bang or a wallop, you just got up and got on with things. You just tried to do the things that you had seen the Meath team do over the previous years.

When I came onto the senior panel in 1994, there was no pressure put on me whatsoever. I used to love the team meetings.

Brendan Reilly had been there a good few years at that stage, but he used to hate the team meetings; he just wanted to go home after training. But I loved them, I loved listening to Bob O'Malley, Martin O'Connell, Brian Stafford, PJ Gillic, Colm O'Rourke… and obviously to Sean and the selectors Mick Lyons and Joe Cassells. If those meetings went on for an hour that was all the better for me. I was just soaking in all that wisdom from all those players who had done it all; it was a great learning experience.

If you are a good underage player and you come into a county set-up and are expected to go straight into midfield or centre-forward that can be hard going, but I was wing-forward and all I was expected to do was play my part, do my bit for the team, work hard – and I was able to do that for a couple of years, before I grew into a more senior role where I was trying to influence the game.

There was no pressure whatsoever playing with Meath.

I would have played with Colm O'Rourke and John McDermott with Skryne and I would have played against lads like Tommy Dowd, Kevin Foley, Colm Coyle… and lads like that while playing senior with my club, so I was well aware of players like that when I went into training.

I do remember Bob O'Malley hit me hard during one of my early training sessions. I was really surprised and annoyed at the time, but someone said to me that he was just letting me know that that is how it was going to be in games and that he was just trying to do me some service… do me a favour almost.

It took me a couple of minutes to work that one out.

Being in there so young certainly developed me physically, but also mentally because all those lads had the mindset of winners.

Everything had gone fairly well in my first year. We won the National League and beat Laois and Wexford to get to the Leinster final, but I didn't play well in that final against Dublin. It was a higher level than I had played before.

In 1995 I continued to develop and again we got to the Leinster final against Dublin. I worked hard in that game, but didn't influence the game too much. I was up against Keith Barr that day; he was a seasoned player, so it was tough.

We had lost the Leinster final by one point in my first year, then we lost by 10 in my second year... it looked like things were going in the wrong direction. Losing by 10 points back then was a huge margin of defeat.

The game has changed now with the amount of scores being kicked, but to lose by 10 points back then was huge, especially when there was only ever a point or two between Meath and Dublin... that was a huge setback for the Meath players, supporters and the whole county.

Colm O'Rourke was fantastic in that 1995 final.

He had Paddy Moran all over him, and the referee gave him nothing, but he was still our best player on the day, along with Colm Coyle.

Then Colm O'Rourke retired. So we were beaten by 10 points with him playing well and now he was gone, so we were thinking we were even further back from Dublin. Obviously, I had my whole career ahead of me at that stage and I was determined to play for a number of years, but I never could have envisaged what was going to come so soon.

Having lads like Martin O'Connell, Colm Coyle, John McDermott, Brendan Reilly, Tommy Dowd still on board in 1996 was huge; they were fellas who had all played on teams that had beaten Dublin. The lads that retired like Bob O'Malley, Brian Stafford, Bernard Flynn, Colm O'Rourke, they were huge losses, but their retirements probably allowed a lot of us to grow a little bit more; but at the same time none of us younger fellas were ready to carry the team the way those lads had.

We did get a bit of room to grow, but we still had the experienced five lads there; they were still the real leaders, the fully grown men who provided the leadership. We also had to change the way we played, especially with Colm gone.

Meath had a very strong full-forward line and the idea was always to get the ball in there as quickly as we could, so when Colm was gone that option went too. We changed the way we played and played through the lines a little bit more, with more of a running game, so it was a big change.

In hindsight, everything makes sense, but moving Brendan Reilly to full-forward... no-one could guarantee that would work out. It was the same with moving Graham Geraghty to half-forward. Tommy Dowd was a brilliant full-forward, great speed off the mark and could kick points left and right close to goals, but he was moved to centre-forward and there was no guarantee that would work out either.

Moving players and putting them in different positions was something that Sean often did. For that Leinster final in 1996 the half-forward line was Graham (Geraghty), Tommy (Dowd) and myself, and Dublin had Paul Curran, Keith Barr and Eamonn Heery... as good a half-back line that ever played the game. They were all seasoned players at that stage, fully grown men, so it was a risk to play the three of us in direct opposition to them.

We went into that 1996 championship off the back of the 10-point beating by Dublin the year before and we were also beaten in the league quarter-final by Mayo, who weren't a household name at the time even though they did go on and get to the All-Ireland final as well.

At the time our line of form didn't look impressive at all, and the Carlow lads were really well known. A lot of them played with Eire Og and they won five Leinster club titles from 1992 on. Lads like the Haydens and Garvan Ware were all really well known to the general public and had won stuff, so that was a big challenge for us. It was no certainty we were going to win that game.

Mark O'Reilly started that Leinster quarter-final and he hadn't even been on the panel the year before. I didn't really know of Mark playing underage, but he came straight in at corner-back. Even Darren (Fay) had been centre-back with the minors the year we lost to Cork and he was a good minor, but you wouldn't have definitely projected that he would go on to become the player he did. Soon, no Ireland manager would play against Australia at that time without Darren at full-back, but 1996 was his first championship start.

Paddy Reynolds and Barry Callaghan also came in for first starts and they were good underage players, but they were just starting out on their senior careers – we were not expecting the world from any of those lads who were just in their first year at senior. It was a good start to win by 24 scores to six against Carlow.

To kick 24 points back in those days was a huge score; our scores came from everywhere that day, even Mark O'Reilly came up and kicked a point near the end. We did a lot of things right that day.

I managed to kick three '45s' and I wouldn't have had the strongest kick off the ground, because when you kick off the instep you end up curling the ball, so you are losing a little bit of distance. I used to struggle to kick '45s' but Colm Coyle challenged me on it and in fairness to Jimmy McGuinness, he gave me a few tips.

Jimmy is technically very clever the way he thinks about football and he got me standing straight behind the ball and trying to kick it dead straight off the laces. It was a high risk technique, it either goes straight or it doesn't – a bit like a golf shot.

I worked on that technique based on Jimmy's advice and I got three '45s' that day which was unusual for me and that was very important to me to know that I was able to do that, so I give Jimmy a lot of credit for his help on that.

There was a little bit of doubt about the team before that Carlow game, but our performance dampened that doubt a bit. We followed that up with a win over Laois and that was crucial too.

Laois were a really tough team; we had a lot of tough games against them in the O'Byrne Cup and the league. We used to meet in the Montague Hotel for a bite to eat before we played them in the league in Portlaoise and when we got back on the bus to go to the game there wouldn't be a word, because we knew it was going to be physical, almost a nasty game.

Laois had beaten us in some league games and they beat us in an O'Byrne Cup final, so to beat Laois by a few points was good going. They came back at us just after half-time, but we handled that well and ran out comfortable winners. To the neutral, it mightn't have looked that impressive, but for us to beat a Laois side that had Hughie Emerson, Damien Delaney and other good underage players... it was a good win for us; and we were making strides at that stage.

Dublin came into that Leinster final in 1996 as All-Ireland champions.

They had changed managers with Pat O'Neill stepping down and Mickey

Whelan coming in. We had a settled team and the two wins over Carlow and Laois gave us a sense of security.

I put myself under severe pressure going into that game. Unlike my start with Skryne, where I had won two county finals straight away, my start with Meath saw two Leinster final defeats, so this was the third one and I put pressure on myself.

I felt when I came onto the Meath team that the media were good to me, building me up to be a brilliant player. I got loads of coverage, but then when we lost the few games I felt the coverage I got was harsh. Now when I look back, it was probably accurate.

When you are 19 or 20 years old, you can be sensitive.

Back in those days the journalists would ring the landline in your house for an interview and most lads generally did talk, that was the way it was done back then. I decided in the week before the Leinster final that I wasn't talking to any journalists leading up to the game.

My mam and dad were over in Atlanta at the Olympic Games that year. Dad's best friend from Navan had been working in Navan Carpets and he moved over to Atlanta and started to work in carpets over there, so my mam and dad went over to him for a couple of weeks around the time of the Olympics.

So, I was in the house on my own all week. The phone rang a couple of times during the week and I didn't answer it once.

Mam and dad came home on the Friday morning before the game and the arrangements were that I would pick them up in Dublin Airport when their flight landed at 10am. I was there on time to pick them up at 10am, but it turned out that they had managed to get an earlier flight and they had been ringing all week to try to tell me that they would be landing at 6am, but I didn't answer the phone!

I landed in at 10am all smiles… there they were, as thick as two doors, waiting for me for four hours and demanding to know why I didn't answer the phone.

They also brought home these nose bands from America. They were all the rage at the time with the athletes at the Olympics to help them expand their nostrils and to be able to get in more oxygen, so I landed out for the Leinster final the following Sunday with one of these on my nose.

It was lashing rain and I'd say it only lasted about 15 minutes. That was my fashion accessory for that day.

I had been in Croke Park on the Canal End in 1986 with my dad and my friends when it was lashing rain and Meath beat Dublin to make their breakthrough, so I was happy enough that it was lashing rain again in '96 because I was always looking for some bit of connection or superstition or omen... the wet day was fine by us. The grass was really long that day in Croke Park, I had never seen it that long before or since and that certainly didn't help. I took two frees in 1994 and missed both of them and lost by a point. Then in '96 it was a wet day, wet ball, long grass... and I missed a couple early on.

They weren't easy ones, but I would have fancied getting them, so that wasn't a good start.

After about 10 minutes Tommy Dowd got a cut under his eye following a clash with Keith Barr, and Graham Geraghty got flattened off the ball... and there were a couple of other flash points, but it was only 0-4 to 0-3 at half-time.

It was a really low scoring game – it finished up 0-10 to 0-8. We got the last four scores to come back from 0-8 to 0-6 down, it was great.

The reason I pick that match from my whole career is because of the noise the Meath fans generated for those 10 scores, particularly the last four.

I had never heard noise like it, it really stands out for me; the hair would be standing on the back of the neck even now looking back at it.

It was such a massive game for us.

For me, until you had beaten Dublin in a Leinster final you were not considered to be a good Meath footballer. You couldn't be compared to the players who had gone before us in the 80s, the players who had performed heroics. There was loads riding on that game for everyone else and for Sean, but for me if we had lost three in-a-row to Dublin it would have been a massive set-back.

The Dublin half-forward line that day included Jim Gavin and Pat Gilroy, both later managers of the Dubs, and they also introduced Ciaran Whelan for his debut that day.

I scored one from play and three frees, but I'd say that was the game I covered most ground in that I ever played for Meath. I was up and down the pitch, tackling and doing whatever I could to prevent a score or trying to get a score at the other end. The highlight reel wouldn't be brilliant for me, there was nothing outstanding or fancy, but I worked really hard that day and for me that was one of my best ever performances from a pure work-rate point of view.

After that Leinster final I remember Sean saying that our lives would never be the same again. It might sound dramatic, but he was right, because we had beaten Dublin in a Leinster final. The supporters were delighted and once you had beaten Dublin you were held in high regard, you were almost in the 'club' with some of the greats.

The Tyrone performance in the All-Ireland semi-final was terrific. We scored 2-15 against a really good team. Graham Geraghty was on fire that day, all over the field we were excellent. Jimmy McGuinness and John McDermott dominated their midfielders, they were super. When you play so well in a semi-final it is a bit of trick to try to do that again in the final. You are almost better off to just fall over the line in a semi-final and have loads of things to improve on for the final.

We didn't hit the same heights in the final against Mayo, but compared to the Leinster final I was as calm as a breeze before the All-Ireland final and replay.

Back in those days the Leinster final was the biggest game of the year. It might sound like a funny thing to say, but you have a lot of neutrals at an All-Ireland final, whereas at a Leinster final you just have the two sets of supporters and the noise, the atmosphere is very different. When the final whistle goes in the Leinster final and the commentator says, 'The All-Ireland champions Dublin are out!'... that is amazing.

There was a huge amount at stake before that Leinster final because we were carrying the baggage of the previous two years. Our reputation and pride was on the line; it was brilliant to win the All-Ireland, don't get me wrong, but the relief after winning the Leinster final that year was just huge.

After '96 we felt we were all certainly young enough to win again. The 1987 team went on and defended their title in '88, and the '49 team won again in '54, so there was plenty of lads around who had won a couple of All-Irelands. I was certainly assuming we would win a second one at some stage.

In 1997 and '98 we always had an excuse for falling short. Between injured players and players suspended, we never had our full team in the '97 or '98 Leinster finals and we always felt that if we had our full team out then we could beat anybody. Maybe it took a couple of years to get the hunger or maybe the discipline back, or maybe it was a bit of bad luck with injuries.

The 1999 campaign was a little bit more straightforward and we were relatively convincing winners in all our games. There was no luck attached to any of the wins, there were no rows, no controversies… the team ended up with seven All Stars so we deserved to win it in '99 and were the best team that year.

The 2001 final would be the one game in my career that I would love to play again, if I could. That was a fine Galway side, with a great forward line. I certainly didn't underestimate Galway, but we just didn't have an edge about us that day where we were out to prove something.

The way we won the semi-final against Kerry was too comfortable, I'd much prefer someone to tell me I had no chance of winning, then I would go out to try to prove them wrong. Everyone we met on the street after that Kerry game kept saying that they thought we would do it; that was grand, but I'd have preferred to have gone out with a bit of an edge. We still might not have beaten Galway, but we would have played better.

It is hard to believe that we haven't been there since.

You would have hoped that the next generation coming along, that would have grown up watching us win All-Irelands in 1996 and '99, and get to the final in 2001… you would have thought that they would have dreamt of doing the same just like we did, when we watched the '87 and '88 lads.

I was lucky to grow up in the 80s, watching Skryne getting to county finals, albeit losing most of them, but they were competing at a high level.

And watching Meath getting to All-Irelands and winning them!

Back then, you'd just go out to the back garden with a football and be kicking points and goals because your dream was to be on the Meath team and winning All-Irelands. Unfortunately, the kids now in Meath don't have those memories to feed off and that's a pity.

DARREN FAY
(& GRAHAM GERAGHTY)

MEATH 2-15 TYRONE 0-12
All-Ireland SFC Semi-Final
Croke Park
AUGUST 18 1996

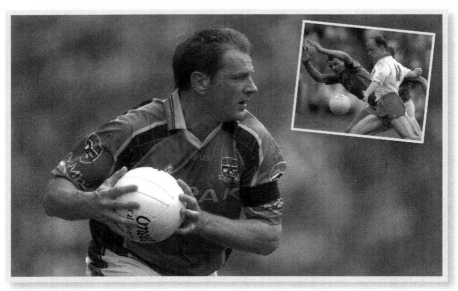

Meath's march to the 1996 All-Ireland title included beating Dublin, and also Mayo after a replayed final, but the team's most courageous performance came against Tyrone (inset).

★ **MEATH:** C Martin; M O'Reilly, **D Fay**, M O'Connell; C Coyle, E McManus, P Reynolds; J McGuinness, J McDermott; T Giles (0-3), T Dowd, **G Geraghty (1-4)**; E Kelly, B Reilly (0-5), B Callaghan (1-3). Subs: C Brady for Kelly, J Devine for Geraghty.

★ **TYRONE:** F McConnell; P Devlin, C Lawn, F Devlin; R McGarrity, S McCullen, S McLoughlin; Pascal Canavan (0-1), J Gormley; B Dooher, G Cavlan (0-6), A Cush (0-3); C McBride, Peter Canavan (0-2), B Gormley. Subs: F Logan for McGarrity, S Lawn for B Gormley, A Kilpatrick for McBride.

THE ACTION

A 10-POINT DRUBBING by Dublin in the Leinster SFC final a year earlier had signalled alarm bells in Meath and there were calls for Seán Boylan to resign as manager.

After hammering Meath in the provincial final, Dublin went on to win the Sam Maguire in 1995 with a narrow victory over Tyrone in the final. Many believed that with Dublin out of the way, the '96 All-Ireland title was Tyrone's for the taking, but Meath had other ideas.

Tyrone started well and hit the first three points from Ger Cavlan and Adrian Cush (two). It took Meath until the ninth minute before Barry Callaghan opened their account, but Tyrone still looked in control as Peter Canavan restored their three-point lead.

Trevor Giles kicked the first of his three points and after Barry Callaghan fisted over and Brendan Reilly curled one over with his left, Meath were level. Cavlan and Cush restored Tyrone's advantage, but then in the 28th minute Graham Geraghty blasted to the net after great work by Reilly and Giles.

Pascal and Peter Canavan responded with points, but points from Geraghty and Giles (free) either side of another Cavlan point had the sides level at the break 1-6 to 0-9. After the resumption Tyrone managed just three more scores as Meath turned on the style.

Reilly and Geraghty pushed Boylan's side two clear before Cavlan pulled one back, but Reilly and Geraghty against pounced to give Meath a three-point cushion for the first time.

Reilly took his tally to five with scores either side of a Giles point to put six between the sides, and with 10 minutes remaining Callaghan made it a seven-point game.

Geraghty added another before Cavlan responded and with two minutes remaining Callaghan fisted to the net from close range after Geraghty's blistering run to cap a magnificent Meath display.

★★★★★

66

I PLAYED SENIOR for Meath in the same year I played minor in 1994, so I had been on the panel for a while before I made my championship debut against Carlow in '96.

I was on the bench for the 1995 championship and after being beaten by Dublin by 10 points everyone was calling for Seán Boylan's head at the time, but lucky enough he stayed on and he built a new team in '96.

I'd say there were about eight-to-10 under-21s on the panel, and a few of the older lads like Bob O'Malley, Colm O'Rourke and Bernard Flynn all left after the 1995 hammering, so 1996 was about building a brand new team with some of the older lads, like Tommy Dowd, John McDermott, Brendan Reilly, Colm Coyle and Martin O'Connell.

Those older lads had already been with Sean for five-to-10 years, so that was the blend he had to work with in 1996.

The reason I picked the All-Ireland semi-final against Tyrone in 1996 is because that was the game when the whole thing really shifted onto the older lads that year – the younger lads had helped the rehabilitation of the team after the disappointment of '95, but the knowledge and experience of the older players brought us the rest of the way.

There were five of us who started the first game of the campaign against Carlow who were only 19 or 20 years old. We were so delighted to get to play for Meath and we would do whatever it took to get the best out of ourselves, but it was a rawness that got us to a Leinster final… an energy. We were full of running, enthusiasm and actually had no fear whatsoever.

When you have no fear you can do amazing things, and that is what won the Leinster title for us that year. The older lads, who were scarred by the previous few years, were a bit disillusioned, but I spoke to Martin O'Connell recently and he recalled that he had been unsure about his future at that stage, but that he had got such a boost seeing us younger fellas flying around the place that he felt he was lifted by us. The older lads knew what it took to get to All-Irelands, and even win them, because they had been involved in 1991 and some of them were involved in 1987 and '88.

They knew how to compose themselves; they knew it wasn't all about enthusiasm and rawness. They knew there had to be a bit of thought put into it.

They led the drive for intensity at training, and us younger lads were always learning from them about how to channel our energy.

When we came through in 1996, the older lads were a bit drained. They had had four or five years where Dublin had been beating them and they hadn't won a Leinster since '91, so it was the younger players who brought the older players through the Leinster campaign in '96. Our enthusiasm was what got Meath through a lot of the early games and the older lads just followed along, but when we got into the All-Ireland series, then, the older lads took over and brought us the rest of the way.

Enthusiasm and youth will only get you so far and that is why the Tyrone game in the All-Ireland semi-final is the one that sticks out for me. Players like Tommy Dowd, Martin O'Connell, John McDermott and Colm Coyle... they were the ones who sowed it into us young lads that we might never get a shot at an All-Ireland series again and we had to be focused.

That Tyrone game was a real shift in the dynamic of the panel.

Even going into the Dublin game in the Leinster final no one gave us a chance, because they had beaten us by 10 points the year before. Outside of the team, it would have been seen to have been acceptable to have a moral victory against Dublin, but inside the panel we knew we had an opportunity and we wanted to do our best and, luckily enough, we won that Leinster.

Against Tyrone we made a conscious decision that it was all up to us now; we didn't have the luxury of having a moral victory against them. Outside of the panel, the supporters would have been happy if we got within a couple of points of Tyrone because they had been unlucky not to win the All-Ireland the year before against Dublin.

They were coming down to Croke Park as overwhelming favourites, but we said to ourselves after the Dublin game that we needed to park the celebrations to one side and we needed to really make sure we gave the All-Ireland series a cut.

Within the panel, moral victories were completely out the window.

Training between the win over Dublin and the All-Ireland semi-final against Tyrone was all focused on the first 10 minutes; we didn't focus on anything after that. Sean gave us a scenario of what was going to happen before the game. He created the scene… that the noise of the crowd was going to be deafening, he kept onto us about that; it was as if he couldn't stress it enough. He wanted us ready for that noise.

He said it time and again, but it was one thing saying it and another thing understanding it. We were first out on the pitch that day in a packed, *packed* Croke Park and when Tyrone came out onto the pitch we didn't even look over to see them. We knew the noise was there, but we were in our own bubble, doing our own thing, so the noise didn't get to us at all; we weren't overwhelmed at all because that was something Sean had prepared us so well for.

We never spoke about anything else other than the first 10 minutes.

We had to make sure our intensity was so high that we would find our second wind within 10 minutes. It was crucial that every player on the pitch was absolutely out on their feet after eight or 10 minutes. Sean always focused the training so that we would be out on our feet after eight or 10 minutes, but then we would find our second wind and be okay for the rest of the training session.

Another huge thing that day was that we lined up exactly as we were picked. It was actually the fourth game in-a-row that the same team started with everyone in the same positions. There was no chopping or changing and Sean insisted that we all lined up the way we were picked.

I went in full-back, Mark O'Reilly went in corner-back, Enda McManus was centre-back and so on. Sean drilled into us that no matter what Tyrone came at us with, we had to stay in our positions.

After the national anthem, Tyrone ran into their positions and Peter Canavan, who had been picked at full-forward, ran into corner-forward… we stood in our positions and held our ground, and that was probably the first bit of the psychological battle.

They fully expected me to switch onto Peter Canavan and Mark O'Reilly to go full-back, but we stuck to our positions and got the upper-hand on them straight away. That was a defining moment for that team.

We had set out our stall and we weren't going to react to what any other team was doing, we were determined to play our own game. For such a young team to have the trust to do that was brilliant. It all came back to the way Sean prepared us for it, but for such a young team to do that against such a seasoned team like Tyrone, who were tipped to win the All-Ireland that year, it was a huge plus for us. Our biggest fear was that, as individuals, we wouldn't be able to get to the stage where we were whacked after 10 minutes and we wouldn't get our second wind.

We weren't afraid of Tyrone or anything they might bring, we were just purely focused on getting to a stage where we were whacked after that eight or 10 minutes! We knew that if that happened, we would be okay .

Sean had stressed to us in the weeks leading up to the game not to be worried if we were losing after those first 10 minutes. He insisted that the scoreboard didn't matter at that stage, it was all about finding that second wind and getting to a level of intensity that would carry us through the rest of the game.

After eight to 10 minutes, we were three points down.

But we never panicked because the three points that Tyrone got were under severe pressure and that set down a marker to them that they were in for a serious game and would have to work like hell for every one of their scores.

Personally, after eight to 10 minutes, my legs were gone, my lungs were gone... it was as if I had nothing left, but I knew in the back of my mind that I would be okay in a few minutes and, once I got my second wind, I never got tired after that.

That is a mental thing, but it is also a physical thing. You can't do the physical thing without the mental side of it. To get yourself to your second wind there is a physical aspect, but to get there you need a strong mental attitude. I could go in for any game and stand at full-back and jog around, but I'd never get my second wind and you wouldn't get the best out of yourself by playing like that.

Against Tyrone, I was determined to make runs that I knew in my heart and soul it wouldn't make any difference if I made them or not. I ended up dropping back a bit. Ciaran McBride, who had been prolific for Tyrone that year, came in full-forward and he started running around the place and I knew that even if I didn't go with him on some runs the ball wouldn't come into him anyway, because I was reading the game.

I knew that even if I didn't make the runs he wouldn't have damaged us, but that might have damaged me so I made sure that I made all the runs that he made and I was making even more runs than him, because I was trying to cut out other balls too.

That might have been a risky game to play, trying to cut out other balls, because that was leaving McBride wide open and it made my job harder to get back over to him, but I had to run around the place and make sure my intensity was one hundred percent. When your intensity levels are at one hundred percent you get to the end of your first wind a lot earlier, that is the mental aspect of the plan. You put so much pressure and stress on yourself to get to that second wind that you are getting tired earlier.

I could see it in the lads faces in those early stages, that everyone was bursting to get to that second wind. I knew that everyone would get there, I knew looking around the dressing-room before the game that every one of the lads would get there.

You look at lads in that dressing-room and you think to yourself that you mightn't like someone that much or you might not get on that well with some of them, but you wouldn't want anyone else in that dressing-room other than those lads, because, you know they are prepared to do the very same thing that you are willing to do when you go out on the pitch.

Whereas a clubmate or a friend or a family member mightn't want to do that, and you wouldn't want them in that dressing-room.

Seán Boylan's Meath teams were notorious for never being beaten and for being capable of coming back in the last 10 minutes, but those teams would never have been able to come back in the last 10 minutes unless they had been able to bring the intensity in the first 10 minutes. You can't build yourself up to get to a point where in the last 10 minutes of a game you then flip a switch, it doesn't happen like that.

The rumours coming down from Ulster and coming out of the Tyrone camp ahead of the 1996 All-Ireland semi-final were that they were going to come down to Croke Park and try to bully a young Meath side off the pitch.

We had prepared for that type of approach and Seán had insisted that no matter what we do to make sure that nobody found themselves isolated at any stage; you can take from that what you like, but for us it meant we always backed up our teammate if anything happened on or off the ball.

We played with such intensity in the first 10 minutes that Tyrone didn't know how to handle our physicality, they weren't expecting that. They thought they would come into Croke Park, bully a young team early on and then away they'd go… so they got a bit of a shock. We played with such intensity.

When you have that level of intensity going for a ball it is frightening what you can achieve, rather than an intensity where you say you are going to kill this fella. If you go out to try to kill a fella, it is never as intense as when you are going for the ball. That day all we could see was the football, we didn't see the Tyrone lads. If you are going for a ball with full intensity you can hit three or four lads unknown to yourself just trying to get there and that was the intensity that Seán brought to our game.

From the outside that might have looked like we were going for lads, but we weren't; we were just going for the ball and couldn't see the players in the way because we were concentrating on the ball that much.

We knew that once we got the first 10 minutes out of the way and found our second wind we could win. Our midfielders and half-forwards tracked back and tackled ferociously in defence and that gave us a lot of space up front, and with Graham Geraghty running onto loose ball with his speed, he had a field day.

Graham got a goal just before half-time which brought us level and that was the crucial score of the game. Even if we had been three or four points down at half-time, I don't think that would have bothered us too much, but being level at half-time showed Tyrone that they didn't get the upper-hand like they had planned. If they had been a few points up at the break they might have been a bit more confident, so I think Graham's goal just before the break was the key score of the game.

In the last 20 minutes we completely opened up. We knew we had that in us, we knew Tyrone hadn't the desire necessary.

Canavan started at full-forward for the second-half. I looked into his eyes and I knew when he was coming into me that he was bet. I still had a job to do and my intensity was still very high and it was never going to drop until after the game, but I knew when he came out after half-time that we had them.

His body language and his eyes were shell-shocked; he was like a rabbit caught in the headlights. He didn't really know how he was going to do what he had to do, and Tyrone only scored three points in the second-half.

It was a complete team performance from Meath.

The full-back line were still under a little bit of pressure in the second-half, there were still interceptions and blocks that we needed to make and get right. They were important and at crucial times, but we did exactly what we were supposed to do. The half-back line did what they were meant to do and feed the midfielders. The midfielders then fed the forwards and the full-forward line, who are there because they are scorers; we scored 2-12 from play, so they also did their job. Every line did exactly what they were meant to do; no one line depended on another pick up their slack – it was a complete team performance and in the last 20 minutes Graham Geraghty and Barry Callaghan opened up and we ran away with it.

We ran away with it professionally because we were very, *very* ruthless. It was the most ruthless performance that I have ever been involved in. It was all about how much can we score, how much can we stop them from scoring right up to the last minute.

That happened right up until the referee blew the final whistle and I didn't even realise the game was over, it went by so quickly.

There was no roaring or shouting back in the dressing-room after the game; we knew the job wasn't done yet. We had roared and shouted after the Leinster final because that was special and really important to lift a trophy, but after the win over Tyrone we were calm because it was only a semi-final of an All-Ireland.

I remember going into the dressing-room and everyone was sitting down. Because we had got ourselves into such a high state of intensity it took lads maybe an hour to come back down. There was no one talking. Seán came in and gave a low-key speech where he said he was proud of us doing a professional job, but there was no one hugging or laughing or anything like that.

It was a job done and we had set down a marker that we were going to be a top team in the country for the next few years and that proved to be the case for the next five years where we were one of, if not the best team in the country – and that was because of the marker we put down in that win over Tyrone.

We played every game after that win over Tyrone with the same drive and desire to lay down intensity levels in the first 10 minutes that no other team could match.

It was crucial that we went on to win the All-Ireland that year to back up that performance. We won the All-Ireland because of that game.

In the All-Ireland finals against Mayo, we found ourselves six points down in both games, but we knew that because of our intensity in the first 10 minutes that we would always be better than the opposition in the last 10 minutes.

If we had played against Tyrone with the same intensity we had played with in the Leinster campaign then we wouldn't have had that kick in us on the two All-Ireland final days where we dominated the closing stages of both games to get a draw the first day and then win it the second time around.

After the win over Tyrone the media went to town about our style, about the alleged sledging we did and about Martin O'Connell's famous 'stamp' on Brian Dooher. That sticks in my mind.

At that time, football was the type of game where, if you got a belt, you got up and you sorted it out yourself. The Martin O'Connell incident, whether it was meant or not meant, it was one of those things that happened and at most it was a bookable offence – so even if he had been booked for it, it would have made no difference to the outcome.

The criticism after that game didn't bother us in the slightest; it was the same after the finals against Mayo. We were so focused on getting the result in those games that anything afterwards didn't bother us at all.

So, after my first full year of championship football, we had won every game, apart from the draw with Mayo, and we won the All-Ireland, so I thought this is great… I hope it's like this forever.

However, you do realise that at some stage it won't always be that way.

All we could do was keep playing the games and keep trying to find those high levels of intensity. The game against Tyrone wasn't my best ever individual performance, but it was the performance that laid the foundation for every other performance after that.

There were games after that where I played better, but I would never have been able to reach those levels without that game against Tyrone. Up to that point I had never given as much of myself on a football field.

GRAHAM GERAGHTY

Graham Geraghty would have the honour of lifting the Sam Maguire Cup as Meath captain in 1999 (above with Seán Boylan), but the thrill of defeating Tyrone en route to the '96 title will live with him forever.

66

IT WAS A dream come through for me, when I came onto the Meath panel after the 1991 All-Ireland final. It was something that I always wanted to do, I always aspired to representing the senior team in Croke Park because I would have followed that team from when they played in the Centenary Cup final in 1984.

As minors, we would have played a lot before the seniors in Croke Park during 1990, so you got a feel for the big game atmosphere – we were winning and we were getting the full experience of a big crowd.

That experience of playing in Croke Park in front of a huge crowd as a minor was enormous. Those games weren't easily won, so to get that big game atmosphere and to win tight games was hugely beneficial for the five or six lads that made it off that team and onto the seniors.

When I went into the seniors in October 1991, I put a bit of pressure on myself because I wanted to perform, I wanted to be on the team. I didn't want to be going in there and just making up numbers, and from talking to some of the older lads who were there at the time, they were looking to the next generation to come in and give the whole thing a boost again – that is what we tried to do at that stage.

It did take a couple of years before we had any significant impact. It was a period of mini-transition and it was 1994 before we won anything, when we managed to win the National League.

It was a bit of a tradition that some of the older lads got a bit of a rest over the early league games, so I got to play a lot of those games over the winter months when they used to play three games in the league before Christmas.

It was a daunting task going into that group of legends and heroes. The first night I went in, I was sitting in the dressing-room minding my own business… when I saw these two feet standing in front of me. And when I looked up, I saw it was Liam Harnan and I thought to myself… *Oh f**k, what am I after doing wrong here.*

Liam looked down at me and growled… 'That's my seat!' so I thought to myself okay, I better move out of here. Those lads were legends and fierce competitors.

When we went out training, I was there to be competitive and I got stuck in probably a bit more than they expected. Some of the older lads mightn't have liked the way I was so competitive in training, but I wasn't going away, I was determined that I was there to stay and I was going to make my mark.

Later on in life, some of those lads, the likes of Colm O'Rourke and Bernard Flynn said to me that when I came in I was a cocky 18- or 19-year-old lad and they were thinking… *Who the hell does this lad think he is?*

However, they were delighted to see that attitude because they knew they weren't going to be let down on the big day by a young lad who was out of his depth. I was willing to give it everything I had and those lads saw that from the start.

My first few years were tough.

I was playing all during the league, but I never really got a chance in the championship until 1994. Many of the older guard were still around at the time and Seán was loyal to them, so I didn't get the proper opportunity in championship until '94. That was frustrating for me because when you are sitting on the bench all you want to do is play and have an effect on the game. It was tough, but when my chance came I took it with both hands.

It was great to win the National League against Armagh in '94, that was my first success at senior level and then I got an All Star as well which capped off an amazing year for me… and I was still only 21 or 22.

The following year was hugely disappointing because we were expected to push on a bit. It was the last year for Colm O'Rourke and Brian Stafford and lads like that; they had given it everything for so long for Meath, so they decided to move over after the Leinster final loss to Dublin and let some of the younger lads try to take over the mantle.

The 1996 team was a very young team with Darren Fay, Paddy Reynolds, Trevor Giles, Mark O'Reilly, Barry Callaghan… all those lads came through from the '92 minor team, they were fresh from a bit of success too and they were mad keen to make an impression straight away.

So for those lads to come into the panel and have lads like Martin O'Connell and Colm Coyle, who had been there for years, was a huge benefit to them.

Brendan Reilly was a quiet fella, but he had great experience too and with others like Tommy Dowd and John McDermott, there were lads with huge names around who were still willing to push it on and do whatever had to be done – we all rowed in behind those lads.

When young lads get in or get their chance, they fear nothing. In 1996, the league wasn't particularly good for us, but coming towards the end of that campaign and in the lead up to the championship, we could feel there was something in the air around the camp. There was certainly something special brewing and we just needed something to kickstart it and, thankfully, that happened in the first game against Carlow.

I didn't think that it was going to be a period of transition, or a two- or three-year project, I felt straight away when those young lads came in that they were ready for the now. I had been watching Trevor Giles from when he was a young lad, even when he was playing under-12 he was sticking his head up in the air to see where he could kick the ball to.

Darren Fay was a Rolls Royce of a full-back. Paddy Reynolds was a real workhorse and would get stuck in anywhere, and Mark O'Reilly was the same. Those lads weren't going to be found wanting, so there was never a worry that they would need time to bed in; everything just came together at the right time.

Ahead of that game against Carlow, when I was leaving the house that morning, my wife Amanda said to me that she thought Carlow might beat us, but I was so confident that I just replied, 'No chance!'

And I told her there and then, that we would win the All-Ireland that year.

I wouldn't say I was being cocky or over-confident; there was just something special about that team, and we went on and hockeyed Carlow, and then just went from game to game.

Going into the Leinster final against Dublin we didn't need any extra motivation because we had been beaten by 10 points by them the year before and they were All-Ireland champions. We were willing to put our necks on the line and that's exactly what we did; we got our result and we were fully deserving of it as well.

There was no resting on our laurels after that win. We enjoyed that night, and probably a few nights after it too, but we were determined to just take each game as it came. We weren't looking at winning All-Irelands, we were looking at the next game – the semi-final against Tyrone.

That game against Tyrone was a massive game for us.

They felt they were done out of winning the All-Ireland the year before against Dublin, and they were feeling sorry for themselves. Everyone was thinking that Tyrone would get back to the All-Ireland final, where they could finally put the ghost to bed and win one.

We approached every game the same way.

We always studied the opposition to see where their strong points were and where they were weak; then we looked at what way we were going to play. There was never the case of sitting back and having a go and seeing what might happen… we were determined to win, we approached that game determined to get to the All-Ireland final.

Only four or five of our team had been to an All-Ireland final before and they weren't taking anything for granted; they wanted to get back there again, so a lot of those lads drove on those ambitions.

Brendan Reilly was phenomenal that year… Martin O'Connell the same.

Colm Coyle was brilliant too and John McDermott was there since 1990, so he had great experience as well; those lads were huge leaders on and off the field.

There was a lot of talk after that Tyrone game about it being a rough game and how tough Meath had been, but I played football for Meath for 17 years and I never saw any teams as physical as the northern teams. They were the most physical teams we ever played against.

We were ready for the physicality Tyrone were going to bring to us in that game and we stood up to them.

There were a few incidents during the game, but I don't think any of them were the winning or losing of the match.

We were determined to come out of the blocks at 100 miles per hour and hit them with everything we had. The first five or 10 minutes of any game at that level – especially at that time of the year in semi-finals or finals – everything was 100 miles per hour and it could be 20 minutes before you'd even get your hands on the ball.

Sometimes you don't know where you are and you can't even catch your breath, it is unbelievable.

That day the atmosphere was electric; it was probably the most intimidating game I ever played in because they were tipped to win that game and go on and win the All-Ireland, whereas we were just a young Meath team that had exceeded expectations and that was as far as we were going to go.

I remember standing with Donal Curtis going through our warm-up, just hand passing the ball to each other when Tyrone came running out onto the field.

I never heard anything like it in my life.

The Tyrone supporters must have outnumbered ours by about five to one, there just seemed to be red and white everywhere. Myself and Donal were only about six feet away from each other, but I couldn't hear a word he was saying to me and I just started laughing, because it was so unreal to be part of it.

The atmosphere was electric and definitely the loudest I have ever felt it – I've played in Croke Park a hundred times since, but I never heard anything like that day.

Tyrone started well and went 0-3 to 0-0 up… and 0-4 to 0-1 up… but I was never overly worried. Most games are not won in the first five or 10 minutes; it is the last five or 10 minutes that you need to perform in and the longer that game went on the more we got into it.

I was happy enough at half-time. We were after growing into the game and we were in a good position. Lads were playing well, so we were very confident. Evan Kelly, Trevor Giles, John McDermott were all brilliant that day.

Darren Fay, even though he'll say it probably wasn't one of his best game… he was still colossal that day in the full-back line along with Cormac Murphy. Martin O'Connell, Coyler… everyone put in their shift.

For me, and I don't mean to be disrespectful to anyone else, I think that was one of the best Meath teams we ever had. We had an all-round team, from one to 15 we were probably a more balanced side. Some of the other teams in the past were probably depending on two or three lads to carry them, but we had such a good all-round side.

We weren't reliant on two or three players, we had great quality everywhere.

I wasn't expecting to get the amount of room I did get in that match. Fergal Logan was marking me and he was quite a fast player… big, tall and rangy, but the amount of space I got that day was a sin really. I was able to set up attacks using pace, so it beggared belief the amount of room I got, but I suppose I did have to work to create that room too.

At one stage a high ball came into the forwards and I was moving at flat out pace and it broke straight down to me. I ran around three or four Tyrone lads, and at that stage I had the momentum and they were flat-footed waiting for the break. It looked good on reflection, but I was just fortune that the break fell kindly for me and we got a score off that – and that was the start of the turning of the tide.

Near the end of the half, Trevor laid the ball on to me and I took a snap shot.

I think the ball bounced before it got to Finbarr McConnell and went into the corner of the net, so it wasn't that it was a rocket of a shot; it was just a bit out of his reach. When you find yourself in those positions, you just have to hit the ball as hard as you can and try to keep it out of the reach of the keeper – sometimes you get lucky and sometimes you don't.

That time, I got lucky.

Everything went right for me that day.

Balls broke in front of me. I found myself in a lot of space which I was able to use to draw in Tyrone defenders and set up other lads for scores as well. I probably could have scored a lot more myself.

I laid off the ball for Barry Callaghan's goal and there were a few other goal chances where I just took my points. In the second-half we were going really well, so we didn't have to be going for goals. At one stage I was going through and I just tipped it over the bar. I probably could have drawn in a defender and set up someone else for a goal, but we didn't need goals at that stage, so we just kept clipping over the points.

That day was one of those days for me when you wake up in the morning and you feel good. When I got to Croke Park I felt good still, and I had this massive burst of energy where I never felt tired and I could run all day.

There are some days where you go out and your legs feel like lead, but that day against Tyrone, everything felt great and of course when your confidence is soaring it is easy to do things and everything falls into place. When you are chasing games, you feel like you are always 60 yards from goals, but when you are going well and full of confidence everything seems so much easier.

The feeling after that game was fantastic.

The most enjoyable part of that whole day for me was going to meet family and the fans after the game because you could enjoy the win. It's different now because I believe you don't have that interaction between the players and the fans any more, which is a pity.

It was very different back then when we used to all go back and meet in the County Club in Dunshaughlin, and after the meal the supporters had full access to the players and the lads used to love mixing with everyone. I loved those occasions, mingling with the fans after a great victory was very, *very* special.

In fairness we had to take the good with the bad, and there were times when it wasn't such fun. The media used to build us up and create expectations, but the fans also used to propel us up and they would let you know if you didn't play well or if you were beaten. The supporters were very important, and you had to be there for them because at the end of the day they will pull you out of holes in Croke Park when they are shouting... 'UP THE ROYALS'... or whatever.

They certainly do give you a lift in those tight situations.

To follow up that win over Tyrone by winning the All-Ireland was fantastic, a dream come through. Everyone knows what happened in that Mayo game and I think it has been blown up a lot over the years. I don't think lads knew what to do when that row started. I had never been in a situation like that before where there were so many players involved.

I think lads were just running around, pushing and shoving, hoping that they wouldn't get a box themselves. Everyone was on the move because there is nothing worse than just standing there... and then someone comes running from behind you and hits you.

Unfortunately 1997 and '98 were disappointing, but then we came again in '99. When Seán asked me to be captain, I thought he was messing for a start. I was honoured to be asked and I tried to tone down the way I played and reacted with referees. I had to do that because I was now the captain, I was expected to lead by example.

Things went really well for us that year. I don't think there was any game where we were struggling. We were confident of winning every game. When pressure did come on us, we took it all on board and used it to help us push on and turn games around.

The final against Cork proved that.

When the chips were down lads stood up and we won quite comfortably in the finish. I never once felt like we were going to lose that game. Even when we missed the penalty nobody panicked, we treated it just like a missed free and moved on... there was a great attitude.

I had Ollie Murphy in beside me in the full-forward line at that stage.

He was some lad to give you confidence; he was always talking about the next ball in and getting a score from it. He was the epitome of that Meath team... he was only 19, but he was like everyone else on that team.

He was the manager, he was the forward, he was a leader... we all were.

The manager is probably the last lad who has a say when the big games start – apart from substitutions – because our players from the 1994 team right up to 2001 were really strong leaders on the field. They used to do things without Seán having to say it to them; they used to make little changes themselves and Seán allowed that, he wanted players to express themselves.

We let the All-Ireland in 2001 get away from us.

We approached it all wrong, not from a management point of view; it was more the players. We got carried away with the semi-final win over Kerry, and it was hard not to do that because we were being built up by the media, by the supporters, by our families and friends… everybody was saying we would win and we started to listen to that.

Things did go wrong for us on the day against Galway as well.

We were only two points down at half-time and I wasn't overly worried. I knew we weren't playing well, but the game hadn't got away from us by that stage so we just needed to buck up and start trying a little harder and things would turn for us, but instead it went from bad to worse.

I remember standing at one stage looking down the field and thinking… *Oh Jesus, just take me off… I don't want to be here!* I would never have said that before, but that was just one of those days where the confidence wasn't there and we always seemed to be 60 yards away from the goals.

Everything went right for Galway that day.

If a ball hit a Galway lad in the face it would bounce into a teammates hands and I don't think they kicked that many wides; everything they kicked went over the bar. The same thing happened for us against Kerry in the semi-final. We built ourselves up for that game, but let ourselves down badly.

I don't look back with regrets.

Sometimes, you look back in disappointment that you didn't win certain games, such as in 2001, but I don't look at life that way really. Things happen for a reason and if you look back with regrets you will never push forward.

JODY DEVINE

MEATH 2-20 KILDARE 3-17
Leinster SFC Semi-Final
Croke Park
JULY 20 1997

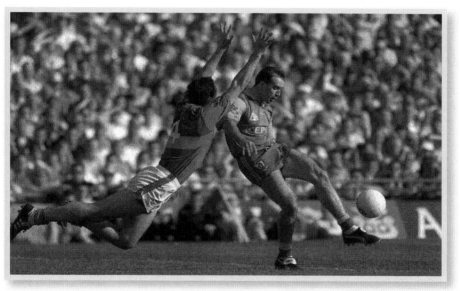

Jody Devine's four spectacular points in extra-time in the 1997 trilogy against Kildare will live with him, and Meath supporters, forever.

★ **MEATH:** C Martin; M O'Reilly, D Fay, D Curtis; P Reynolds, E McManus, C Coyle; J McGuinness, J McDermott; T Giles (2-8), T Dowd (0-2), G Geraghty (0-1); PJ Gillic, B Reilly (0-3), O Murphy (0-2). Subs: M O'Connell for McManus, N Nestor for McGuinness, **J Devine (0-4)** for Gillic. Extra-time: E Kelly replaced the sent-off G Geraghty, McGuinness for Coyle, McManus for O'Reilly, K Cahill for McGuinness.

★ **KILDARE:** C Byrne; M Ryan, D Dalton, S Dowling; A Rainbow, G Ryan, K Doyle; N Buckley (0-4), W McCreery (1-0); E McCormack (0-4), D Kerrigan, T Harris (1-0); P Graven (0-6), M Lynch (0-1), B Murphy (1-0). Subs: D Earley (0-1) for McCreery, B Fahy for Harris, P McCormack (0-1) for Doyle.

THE ACTION

THE HEADLINE ON the Meath *Chronicle* said it all.

DEVINE INTERVENTION it screamed after Jody Devine was sprung from the bench to rescue Meath from the jaws of defeat in their Leinster SFC semi-final replay against Kildare.

After a drab drawn encounter a couple of weeks earlier, Meath and Kildare met in Croke Park for a replay of their semi-final and produced a pulsating thriller that epitomised the typical never-say-die spirit that saw Seán Boylan's sides become stuff of myth and legend.

Those powers of survival were never more severely tested than that warm summer evening in Croke Park as Kildare threatened on several occasion to pummel Meath into submission, but Boylan's side never gave up and even when they were six points down at the break in extra-time there was still a sense that Meath were alive.

It took three minutes into the resumption of play in the second-half of extra-time before Meath's recovery commenced. It still looked like a lost cause when Trevor Giles converted a free and Tommy Dowd added only his second score, but then Devine struck. Three majestic points, kicked with the aid of a slight breeze into the Canal End goals closed the gap to 2-18 to 3-16 and there was still plenty of time left.

Giles brought his personal tally to 2-8 with his fifth successful free to remarkably restore parity, and when Devine took possession two minutes later it was inevitable that he would find the range and edge Meath in front for the first time since Giles had made it 0-4 to 0-3 in the 19th minute.

Moments later Devine had a chance to put two between the sides, but his effort dropped short and on the counter-attack Kildare won a disputed free close to the sideline, and from Niall Buckley's dropping ball Paul McCormack got the vital touch to deflect the effort over the bar and ensure a third day out would be necessary before Meath would eventually advance.

★★★★★

66

AFTER THE DISAPPOINTMENT of the hammering by Dublin in the Leinster final in 1995 there wasn't much expected from Meath for a few years. Nobody was rating the new young lads coming through, but that was because most of the people outside of Meath didn't know who they were.

After the win over Carlow at the start of the 1996 campaign, people started to sit up and take notice of lads like Darren Fay, Mark O'Reilly, Paddy Reynolds, Trevor Giles, Barry Callaghan and Ollie Murphy, so when we beat Dublin in the Leinster final that year it was a bit of a surprise and, of course, we went on to win the All-Ireland. The defence of our titles in 1997 began with a game against Dublin and they were out for revenge after surprisingly losing to us the year before when they were defending All-Ireland champions.

That was a great win for us that day.

Paul Bealin missed a penalty, but there was never much between Meath and Dublin back in those days; it was always very, very tight no matter if we were on top or if they were on top, they were always close games.

We had eight different scorers that day and in our forwards you had lads like Graham Geraghty, Trevor Giles, Tommy Dowd, Ollie Murphy, Evan Kelly and Barry Callaghan… they were all lads who could chip in with scores, so we were never relying on just one lad to get us five, six or seven points.

If you look across the spread of scorers in nearly all the games we played in that time, we would always have had at least five or six different scorers. So it was hard to break into that forward line.

Some of the training games we had to try to force our way onto that team were tough; the competition was fierce and I often went to the management asking what did I need to improve on to get onto the team. Seán always used to say to me to keep working hard and he always said that I gave a different dimension to the team coming off the bench when things needed to be changed.

At that time I was just glad to be on the panel because the strength of the forwards available was unreal. It was hard to even get on the panel. I always wanted to start, but I was delighted to be there and if I couldn't start, I always wanted to make sure I made a contribution when I came on.

Without doubt there were times I got frustrated with my role and I often asked the management what more can I do? They always gave me advice about what I needed to do, but the view was almost always that I might help change a game off the bench for the last 20 minutes or half an hour.

I was vying for the No 10 or 12 jersey, which meant I was up against either Trevor Giles or Graham Geraghty, so I certainly could never say the two lads picked ahead of me were worse than me, because in my opinion those two lads are two of the best players I ever played with.

If you look at the 1996 side, the half-forward line was Graham, Trevor and Tommy Dowd – I was up against them, so best of luck trying to dislodge one of those legends of the game.

The class of player I was competing against were the envy of every other county, but that is the way it was, so I had to buy into the decision of management. It wasn't about my own personal game, it was all about Meath; that was the main thing for me.

In the inside forward line you had Brendan Reilly, who probably never really got the credit he deserved… you had Barry Callaghan, who broke through in 1996 and he was as good a corner-forward as we have had.

Ollie Murphy was still young in 1996 and '97 – it was Colm Brady who was the other corner-forward in '96 and he operated further out the field, so anyone that was ahead of me deserved their spot.

Evan Kelly was another lad who came onto the panel and could have started a lot more games too; we were lucky to have really good forwards.

After beating Dublin in the Leinster quarter-final everyone was talking us up again, but I missed out the first game against Kildare… I wasn't even togged out.

Between that Dublin game and the first game against Kildare, I was sick with conjunctivitis. I was at the game, but I didn't tog out because I had been sick and I wouldn't have been well enough to offer anything to the team.

Because I wasn't involved, I don't really remember much about the first game. It finished 0-12 to 1-9, and Geraghty and Giles finished with seven points between them, so how on earth was I ever going to start ahead of them two?

Tommy Dowd, Ollie Murphy, Brendan Reilly all scored as well that day, so that just goes to prove the spread of scorers we were capable of.

After the drawn game I had two weeks to get myself back into the frame ahead of the replay. The panel of players at that time were a lot smaller than what you would have now. We probably only had 25 or 26 lads on the panel, so I wasn't worried that I wouldn't be on the panel for the replay – if you were showing well in training that would be enough to get you into the matchday 15 or get you chosen as a sub.

The fact that it was only conjunctivitis I had didn't take much out of me, it wasn't like I had pneumonia or something that would have left me gasping for breath, so as soon as it cleared I was back in training straight away on the Tuesday or Thursday after the first game.

Everybody on the panel wanted to be on the team and after beating Dublin in the first round the team didn't perform to their best in the drawn game with Kildare, so everyone felt they were in with a fair chance of getting a start in the replay.

The in-house games at training were as competitive as anything you'd play in the championship. Seán would be refereeing, so you knew the whistle wouldn't be blown that much. We were expected to work hard; it was very competitive and that really stood to us in the latter stages of games.

Our training sessions were an hour, an hour and a half… non-stop, full blast… flat out. There was no let up at all – what you do in a training game you would then automatically bring to a matchday situation and that stood to us.

After being named on the bench for the replay I was just the same as all the other subs and I was hoping that I would be called upon. I came on with about six or seven minutes left in normal time for PJ Gillic, who had come back onto the panel after not being involved in 1996, and luckily we managed to force extra-time with Trevor getting a late goal after missing a penalty just before that.

Kildare were very strong at that time… Niall Buckley in midfield, Glenn Ryan in their backs… Davy Dalton was full-back, so they were good, although their forwards probably let them down at times as they weren't as accurate as they should have been.

They had us under serious pressure at certain times in those three games, but they didn't take their chances and they left us in the games, which was a dangerous thing to do to those Meath teams.

They were 1-7 to 0-7 clear at half-time and then added a second goal after the break. Then Graham Geraghty got sent-off, but we got back into the game when Trevor scored a penalty. Late on he missed another penalty, when we were three points down, but Davy Dalton kicked the clearance straight out over the sideline and when it was sent back in there was a bit of a scramble in the box before Trevor palmed it to the net – he scored 2-8 that day.

I didn't see the incident that led to Graham getting sent-off.

We were told it was because of an off the ball incident with Glenn Ryan. That left us down to 14, but we rallied well.

In extra-time they went ahead again and it was 3-16 to 2-13 at half-time of the additional period, but we didn't panic because we knew there was a breeze blowing into the Canal End at that time and we would have chances.

When played resumed we just got on top again and scored six or seven points in-a-row. I got four of them so that's what makes this game extra special for me.

When we were five points down I think I managed to kick three points in-a-row, then Trevor converted another free, and I managed to get another one to put us in front. We were totally dominant for that 10 or 15 minutes of extra-time, it was one of those periods where everything went right for us.

We knew we had a chance at half-time of extra-time.

We were back to 15 men with Evan Kelly coming in to replace Graham and with the wind behind us we knew we just had to keep kicking over the points, so after Trevor kicked a free and Tommy Dowd got a point, I just swung my boot at the first chance I had and it went over.

Then the second one went over, and so did the third one… we just kept tipping away. It was the intensity from our training sessions that kept us going in that spell; we had that never-say-die attitude and Seán was a great believer in just keep going and going.

My fourth point put us ahead and I thought we'd win it then, but there was some controversy over Kildare's late equaliser.

The referee Pat O'Toole was injured and had to be replaced by John Bannon, who missed a couple of things. The Kildare equaliser came when Trevor was adjudged to have shouldered a lad out over the line. Before that, the referee missed a clear push by Martin Lynch on Darren Fay and when the ball came out to the sideline, Trevor shouldered a fella over the line, but the referee gave a free to Kildare instead of a line-ball to Meath.

The free was lobbed into the square and I suppose it could have ended up in the net, but Paul McCormack got a touch to deflect it over the bar – that looked like a square ball too, but there were definitely two incidents before that where we should have had a free out and a sideline ball.

The game finished level and so it was on to a third game, which turned out not to be near as good as the first replay. The third game was played on a wet, damp day.

We were in control for most of it and we were always a few points ahead and we stayed on top throughout.

Plenty of people probably thought I'd start the third game after what had happened in the second one, but how would I get in ahead of Trevor or Graham. The half-forward line didn't change that much from Trevor, Tommy and Graham.

They started Nigel Nestor in the half-forward line instead for the third game. I had always thought I could start every game if I was going well in training, regardless of the fact that I had scored four points in the previous game. However, I was always competing against Graham and Trevor… and then PJ Gillic came back in in 1997 and he often started at half-forward.

That is the competition you are up against when you are part of a great squad.

Looking back, those three games against Kildare probably cost us the Leinster final because in the final game against Kildare we had Darren Fay and Mark O'Reilly sent-off and, with Graham also suspended, we were down three huge players and very depleted for the game against Offaly.

We didn't have a big squad at the time, and we had a couple of knocks going into that Leinster final too. We still went into the Leinster final as favourites because we were All-Ireland champions and we were after beating Dublin and Kildare – Offaly, under Tommy Lyons, were an unknown package coming in under the radar.

However, Offaly were that little bit fresher than us and the toll of the three games against Kildare had taken a huge amount out of us – we were still a bit dazed in the first-half of the final and it was a disappointing end.

Those were amazing times for Meath.

It was great to be part of the Meath squad and it was nice to come in and play my part and do well, but all I ever wanted was for Meath to win. If I made a contribution to that then great, but at the end of the day it was always about the team winning.

My regret from that game against Kildare was that the easiest chance I had, I kicked it into the goalie's hands. I should have taken another step or two and shot from closer, but that dropped shot is a big regret because if that had gone over the bar or even just gone dead, we might have won that second game and who knows what would have happened from there.

Being involved with the Meath senior squad for 10 years, I have no big regrets. Being involved in the National League win in 1994… winning three Leinsters too!

OLLIE MURPHY

MEATH 1-14 DUBLIN 0-12
Leinster SFC Final
Croke Park
AUGUST 1 1999

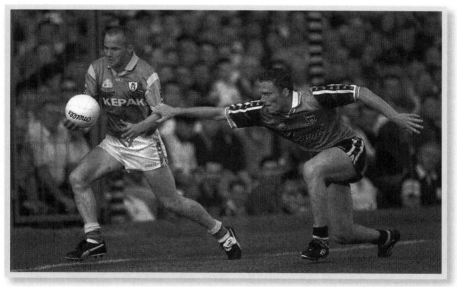

Starting his senior county career in London's colours, Ollie Murphy never imagined he would be routing Dublin in green and gold in 1999 (above) in an All-Ireland winning season.

★ **MEATH:** C Sullivan; M O'Reilly, Darren Fay, C Murphy; P Reynolds, E McManus, H Traynor (0-1); N Crawford, J McDermott; N Nestor (0-1), T Giles (0-5), D Curtis; E Kelly, G Geraghty (0-2), **O Murphy (1-5)**. Sub: R Kealy for McManus.

★ **DUBLIN:** D Byrne; P Moran, P Christie, P Andrews; P Croft, J McGee, K Galvin; C Whelan (0-1), B Stynes; E Sheehy, D Farrell, D Darcy (0-6); J Gavin (0-5), I Robertson, J Sherlock. Subs|: R Cosgrove for Farrell, D Homan for Cosgrove, P Ward for Sheehy.

THE ACTION

MURPHY'S LAW WAS enforced at Croke Park as Meath claimed their 19th Leinster title with a convincing victory over old rivals Dublin.

The dramatic acts of years past weren't repeated and free-flowing football was a rarity, but it mattered little as the 56,315 attendance were treated to one of the finest ever individual displays by Carnaross clubman Ollie Murphy.

The corner-forward made light of Tommy Dowd's absence due to back surgery and broke Dublin's hearts with a personal haul of 1-5, all of which came from play.

Murphy will long be remembered for this performance.

The goal, which came after a remarkable pass from Trevor Giles in the 59th minute, gave Seán Boylan's warriors a 1-12 to 0-8 lead and ended any faint hopes a poor Dublin side had of making a comeback.

The thrills and spills which go hand-in-hand with a Leinster final weren't evident on this occasion and, for the most part, the game lacked panache – the one exception being Murphy.

The attendance watched in awe as the Carnaross clubman dug deep into his bag of skills and produced a classic attacking display which, according to the *Meath Chronicle... made his marker, Peadar Andrews look like a Morris Minor alongside a Rolls Royce.*

Murphy's celebrations in front of Hill 16 after his stunning 59th minute goal will long be remembered by Meath supporters.

Graham Geraghty lifted the seventh Leinster title of Boylan's reign to the delight of Meath supporters, who dutifully obeyed the new rule which forbids patrons from invading the pitch after the game.

★★★★★

"

WHEN I GOT brought onto the Meath minor set up in 1992, we had the best underage sides in the country. We were contesting under-21 and minor finals year-in and year-out, and success seemed normal at that time for Meath underage team.

It was great to be a part of that All-Ireland winning minor panel in 1992.

I had a great minor season in 1993 when we got to another All-Ireland final and I also won the intermediate championship with Carnaross, so I felt I was flying and then in '94 I went for trials with the Meath under-21s, but I didn't get a call back. I was very disappointed.

My clubmate Conor Woods had a great year with the minors too and he got called back to go in with the under-21s, so that compounded my disappointment.

Conor deserved it. He was a big fella and an excellent player, and he was entitled to the call back. I was always quite thin and small when I was younger, so that probably went against me, but I was still very disappointed.

So when the opportunity came to go to London, I just thought why not… so away with me. I just wanted a bit of adventure more than anything else at that time, and London seemed ideal… and looking back on it, it probably wasn't a bad thing. It probably helped me progress as a footballer.

It was great to get away for a year and see things from a different angle and realise that there was no reason to be disappointed with not making the under-21s, because I always loved football and once I was playing that was the main thing for me.

Ollie Lynch from Trim was my contact in London.

I saw an advert in the paper that Tara were looking for players, so I gave Ollie a ring and as soon as I got talking to him I knew he would be great craic and I would be safe enough with him. He is a savage for football.

The lifestyle in London was tough enough because I worked long days, and early on the football was poor enough fare, but when the championship came around it certainly improved as teams produced their best players. The leagues were a bit wishy-washy, but championship football was a good standard.

I ended up making my senior county debut for London and not for Meath, as I might have hoped, so that was a big shock to me.

I was at home with Ollie (Lynch) one day and a fella rang to see if I would go to play a match with London against Tipperary in the McGrath Cup, I think it was. I was completely shocked, but it was a great feeling to get selected and I was delighted because it was acknowledgment that I was doing well enough to be called in.

When you go somewhere new like that you really want to prove yourself, so I worked hard on my football and it probably helped that nobody knew who I was at that stage so I kind of went in under the radar. It could have just been a first year bounce, I'm not sure if I'd have lit it up as much if I had stayed another year.

I definitely enjoyed playing in London and I got loads of scores.

It was great for the club too because they hadn't been doing that well and they got a bounce out of it. The Tara's are a great old club in London. They have a great mix of people from all over Ireland.

Once the championship was over in London I headed home because I wanted to play for Carnaross. At that stage I never dreamt I would have got a call up for Meath. I hadn't made the under-21 panel 12 months earlier, so getting called up to the seniors wasn't even on my radar.

I knew I had played well in London, but it wasn't in my head at all that I would go home to play county football. I just wanted to get home to play for Carnaross.

Even though I didn't make the under-21 panel that time, I was still only 18 so I still held ambitions of playing for Meath again, but coming home from London was just all about getting back to Carnaross for me.

I had been setting my target to get on the under-21s in 1995, so to get a call up in late '94 to go in with the seniors was amazing. Joe Cassells rang me and asked me to go in – I thought it was someone taking the mick.

There was a group of players brought in around that time. Lads like Barry Callaghan and Darren Fay were all called in and they were barely 19, so there was a conveyor belt of players coming through. The management were looking for players to fill holes, looking for lads to start.

It certainly wasn't a case of just bringing in a few lads to develop them slowly.

Some people might look back at that time after 1991 and think it was a tough time for Meath football, but if you look at the bigger picture and delve a bit deeper it wasn't such a bad time at all. I'm sure Seán Boylan was probably salivating looking at all the genuine good footballers coming through.

It worked out great for him in the end. He had a huge amount of retirements around 1994, '95 and then, next thing, he had a huge amount of young footballers around to come in and fill the void.

With so many retirements it was a great opportunity for a young player like myself to get in there and try to stake a claim, so it had to be taken. There were still some big names around the panel and they were as ambitious as the young lads who came in, so it worked out well.

It was a dream going in to the Meath panel at that time.

I was going in and training with lads that I had followed on buses to watch play year-in and year-out for the previous 10 years. I was looking at them gooey-eyed, shocked and in awe of them, but that didn't last too long either because I was an ambitious young footballer – I had to knuckle down and get stuck into it.

The training was some step up.

Their idea of running a lap was totally different from running a lap in Carnaross or London. I was very fit when I was younger, so I could have trained twice a day, every day, without it causing me a thought, but I was still a bit light at that stage so the physical end of it was a bit tough.

I could have been knocked off the ball a bit easier than I would have liked at that time.

I ended up in competition with the lads who were my own age... lads like Ray Magee, Barry Callaghan, Evan Kelly, those type of lads. I always kept one eye on those lads to see how they were going. At the end of the day, even though they were your teammate, you were still in competition with them for places on the team.

Tommy Dowd was another player I looked up to.

People would often have commented that myself and Tommy's styles were very similar and that is a nice compliment. From the early 90s to the mid-90s, Tommy Dowd was unbelievable, he was almost carrying Meath on his own and was winning All Stars for fun.

You don't really look at lads when you are playing and say, 'Yeah, he's a role model', but looking back Tommy Dowd was someone I used to look at and think he had something that I would like to have... he was brilliant.

I wasn't allowed play in the 1994/'95 league because I had played in London, so I didn't make my Meath debut until the O'Byrne Cup against Westmeath. I did well in that first game, so I was delighted with myself and I debuted in the championship against Offaly in Navan, but that didn't go great.

I had started instead of Colm O'Rourke in that game, but I didn't do well and he came on for me and scored a goal and a few points, so you could say I was disappointed with that championship debut.

The hammering by Dublin in the Leinster final that year was very disappointing for all of us. A lot of the older fellas, who had put in 10 or more hard years, looked at the players coming behind them and felt it was time to hand over the reins to us and leave us at it, so a lot of them stepped aside.

The 1996 period was so exciting with the young lads all playing and doing so well. I was only a bit part player at that time, coming on here and there, but it was great to come on as a sub in the last few minutes of the All-Ireland final, it was so exciting. Obviously I'd have preferred to have started, but you will take coming on in an All-Ireland final any day of the week.

We had a small, but a great squad that year.

There were times when you might have a few lads injured or carrying a knock and you could only have 21 at training, but it was savage competition for places and it was a great group.

Coming up to the All-Ireland final in '96 there was a question mark about the corner-forward position and I would have been in the mix, but Colm Brady got the nod and won the berth that day. But the competition for places at training remained savage.

I remember saying to Colm Brady one time at training that I thought I was going to die because the training was so tough and intense. Little did I know at that time that the corner-forward spot on the team was between me and him. I think management were pushing the two of us hard to see who would last the pace longest and obviously with Colm being the fittest man in the world, he won that race.

I was delighted for him because he had a lot of injuries in his career and he deserved that for all his hard work.

The following couple of years were disappointing for various reasons, but then in 1999 it started to shape up nicely again.

We started off with a win over Wicklow and even though I only managed to score a point that day you have to remember who was on the full-forward line with me – Graham Geraghty and Tommy Dowd – and they scored 2-6 between them.

In hindsight, that was some full-forward line. I was very definitely number three in that full-forward line. If Seán ever wanted to change anything in that full-forward line, let's face it, I was always going to be the first one to go!

Playing in a full-forward line with two All-Ireland winning captains, if anything went wrong I didn't stand a chance – then you had Barry Callaghan, Ray Magee and Richie Kealy waiting to get into one of those spots too.

When you think about it, we really should have won more with players like that at our disposal.

In that game against Wicklow I passed a few balls to Geraghty and Dowd, and put them in for scores and only ended up getting a point for myself, but the next day out against Offaly they set me up for a few scores which was great for my confidence – I ended up with 1-3. Tommy also scored four points from play that day against Cathal Daly, and Daly was a hell of a good corner-back... nobody gave Cathal Daly a skinning, but Tommy did that day.

Preparing to play Dublin in a Leinster final then was amazing, but there was a big shock in the build-up because Tommy Dowd got a back injury and needed to have an operation... so there was a lot of talk about that. The speculation was who could step up and fill Tommy's boots. After being number three in that full-forward line, I was now expected to rival Graham for the number one spot and step up to the plate. I remember doing a few interviews at that time; no one was afraid to do interviews back then, and we talked about that scenario of filling Tommy Dowd's boots and being confident at the time I said that maybe I will or maybe I won't, we'd have to see how it goes.

I was coming off the back of having a great game against Offaly. Seán was a great man-manager, he never said too much, but at the same time he always said enough that needed to be said.

Trevor Giles was a big, big player at the time and while he would never admit to it he did a bit of man-management with me and was a huge help to me. He reminded me that it was a big opportunity for me and that I didn't need to try to beat Dublin on my own.

He urged me to take my opportunity; it was almost like he could see the future coming, that I was ready to explode.

Trevor is a very unassuming character, but he has a sharp tongue as well. He could put you on the backfoot or rise you up to the sky; he was always very positive to me because he recognised my potential. We were only as good as our weakest link, so if I was going good, then Trevor was going good.

I was buzzing at the prospect of accepting the extra responsibility with Tommy being missing. Training was like an out of body experience. At times it felt like you were going through the motions, but it was all at 100 miles per hour. I felt great and I felt anything was possible.

I wasn't over-confident because I had had too many disappointments in the past to allow that creep in on me, but everything came together for me in that Leinster final – it was the perfect storm.

One of the best things I recall about that day was that we had great craic going up to Dublin on the bus. Sometimes we had a minibus or a couple of different buses, but I always tried to veer towards Jody Devine and Jimmy McGuinness.

I remember going up on the bus to that Leinster final and Enda McManus was great craic. Enda could be a quiet fella, but he was in great form and you would swear we were just a bunch of lads heading off to a concert. All we were missing were a few cans of Bulmers.

I think we had a water fight on the bus and Pat Kelly, the bus driver, was going bananas trying to get us to calm down before the big game.

We were going to that game coming off the back of losing the previous two Leinster finals to Kildare and Offaly, so there was no real pressure on us. We knew we just had to go out and do our stuff. Our confidence was high, but we weren't over-confident.

We were ready!

It is a very hard science to explain. There is no equation out there, but when you are ready you just know it.

Playing Dublin in a Leinster final is different to playing anyone else in a Leinster final and we went into that game almost at full strength, with the exception of Tommy Dowd. We had savage reserves and had men on the sideline who were All Stars in the making. We went into that game with nothing to fear;

the only person you had to fear was yourself, so all you had to do was get yourself ready… and I was totally ready for that day.

Peadar Andrews was unlucky that day to come up against me considering where I was coming from, where I had been and the experience I had behind me. He came into that game fairly fresh as a young player, so it turned out to be an unfortunate day. In fairness to him to recovered well and came back to win a few Leinsters.

I was running so freely that I felt no one was ever going to catch me.

I could put it onto my left foot or onto my right foot and I could kick freely. I always felt it would go over the bar. I did hit the post once, but I think it came back out to one of our lads and he put it over the bar.

Our half-back line that day were excellent. Hank Traynor and Nigel Nestor, who played in the half-forwards, were two very unsung heroes and both of them scored that day. Nigel Crawford was fresh to the scene and he was playing great football at that time too. Everyone clicked that day.

After the final whistle, I was on top of the world.

It took me a while to come down from it. I was so much in the zone that it took me two or three hours to come back down and relax and enjoy the evening.

I saw pictures of myself afterwards and my eyes just were so focused even hours after the game. It just showed the thought and preparation that went into that game, preparation that I never even considered, but I was still very much in the zone a couple of hours after the game.

Going into the All-Ireland semi-final against Armagh training was going so well, I was running so freely. I was doing drills against Darren Fay and doing well. You would be afraid of your life going up against Darren in training because he approached training the same way he approached a game; he was always deadly serious, a fearless warrior who would put his head in where you wouldn't put your boot.

Even in those drills against Darren I was doing really well and that is how I was measuring myself, because if I can do it against him – and he's the best in the country – then I can do it against anyone. So I was flying at that time. Hank Traynor was another one… you knew if you did well against them in training, then you were in business.

So heading into the Armagh game I was really in the zone, but then a few minutes in disaster struck.

Armagh were a good team, and they got to a few All-Irelands after that, so they were an excellent side and that day they got a good start against us. Then I remember when I was running backwards I heard something crack in my knee and, two minutes later, I'm back in the dressing-room... lying down with a load of ice on my knee and hoping we would win. Thankfully the boys came through it.

Directly after that All-Ireland semi-final I was so down in the mouth because I thought my season was over, I was going to miss the final against Cork. I couldn't believe I was after coming this far and then this happened.

Ray Magee came in for me against Armagh and kicked a couple of points while others were struggling and he played well, so he was ready to go and take my place if injury ruled me out of the final. Ray was that good that year that if he had played in my place in the All-Ireland final he probably would have won an All Star, that's the thin line that existed.

It turned out I had torn a bit of cartilage and did a bit of damage to the bone in my knee; it was really, really sore. The Cork captain Mark Landers had also hurt his knee in their semi-final win and he went for a small operation the next day and managed to play the final, but I went down a different route.

The day after the win over Armagh the Meath medical team finally caught up with me. I don't remember where I was, but I'm sure I was feeling sorry for myself somewhere drinking a pint. They told me to stop whatever it was I was doing and get my arse up to Micheal O Muircheartaigh's son Eamonn... straight away.

I didn't have a car at the time, but James Reilly picked me up and brought me to Eamonn, who has a special machine for treating those type of injuries – and I basically became a professional footballer for the next few weeks.

I was working with Mercury Engineering at the time and I had a really good manager called Frank Matthews, who was a Meath man, so he made sure I was able to get the time off to go for the treatment I needed. I got physio twice a day and I was getting my meals handed to me – I was like a Dublin footballer nowadays. It must have cost the County Board a fortune to get me fit to play in that final! I was getting taxies to and from specialised training and treatment – only for the Board I wouldn't have made it back in time.

I was worried that even if I did recover I mightn't be fully fit and Seán had Ray Magee, Barry Callaghan, Richie Kealy… all chomping at the bit to get the start. However, Seán put my mind at ease and told me that the No 15 position was mine and that he wouldn't take the opportunity away from me so long as I put in the work and worked with them. It was a joint effort with all the support I got. Ann Burton took time off work to help me too – everyone went above and beyond.

I was probably a bit naïve thinking people were taking time off work to help me get better, but they all knew the bigger picture. They knew this was an All-Ireland final and they wanted Meath to have the best chance and they left no stone unturned. I wasn't as fit as I could have been going into that final, but I was fit enough to play. My mind was in a good place because I had worked so hard, day-in and day-out, to get there.

It was great to win and I scored the goal in the All-Ireland final. When I look back I could have had another point or two in that game, but I just wasn't as sharp as I would have expected myself to be. I ended up with an All Star that year and was nominated for Player of the Year… it was an amazing time.

I had a phenomenal year in 2001.

We played some savage games of football. We had epic games against Westmeath, Kildare, Dublin and Kerry. Those Westmeath games were mad and they really came of age that year and haven't fallen away since.

We had so many great players; there is a feeling that we probably could have won a bit more, but we all started so young that we probably burned out a little bit quicker. We had had a lot of underage success, so a lot of those lads had played in minor and under-21 finals and had a lot of hard years under their belts despite being so young and had quick burnout. That aspect of it was a bit disappointing, but that's amateur football for you and that's how it goes. I absolutely loved my time in the Meath jersey. If I could have my time back, there are a lot of things I would do differently and stew on, but that's easy in hindsight.

I had a great innings.

I just love football. I'm as happy at a Junior B match as I was in a senior All-Ireland final. Even going to watch the kids playing now… it has been a great cycle and I love it all.

99

STEPHEN BRAY

ST PATRICK'S CS NAVAN 0-11 ST PATRICK'S ARMAGH 1-6
All-Ireland Colleges SFC Final
Breffni Park
APRIL 16 2000

Stephen Bray had many spectacular scoring displays in Croke Park (above against Dublin in the 2010 championship), but Breffni Park in Cavan, as a secondary school student, is a ground which holds a most precious memory.

★ **ST PATRICK'S CS NAVAN:** R Kenny; I Matthews, K Slattery, S Gough; R Reynolds, B McCormack (0-1), R Conaty; S MacGabhann, C Blake; D O'Toole (0-2), S McKeigue (0-1), **S Bray (0-2)**; P O'Brien, P Treacy (0-1), I McCormack (0-4). Subs: M O'Rourke for Blake, J Sheridan for MacGabhann.

★ **ST PATRICK'S ARMAGH:** J Hearty; R O'Neill, C Rafferty, S Lennon; F Moriarty, P Grimes, K Beagan; B Comiskey, M Slevin; L O'Hare, S Cavanagh (0-1), B Mullen; M Mackin, R Clarke (1-5), B Smyth. Sub: S McElvanna for Smyth.

THE ACTION

COLM O'ROURKE ADDED another feather to his already blooming cap as he guided St Patrick's Classical School, Navan to a superb All-Ireland Colleges SFC crown and the Hogan Cup with victory over a star-studded St Patrick's, Armagh side at Breffni Park.

The Navan school finally exorcised the ghost of 1991 when they were unluckily beaten by St Fachtna's Skibbereen in the final. This time it was all very different as the Meath school lead almost from the start to seal a tremendous performance.

From the 11th minute when St Patrick's CS got back on level terms at 0-2 each, following points from Shane McKeigue and Ivan McCormack, they never looked back and raced clear, eventually taking a 0-5 to 0-4 interval lead following further scores from Philip Treacy and two in-a-row from Stephen Bray.

A blistering 10-minute spell at the beginning of the second period saw St Patrick's CS move five points clear with Brian McCormack, Ivan McCormack (two) and Darren O'Toole on target and ever closer to that elusive first Hogan Cup. However the Armagh side refused to lie down and battled back well.

Galway referee Mick Curley awarded St Pat's, Armagh a penalty and despite a brilliant stop from Ronan Kenny, Armagh's Ronan Clarke followed up to fire home the rebound.

Sean Cavanagh added another point shortly after to cut the deficit to the minimum, but St Patrick's CS, Navan were not to be denied and when Ivan McCormack fired over to put a two point gap between the sides it signalled Curley's final whistle and prompted huge celebrations amongst the Navan faithful.

★★★★★

❝

THE FACT THAT you are in school and have been living in each other's pockets for the previous five years, and seeing each other every day, created a special bond and made winning the All-Ireland Colleges title for the first time for St Pat's one of the memorable experiences of my time in football.

We had a great group of lads and it was such a unique achievement. We had won the North Leinster League final the week before Christmas in 1999 against St Mary's Mullingar and there was a stroke of good fortune about that when the team we were playing won a free about 14 yards out. As that free was being kicked, Kevin Slattery took a run at the kicker and managed to block the ball. Luckily enough the referee didn't ask for the free to be retaken and the game went into extra-time, and we went on and won that final.

It was on incidents like that that big games swung and after that game we had belief that we could do something special.

As a group, most of us played juvenile together in first year and then on to junior in third year. We probably had a slightly different team at senior level because we had the pick of the best lads from fourth and fifth year combining with the Leaving Certs – whereas at juvenile and junior level the team was mostly focused on just one year and there wasn't that same mix.

We didn't do great in 1999, but we had a decent crew of lads going into 2000 who were all underage again, so as well as getting great experience with our clubs we were all starting to play a bit of adult football, so that stood to us.

We had a good few O'Mahonys players involved on that team and huge amount of the credit for our progression must go to Paddy O'Brien and the impact he had on our football careers.

Paddy was basically 'Mr Juvenile' in O'Mahonys. From eight or nine years of age, when we first started going up to O'Mahonys, it was Paddy who brought us through the grades to under-12s where Cathal O Bric then had a big influence on us too as he took over my age group for the next few years.

As you get older you really appreciate the people that volunteer their time and do it for nothing. The big thing, from my perspective, about Paddy was that he gave every single underage player that came into the club an opportunity; they were encouraged all the time and no matter what, Paddy was there – he left no stone unturned for any young lad that came through the club.

He did massive work for Navan O'Mahonys and we can be very grateful for the lads he brought through and the successful teams we ended up having because of him.

When we went into St Pat's then, Colm O'Rourke became our coach and he was a huge role model too, a superstar in our eyes. Even the year we won the Hogan Cup, he had managed Ireland in the International Rules win in Australia the previous November; then he was coming back to manage us, and that was massive for us at the time.

Colm is a complete football man.

Like every good manager and good person involved in football, he was really passionate about it and driven to try to get the best out of us all. He trained us hard, focused on the skills; he was a massive influence and really knew his football.

He never over-complicated things for us. We trained pretty much every lunchtime from Monday to Thursday and we did that right up to the Hogan Cup final – we did that every year for the best part of five or six months of the year.

He also showed us great respect.

As the weeks and months rolled on in school, you got away with blue murder once you were playing football. Because we trained every lunchtime I'd say there were very few after-lunch classes that we made between 1.30pm and 2.05pm… we were always late for those, but we were forgiven because we were on the football team.

There was a great atmosphere and it was great craic. All that was brought by Colm O'Rourke; he was part of successful teams himself and knows the importance of a happy group. He was a pure slagger himself, he was always trying to rile someone up. Even though he was a teacher, we always had good banter with him and as well as that, he was someone we had huge respect for and he was someone we didn't cross the line with either.

Tommy Diver was the other coach of that team. He was much quieter. He was a Donegal man and had a great influence on the lads as well. He spoke more one-to-one to lads and encouraged us to work on certain weaknesses. Tommy was Colm's assistant and they worked very well together.

We won our first game in the Leinster Championship against Coláiste Choilm from Swords by 6-18 to 0-1, and then we beat St David's of Artane by 2-11 to 2-2. In the semi-final we played Good Counsel, and that was the game that really sparked our belief.

Good Counsel were from Wexford and they had won the All-Ireland the previous year. They were the team to beat and were being touted by almost everyone as the team to win it again because they had a lot of the 1999 team still knocking around in 2000.

That ended up being an outstanding game – we beat them 1-13 to 2-9 after extra-time; that was a great buzz. The rest of the championship was pure momentum, we got on such a roll after that win that we believed we could go all the way.

Obviously we didn't look beyond any of the next games, but it was in the back of the mind that we could achieve whatever we wanted if we worked hard enough for it. The win over Good Counsel proved what we were capable of and instilled a belief of… *Why couldn't it be us!*

We played St Mel's in the Leinster final in Cusack Park, Mullingar. We were much the better team that day and that game was much easier than the Good Counsel game. The game against Good Counsel was a savage game in the depths of winter and the standard of football was so good, it made the final seem a lot easier. We beat St Mel's by 0-15 to 1-9.

We were all 17 or 18 years of age, so we weren't total green horns let's say, so we got to go out after most games as they were on Sundays that year. We ended up at the nightclub in Athboy after most games and those nights out together were the making of us too because we celebrated victory together and that built great camaraderie and also great memories.

We had players from Dunderry, Simonstown, O'Mahonys, Seneschalstown, Walterstown… loads of clubs, but we all got on so well that that was such a huge part in our success. We were all playing for the one team when we played for St Pat's and realistically that was the academy of Meath football – there was an opportunity there for every young player to do well and use the school as a stepping stone for further things.

Earlier in the year, probably before the Christmas of 1999, we had a weekend away in Galway and still over 20 years on you look back on occasions like that with such great fondness and memory.

We stayed in St Michael's, a boarding school in the city centre, and we played them in a game on the Saturday we arrived down there. That night we got to go out and, because Colm was so well known after the International Rules success, a couple of the Galway lads that were on the Ireland team came down to meet him. So here we were, a group of Leaving Cert students out with Colm O'Rourke and mixing with Ja Fallon, Michael Donnellan... lads like that.

For young lads it was great craic and an amazing experience for us, nothing bad happened and everyone was very well behaved. We were in awe, out with lads that we had seen over the previous 10 years on our TVs during the summers, big high profile players.

Then, we played St Jarlath's in Pearse Park, Longford.

That was a much tougher assignment and was a fairly tight game before we managed to get through by 3-7 to 0-13 and went on to face St Patrick's from Armagh.

Back then, there was no such thing as video analysis or seeing too much of an opposition. In those days the MacRory Cup was a big thing, so as I jog my memory I think we did watch the MacRory Cup, but we would have played a lot of northern teams all the way along with St Pat's.

Colm focused on playing those teams because of their standard of football and the quality of their schools, so we played loads of challenges against teams from Newry and Tyrone in October, November and December before the championship would kick off in the new year.

We had never played St Patrick's, Armagh before, but we knew that being Ulster champions they were a very good side. For us nothing really changed. We just trained Monday to Thursday – there was no big hype going into the game and while there was previews of the game in the paper it was nothing like it would be now.

As I said, we didn't know a whole lot about them before the game, but we were aware of lads like Sean Cavanagh and Ronan Clarke. Clarke was a big physical presence at that stage and from watching the MacRory Cup final we could see what they were like and realised that they were just as good as we had heard they were.

The Armagh lads were featured on BBC in the lead up to the final and they were filmed at training. They were shown doing gym work and we were thinking...

Jesus, what are we in for here? That type of work would have been unheard of for us. Colm always told us to do press-ups, sit-ups… that type of strength and conditioning stuff at the time, but weights were not thought about at that stage.

So when we were watching these Armagh lads lifting weights in the week leading up to the All-Ireland final, we were amazed at it.

We got to play in some great pitches and stadiums that year and the final was played in Breffni Park. The disappointing thing for us was that the Hogan Cup final was normally always played in Croke Park, but because of the redevelopment of the stadium they couldn't hold the game there and so we had to play in Breffni; that was the only disappointment, but there was still great excitement ahead of the game.

The Armagh side started well, but I don't think there was ever a sense of panic. We really believed in ourselves and once we were within touching distance of them we were happy. We had a strong never-say-die attitude built up in the panel – there was a real belief in the team and we just played the game that was in front of us. If a team got a bit of a run on us we just kept plugging away.

We had plenty of good forwards and we had confidence that anyone of us could step up on the day. We had a great scoring threat.

I never once felt like we were going to lose that day, not a chance. Even though they got a good start, I always felt we were comfortable and we were always strong at the back.

That day was very wet, so it wasn't a great day for forwards and it was far from ideal for football, but we got a few great scores early in the second-half to push us clear and we were definitely the better team.

Their big players didn't reach the heights they might have expected. They weren't as balanced as we were, and they had a few standout players who did go on to bigger and better things, but outside of those few lads they weren't as strong as us.

Even when they were awarded a penalty late on, I can't say that doubt ever entered my head. I always felt we were going to win that game.

There was a savage buzz after the game, an amazing sense of achievement because we had all played together for so long. It was only afterwards that we realised just how big the occasion was; we were in our own little bubble and not too many people were passing much remarks on us, but after the game it was huge, and there was enormous pride for a lot of people.

For Colm it was so special.

He had gone to school in St Pat's and had been teaching there his whole career, so to bring a team to a Hogan Cup was a huge achievement. For the clubs surrounding the school as well, it was great. We were blessed to have so many good players around at that time from all the different clubs and that fuelled the success.

I was surprised that more of that team didn't go on to make an impact on the inter-county scene. The biggest step is going from being minor to 22 years of age.

There is a lot of change in your life in those years, between going to college, finishing up your underage playing career, and trying to find your way in life… those years lead to a lot of uncertainty.

You really have to knuckle down and work harder than you have ever worked before. Just because you were a decent minor player or won a Hogan Cup, it doesn't mean anything because there is a much higher standard of player at 20-plus-years-of-age.

A lot of that St Pat's team could have made it.

A few of them were very unfortunate with injuries, but the big thing is the transition from underage to adult, it is so difficult.

I was very lucky that we had a decent club team and a strong group of players coming through that helped keep us together and keep the focus, so that the transition happened a lot easier.

I was overage for minor in 2000 – my birthday is late-December – but I went on to play under-21 that November and we won a Leinster title the following spring, so that also helped me transition from underage to adult.

When I look back on my career, getting to the All-Ireland semi-final in 2007 was a brilliant achievement. We got on a very good run and I had a run of consistency from the get-go in the league and championship. I got great belief from that year. In every game I was getting better and stronger. I felt I could lead the line myself and I wasn't relying on other individuals any more.

I got to the stage where I just believed in myself so much more.

Colm Coyle took over that year and he always had great belief in me. He was a selector in 2004 and '05 and I made my championship debut in '05 0 then he was made manager in '07, so I fed off his belief in me.

I worked really hard in the pre-season and Coyler put a great set-up in place where we worked with DCU on our strength and conditioning, testing and analysis; that stuff wasn't really done within our group up to that stage.

I totally bought into everything he was trying to do and I trained hard. I had been getting frustrated up to that year because I had struggled to get a consistent run because of injuries, but it changed in 2007 and everything fell into place. I had no injuries, we picked up good results and I had a rub of the green along the way.

I was lucky that we got on such a good run and we had played so many good matches, and getting to an All-Ireland semi-final certainly helped in getting me the All Star that year.

I didn't really look back on those years when I retired, but more recently I have reflected back on it. Watching the Seán Boylan documentary and hearing him say that he believed there was an All-Ireland in the team that was coming through when he finished up in 2005 makes you think what might have been.

Maybe he might have been the missing piece that could have provided the years of experience that the management set-up in those years didn;t really have. The problem for us was that in those years we had too much change in management and we couldn't get any consistency going. I believe there was enough ability in that team that we could have potentially nicked an All-Ireland.

Another big day for me was the Leinster semi-final win over Dublin in 2010. I scored two goals that day, the second one into the Hill… those are the occasions you dream about. That is what you start off playing the game for, that is what you always aspire to do, so when it actually happened it was a brilliant buzz.

I had been on the losing side against Dublin a fair bit up to that stage, so to be able to prove that we were good enough to beat Dublin was a great feeling.

It is frustrating to think that we didn't achieve something more significant. The Leinster final still annoys me a bit, but the Dublin game is still a class memory, especially when you see what they went on to do since then. A lot of the players that played for them that day went on to bigger and better things.

We missed an opportunity in 2010 to push on.

In those years we should have picked up something more significant than we did. In 2010 you had Kildare and Down in an All-Ireland semi-final, and Down then putting it up to Cork in the final, but we felt we should have been there.

It was very frustrating because then we went and chopped and changed again, and brought in a manager with totally different ideas… and we were back in the starting blocks again.

I'd love to have seen what would have happened if we had some consistency in our management, or even if Seán Boylan had come back at that time.

Who knows… it's a lot of what ifs!

99

ANTHONY MOYLES

BLACKHALL GAELS 2-9 SIMONSTOWN 1-9
Meath SFC Final
Páirc Tailteann
SEPTEMBER 21 2003

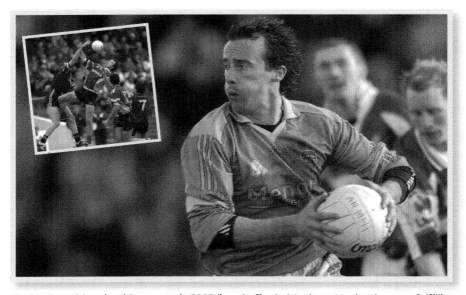

Blackhall Gaels' senior title success in 2003 (inset) afforded Anthony Moyles the most fulfilling afternoon of his football life.

★ **BLACKHALL GAELS:** M Whelan; D O'Brien, P Nestor, B Moyles; G Beirne, S Nally, A Dalton; **A Moyles (0-2)**, J O'Brien; B McKeon (0-2), M Ferris (0-1), D Beirne; R Cox (1-1), T Brosnan (1-1), M Crampton (0-2). Sub: O Creevey for J O'Brien.

★ **SIMONSTOWN GAELS:** G Lynch; S Leddy, R McGrath, M Byrne; C McGrath, H Traynor, B Flood; P Meade, A Meade (1-0); S Kennedy, E Kelly (0-2), S Kenny; R Brady (0-1), N Kearney (0-3), J Lunney (0-3). Subs: E Donoghue for Leddy, S O'Neill for Flood, C Kenny for P Meade.

THE ACTION

IT LOOKED FAR from likely when they trailed by nine points at the break, but Blackhall Gaels turned in a storming second-half display to turn matters around dramatically in an exciting Meath senior football championship final at Páirc Tailteann.

Simonstown Gaels looked well on the way to completing a Navan double – after O'Mahonys had taken the intermediate title – when 1-7 to 0-1 to the good at the interval, but then their opponents were very much the masters on the restart.

Blackhall appeared to be badly missing their suspended county player Nigel Nestor in the first-half but their opponents were equally slow in starting. However, a goal from midfielder and captain Alan Meade on 14 minutes had a galvanising effect on Simonstown.

With Evan Kelly and Ned Kearney showing up well in attack, they built up a nine-point advantage. It took Blackhall 27 minutes to get on the scoreboard, with Mark Crampton punching over the bar.

But it was so different after the change of ends with midfielder Anthony Moyles coming a lot more into the game and full-forward Tadhg Brosnan also leaving his calling card.

Twelve minutes into the second-half, Brosnan had a shot blocked out when the full-forward looked certain to finish to the net. However, Robert Cox was on hand to beat Gary Lynch with a low shot and Simonstown's lead was down to three points, 1-8 to 1-5.

Cox's goal was soon followed by points from the same player and Mark Crampton. Then they hit four wides before Moyles levelled matters with five minutes to go. Barry McKeon put them ahead with a shot from 40 metres and that was followed by the winners' second goal.

A cross from the left by Moyles was flashed to the net by Brosnan and the issue was more or less decided. John Lunney replied with a point at the other end but it was too little too late and the final whistle sounded on the kick-out.

In their player ratings from the 2003 SFC final the *Meath Chronicle* gave Anthony Moyles a nine out of 10 mark, with the comment... *Few could argue with his selection as Man of the Match.*

★★★★★

"

OUR JFC WIN with St Paul's in 1999 is still my greatest moment because getting to play with my brothers and winning that final was fantastic, but the SFC win in 2003 was so special too.

I had played with the Meath juniors in Tullamore against Offaly in 1999, but that was my final year in college and typically a few of us had arranged to go to San Diego for the summer where we had jobs lined up; the usual students trip to the States type of thing. So after playing for the Meath juniors, I left to go to the States and what a year it turned out to be, not only for the juniors, but also for the seniors. I had also been asked to go in and train with the seniors, but I didn't go – so how sick was I sitting watching all the matches as Meath won the All-Ireland?

Even if I had been No 35 on the panel that would have been some journey, but we had our minds made up to go to the States for the couple of months and that's what I did.

However, to get back and play for St Paul's and win the JFC was brilliant. I remember being so nervous for the quarter-final because I wasn't back yet for that game... I didn't get home until the semi-final.

We had gone on some run with St Paul's. We won the JFC, and went from Division 5 almost to Division 1; we were a real band of brothers at the time. It was a small group of just 20 or 25 lads, so we found it tough in intermediate in 2000.

Both my brother Barry and I were trying to push on a bit and we were training more than just the two nights a week. The demand of being in with the Meath seniors and trying to help keep St Paul's in intermediate meant we needed to be doing more.

There was a very frank discussion amongst the players after 2000 and it was a case of... *Are we prepared to push on to training three nights a week to improve?* Some lads were starting young families and others were starting businesses, so the sense was that the group were happy to keep doing with what they were doing and that that was enough.

Myself and Barry had questions to ponder ourselves then.

Our ambitions were to be the best we could be. Barry was with the Meath juniors, I was with the seniors, so we said to the club that we may have to move on.

St Paul's understood where we were coming from. They knew we wanted to push ourselves to a higher level and they gave us their blessing.

Dunboyne were our first port of call because we had played underage with them as part of the St Peter's & St Paul's set-up, and we played hurling with Dunboyne. However, that move fell apart – I could write a book on that story alone.

I was good friends with Nigel Nestor through the Meath team and he said to me that if nothing happened with Dunboyne that myself and Barry should go and meet Leo Turley, who was the Blackhall Gaels manager at the time.

So we went to the County Club and met Leo, and we really liked the cut of Leo's jib and what he had to say. He said he had a three-year plan to go from intermediate to senior, consolidate in senior and then win the senior championship in year three.

To be fair to him, that's exactly what he did.

So we joined Blackhall Gaels in 2002 and what a roller-coaster of a year that proved to be for both me personally and for the club.

I got sent-off in a preliminary quarter-final game against Ballinlough in Simonstown in what was a case of mistaken identity. There was a bit of a schemozzle in the last couple of minutes and I got gate along with one of the Ballinlough lads, Gary McDonnell, and he was laughing on the way off saying, 'Jaysus... you didn't do a whole pile in that row!' I just turned and said, 'I did nothing'.

We had a great chairman in Blackhall at the time, a man called Micheal Lillis, a wonderful man, and he told me that the club would appeal. I was very upset in the dressing-room after the game, but Dudley Farrell, who was the referee, was sound and he told me he'd do what he could to rescind the red card – that he would be putting in his report that he had got it wrong.

So as far as I was concerned, and looking at it from a naive situation where I assumed justice would be done, I was calm. Micheal Lillis said the club would do all they could and as far as they were concerned it was an injustice and I shouldn't have been sent-off.

So the following weekend we were to play the three in-a-row chasing champions and local rivals Dunshaughlin in Dunboyne. The big story was if I would turn up and come out of the dressing-room and of course I did. We went on to win the game which was a pretty ding-dong affair. So we had beaten the champions, who hadn't been beaten in such a long time; we were obviously thrilled.

Then the fall out started straight away after the final whistle.

Prior to the game, I asked the people that mattered were they sure it was okay for me to play and Micheal Lillis and Leo Turley said that I was playing – so in their eyes and my eyes, and in anyone's view who had anything to do with Blackhall Gaels, it was an injustice and it should have been sorted ASAP.

Then after the game the real fun started.

The club were threatened with being banned for a year, and I was in line for a year-long ban, maybe a bit more. There were bans being threatened all over the place and we had to go down to the Leinster Council to plead our case.

To be fair to Barney (Allen) and Fintan (Ginnity), God rest him, they were great at the time. It was one of those things where the rulebook got in the way of commonsense, but eventually at around 1.30am the Leinster Council decided they couldn't rule on the issue – so they kicked it back to Meath GAA and told them to sort it out. Then the possibility of a replay was put on the table, so everyone decided for the sanity of everyone involved we would agree to a replay.

That was played a week later and, unfortunately, Dunshaughlin beat us. I hit the crossbar in the last minute and if it had gone in, we would have won; but we lost and Dunshaughlin went on to win the championship.

That whole sequence of events was never done, dusted and forgotten about. We always took whatever motivation we could get and certainly in 2003 we had what had happened in '02 in our minds the whole way through.

We had a good team and we were a team that was coming of age. We had a fair bit about us, but certainly what had happened the year before was used as a motivational tool in the sense that we knew we were after beating Dunshaughlin in the first game, and then nearly getting them the second day… we knew we were right up there, so it was a matter of putting in the effort, getting focused and doing the job, which fortunately we did.

For an amalgamated club the lads were very, *very* close.

There was a great bit of slagging between the Batterstown and the Kilcloon lads, and they were very open to myself and Barry coming into their set-up, we were always made to feel very welcome.

We were a very solid team at the back. We had Paul Nestor, my brother Barry, the Daltons, the Beirnes, we had a really solid backline. We also had great power in certain areas. Lads like Tadhg Brosnan were crucial. Tadhg was only a young lad, but he was a bit of an enigma in regards to what he could do on a pitch. He could try anything and when his confidence was up it would come off. Then we had Mark Crampton as well.

We had a good, solid base, and we were very, *very* fit. We felt we could out-work anyone. Our work-rate was a massive thing. We harried and hassled teams and really got in people's faces and we believed in ourselves.

That 2002 run made us believe that we belonged at the top table with the likes of Skryne and Dunshaughlin at the time.

Despite all those things going for us, St Patrick's should have beaten us in the quarter-final in Skryne. We were absolutely blessed to get out that day when Mark Ferris hit an unbelievable free from beyond the '45' to rescue a draw. Then when we got to the replay, we won fairly well, but St Pat's had us in that first game and we were fortunate.

We started the championship well with wins over Simonstown and Seneschalstown, but then we were beaten by Skryne. We just didn't perform that day; we had a couple of injuries and Skryne were a very good team. Maybe the rivalry got to us – we were really below par, but it was a nice kick up the backside to get at the time because it was early in the campaign. We knew we could afford to slip up once, but a second slip up would be costly... so that was our slip up.

We bounced back against Dunderry, and then struggled to get past Ballivor. Most teams that win championships reflect on semi-finals or finals, but there are games from earlier in the championship that you manage to win by the skin of your teeth. It is very rare that a team skates their way through a championship, no matter how dominant they are and we were no different.

There was never a feeling in that Blackhall Gaels squad that we were getting ahead of ourselves or that lads were too cocky. We always felt we would work to a certain level, but at times that didn't work for us and we suffered lapses in performances and nearly got caught.

We improved to beat Ballinlough, but then had our struggles again in that quarter-final against St Pat's. We lost Nigel Nestor to a red card in that game and he was a massive loss for us – that weighted heavily on us because Nigel was in his pomp and he was playing really well, so that was a sickener.

We had a few young lads coming through and they stepped up in Nigel's absence. John O'Brien was a big man and he was a great foil for me in midfield because he was such a horse of a man. Most teams generally had a lad in midfield who was able to do a bit of sorting out and John was well able to handle himself. Even though he was only 18 or 19 at the time, he was a huge man with a big pair of hands and he was well able to disrupt.

Then it was Dunshaughlin in the semi-final.

It couldn't have worked out any better. There was a real sense of revenge is on the cards, and being without Nigel added even more to our motivation.

The manager Leo Turley didn't have to try to get us motivated for that game; everyone knew there was a job to do. We said to each other that we wouldn't bring the emotion of the year before to the game… just remember there was a job to do.

We were so determined in that game. There was a kickout at one stage that broke in front of me and George Beirne pounced on it, and someone just pulled on the ball and he got kicked on the head, but he still grabbed that ball and came up with it. I knew there and then that we wouldn't be beaten that day – it was just one of those days.

It was complete bodies on the line sort of stuff.

It felt like the Dunshaughlin lads could feel our intensity that day. No matter what the Dunshaughlin lads did that day they weren't going to get the better of us. They were the best side in the county for getting down in the trenches and battling it out, but our name was on it that day and we were always going to win it.

The emotion of that semi-final was draining. It wasn't draining in the sense that we thought about it too much beforehand or even during the game, but after it there was definitely emotional drainage because of the reputation Dunshaughlin had at the time… they were the kingpins of Meath football.

Also after what had happened the year before, there was a sense that we were putting them to the sword. Sometimes when you build something up that much, after the event you can get so deflated and just look for the next challenge.

Going into the final it wasn't like we feared Simonstown because we honestly didn't. Everything had been so focused on getting ready for Dunshaughlin and we had put such a huge effort into winning that game that had been huge for us.

Prior to the final we had trained really well; we were really looking forward to the game against Simonstown, it wasn't that the semi-final took anything out of our legs, but if you were to put our first-half display in the final down to anything, then maybe it was the fact that our minds were a little tired from the semi-final win. I'm not one hundred percent sure to be honest.

We had beaten Simonstown earlier in the championship, but we were never a team that got ahead of ourselves. Leo Turley never believed in that and with the individuals we had in the team you'd get a fair skelping if you started talking that way.

We believed in ourselves as a squad. If anyone was getting ahead of themselves, anyone not training well, anyone acting the goat… then the sessions would be stopped and we did our own disciplined runs. The manager used to just stand there.

We were a very self-motivated and self-managed group.

We certainly didn't get ahead of ourselves before the final. Simonstown were an excellent side. They had the two Meades, Seamus (Kenny), Evan (Kelly), Ned (Kearney), the McGraths, Lunney in the corner… they had a savage team. They had a side full of names and lads who could hurt you from any position.

We started that game poorly and gave the ball away so much, it was shocking stuff. We looked nervous and we just didn't work hard enough. We probably felt that things would just happen, so instead of really getting into the trenches, we sat back waiting for it to happen.

I gave a terrible pass across the field to Paul Nestor but it got intercepted, and Evan Kelly really should have got another goal. There were so many small little things that made such a huge impact, but then near the end of the half Mark Crampton should have got a goal, but he stuck it over the bar.

It might have only been a point, but the football we played in the lead up to that score was the first time we had strung a few passes together. That point was our only score of the half and it was a boost, even though it was our first of the day.

I'd say you wouldn't even have been able to lay a bet on that game at half-time.

We went in at half-time 0-1 to 1-7 down and we were sitting there with our heads down; there was a bit of shouting going on, but Turley came in and said he'd leave it up to us because it was absolutely cat malogen… and he just walked out again.

There were no speeches or roaring from him.

We were just sitting looking at each other, shocked, but we had enough leaders on that team and we were determined that we would not go out and give a repeat performance of our first-half display.

We started to attack the game. We became more aggressive both with and without the ball – we held onto it and started to make them chase us, and we started to play football and string passes together.

They had a great opportunity after a lovely spell of football where they should have got a second goal, but then they started to panic and they kicked ball away and gave it back to us. We really started to grind them down; it was amazing how quickly the momentum changed, even though the scoreboard didn't change that much.

Then we started to get one score, then two and three... they were still well ahead of us, but you could see the shock on their faces. Then Robert Cox got the goal and we really started going at them. To be honest, there was only ever going to be one winner after that and when Tadhg Brosnan flashed the second goal we were in control.

We put up a rearguard action and were determined not to concede any more goals, so we knew with a few minutes to go we had it won. Then I got a point with my left foot and we added another immediately after that, and it was like a knife through their hearts. They couldn't get the ball beyond halfway and we really attacked their kick-outs.

Almost every single time we attacked their kick-outs we won the breaks and got scores. We probably should have won by more, we could have had another goal or two.

I played football for a long time, but I very rarely got that feeling of real contentment after games. I remember 1999 with St Paul's and that was a different vibe, but after the 2003 final I remember sitting on the bus coming out of Navan... I was on my own, the lads were all roaring and shouting and having the craic. And I was just thinking to myself that this was the best I have ever felt... *This is the pinnacle.*

I was really emotional at that time and I remember thinking... *This is what all the hard work is for.*

All the training on my own, all the hard work we had done as a team, everything that happened to get us to that day was all encapsulated in that moment on the bus for me.

There was a massive amount of emotion in the dressing-room after the game because of the way we won it.

We couldn't believe what we had done because at half-time we were dead and buried, but it was that moment on the bus when I got a chance to sit back and watch everyone celebrating that made it the best moment of my career for me.

KEVIN REILLY

IRELAND 48 AUSTRALIA 40
International Rules First Test
Pearse Stadium, Galway
OCTOBER 28 2006

Kevin Reilly didn't achieve everything he wanted with Meath, but almost a decade as Ireland's full-back against Australia (above) showcased him as probably the best No.3 in the country.

★ **IRELAND: K Reilly**, G Geraghty, A Moyles (Meath); K Donaghy, P Galvin, A O'Mahony, M O Se (Kerry); J Bergin, K Fitzgerald (Galway); A Brogan, S Ryan (Dublin); S Cavanagh (Tyrone); R Clarke, S McDonnell, K McGeeney (Armagh); N Murphy, A Quirke (Cork); C Begley (Brisbane Lions & Laois); T Kennelly (Sydney Swans & Kerry); B Coulter (Down); D Earley (Kildare); T Kelly (Laois); K Lacey (Donegal); S M Lockhart (Derry); P Barden (Longford).

★ **AUSTRALIA:** C Bateman, C Brown (Hawthorn); R Crowley, D Mundy, B Peake (Fremantle); A Davey, J McDonald (Melbourne); N Davis, B Hall, R O'Keeffe, Schneider (Sydney); B Fevola, M Lappin, K Simpson (Carlton); S Fisher, B Goddard (St Kilda); G Johncock (Adelaide); D Pearce (Port Adelaide); A Raines (Richmond); Selwood (West Coast); J Sherman, M Voss (Brisbane); D Fletcher, B Stanton (Essendon).

THE ACTION

SEÁN BOYLAN'S IRELAND outscored Australia by 12 points in the final quarter to clinch a 48 (1-12-6) to 40 (1-9-7) victory in the International Rules First Test at Pearse Stadium, Galway.

The last-minute combination of an over from Steven McDonnell and Joe Bergin's goal saw the Irish win out. The success maintained Australia's record of not having won a Test match on Irish soil since 2002.

Ireland led 16-4 after the first quarter, but a goal from Sydney's Ryan O'Keefe had the Aussies 33-29 ahead by the end of the third.

Sean Cavanagh and McDonnell, who top-scored for Ireland with 15 points, missed goal chances before O'Keeffe fired past Alan Quirke on 52 minutes.

The sold-out signs were up well in advance of the tie in Salthill as 30,000 spectators thronged the seaside venue.

Ireland's accurate kicking helped them get off to an imposing start as they struck four overs and a behind inside the first quarter. Laois' Tom Kelly and Armagh man Kieran McGeeney, back in the hybrid game and chosen as captain, were particularly prominent in the opening exchanges as Boylan's men sought to put down a marker. The Aussies improved as the game went on, with their tight defence in the second quarter a factor in them trailing by only seven points – 21-14 – at half-time.

At the end of the third quarter, the Australians were four points in front. Ireland got off to the worst possible start in the fourth quarter when Meath's Graham Geraghty was given his marching orders after earning the game's first yellow card.

With the minutes ticking down, overs from Bergin and McDonnell got Ireland back in contention and the latter then swerved onto his right to thump over his fourth over to give Ireland the lead again.

A rushed kick-out which saw Adam Selwood dispossessed, fell to McDonnell and he picked out hometown hero Bergin who failed to panic in acres of space, and drilled home the clinching goal.

★★★★★

❝

I WAS LUCKY enough to have had two years at underage level in the International Rules because they held an under-17 tour in 2004 and then they moved to under-18 for the second year, so that worked out brilliantly for me.

I was playing underage football for Meath at the time and I was selected to go for four or five Leinster trials for the International Rules team in Portarlington. From there a Leinster panel was picked for an under-17/18 Interprovincial Series and myself, Cian Ward and Dean Barrett got picked for the Leinster panel – then myself and Dean got selected for the Ireland panel.

After playing the Interprovincial Series, the trial process for the International panel continued and from there an extended panel was picked and we went for more trials in Ballymun; it was a very comprehensive process from start to finish and eventually it was whittled down to 24. It was a great opportunity to pit ourselves against the best the country had to offer.

When we went to Australia in 2004 we went for three weeks over the Easter holidays. I was in Leaving Cert at the time, so it wasn't ideal preparation for my exams to spend the two weeks of the Easter holidays and another week after that in Australia playing football, but it was a very, very enjoyable trip and it was never something I could turn down. I didn't have to think twice about going; I jumped at the chance, it was a fantastic experience.

I know there are mixed views about the International Rules series as a spectacle and a competition, but as players it was a fantastic honour to represent our country in the sport that you love. We were playing with the best from all over the country and it was a great honour to be selected among them. And we were playing against professional sports people too.

As an amateur sportsman it gave us an opportunity to pit ourselves against the best players from a professional sport; as a competitor that is where you want to be. You want to see where you stack up and how you can fare against the best.

Unfortunately, we weren't contesting All-Ireland finals with Meath at the time, so this was the next best thing. To play with the best players against the best quality opposition, that was where you wanted to be. It is a fantastic honour to represent your country at anything, let alone the sport that you love.

Because I made the under-17/18 International Rules team it put me in the shop window for the Meath senior selectors. It certainly increased my profile and people heard about us a little bit quicker because of it.

I played three senior games for Navan O'Mahonys at full-forward before I was called into the Meath senior set-up to play as a full-back. I hadn't played full-back at adult level for my club before I played full-back for my county, which was interesting enough – Seán must have seen me somewhere else.

I did play full-back on the St Pat's team that won the Hogan Cup, and at minor with Meath I alternated between centre-back and full-back, so it wasn't completely alien to me to play full-back.

I have Paddy O'Brien to blame for me being a full-back. The fact that my older brothers played in the full-back line that is where Paddy felt I was destined to be for the remainder of my career, with a brief dispensation to move further outfield at times.

Getting called into the Meath senior panel was the stuff of dreams. It was something I grew up dreaming about; for me I always aspired to be in that dressing-room and to finally get that opportunity was amazing.

I remember sitting at home a day or two after an under-21 final when the call came from Declan Mullen, one of Sean's selectors, to ask me would I be interested in going in? I couldn't believe it, the excitement was amazing… it was like all my Christmases had come at once.

To get the opportunity to train and play with those players was a dream come through. At that time Meath still had that core group from the mid-to-late-90s, like Trevor Giles, Darren Fay, Ollie Murphy, Graham Geraghty… those lads were my idols growing up and next thing, I knew I had the opportunity to train with them… it was amazing.

I went in for October 2004 and trained in Beaufort College in Navan, where we did a lot of strength and conditioning work. Seán was ahead of his time in those methods and we worked hard. It was tough for me and the selectors used to have to help me lift the weights up and down because that was the first time I was exposed to that type of training. There was one time I was trying to do a shoulder press and I was struggling to get the weight above my head and I looked over… and there was Seán just staring at me.

I just started laughing; it wasn't for a lack of effort or enthusiasm.

I just couldn't lift it.

We were due to play Kildare in a game in the January of 2005 and I had broken my nose again, for the third or fourth time, in a trial match a couple of weeks earlier and, to be honest, I think I was about to be dropped off the panel at that stage. Seán came to me that week and said, 'We are going to give you a game at full-back against Kildare, but after that I just want to say thanks for your involvement... we will be in touch again'.

So I assumed that game against Kildare would be my last for Meath. But I went out and played the game; I ended up marking Dermot Earley. I thought I had a fairly decent game, apart from a brief 10-minute sin-bin which wasn't my fault as always.

The Tuesday night before the game Seán told me they would organise to get my nose fixed, as a kind of parting present, but the Tuesday after the game he asked me would I mind putting off the operation for a while because he decided he wanted to keep me.

I took his arm off at the chance to stay on and, as it turned out, it was only two years ago that I finally got round to getting my nose fixed.

I managed to start in the championship that year against Dublin at full-back and I more or less started every game that I was fit for after that.

The training methods that Seán had were phenomenal. The care he showed for the players and the standards that the players set for themselves were brand new to me. They all demanded really, really high standards in everything that they did, so to learn and play with players of such a high calibre was a phenomenal time for me.

There was one night when we were training out on the back pitch in Páirc Tailteann, doing a simple tackling drill and Trevor Giles was out in front of me. Like any self-respecting full-back I was probably holding onto his jersey and giving him a little bit of niggle, but the next thing I knew, the elbow came back and clocked me on the jaw.

And I got this look to say, 'You don't do that to me!'

Whether I was stubborn or ignorant, I didn't let that deter me. I gave him respect, but I did it again just as quickly because at the end of the day, whether it was a training session out the back of Páirc Tailteann or a championship match in Croke Park, it was all about getting to the O'Neills first and you had to do whatever it took to be there first... so long as it was within the rules of course. They were the standards that were set by that group of players.

Growing up, Darren Fay would have been one of my idols and he was one of the players that I aspired to become. I was always learning off him and observing him. Whenever he spoke, I always listened to how he would approach the game.

He often spoke to me about how the game was about angles and trying to narrow the angles of where your direct opponent could run... limit his opportunities or narrow down the angle at which the ball could be kicked in. That was an interesting perspective that I took with me. By positioning, you could influence the kicker and you could negate the amount of room that the forward might have, that was the big thing I learned from Darren Fay.

Getting called up for the International Rules series in 2006 was a bolt from blue because I was so young. Myself and Colm Begley were both called into the squad and Colm had been with Brisbane so that was no surprise. The two of us were the youngest players ever to be called up to the senior International Rules squad, so it was surprising.

It has been well documented that Meath had a mediocre 2006, the year after Seán left. In July that year we were beaten by Laois in the championship and by the following Thursday there was five or six of us over in the States, in Boston. I was playing football there for seven or eight weeks before I came back to play against Trim in the Senior Championship quarter-final, so I spent most of that summer in Boston.

A week or two before I was due to come home I got a phone call from Seán Boylan, who had been announced as the Ireland manager for the series, asking me if I would be interested in attending the trials which would be starting in a couple of weeks' time.

Those opportunities don't come around too often, so I almost took Seán's arm off to have that opportunity.

Having played the game at underage I had a fair idea and understanding of the rules and the way the game can be played and should be played. There were a few incidents in 2005 which threatened to mar the game, but those incidents were the exception and it never crossed my mind to not want to be involved in '06.

I wanted to compete against the best, with the best players from around the country and the International Rules series gave me that opportunity.

Anthony Moyles and Graham Geraghty were also called up to that squad by Seán and Graham used to collect me and bring me up to the training and trials in Westmanstown.

I marked Kieran Donaghy for most of the trial games and that was always a really good tussle. In the International Rules, high fielding and the mark are key elements of the game, so if the forward managed to catch the ball cleanly then that was the end of the contest, whereas in gaelic football the contest only begins when the ball is caught.

I loved the fact that you had to get there first, that you were held to a higher standard. As a full-back in that game if you are not first you are last… and if you dive in and miss, then you were leaving the goals wide open.

I loved the appeal of playing high-stakes football.

Getting picked on the squad was brilliant and that First Test in Galway was special.

It was a fabulous occasion for a 20-year-old to be involved in a set-up like that. One of the proudest moments I've ever had in sport was standing listening to the National Anthem with that group of players as you wear that Irish crest on your chest… wearing the Ireland jersey and representing your country in a sport that I loved, it was amazing.

I was extremely proud.

As well as the responsibility and pride of wearing the Ireland jersey, I was also aware that I was representing all the other footballers that played gaelic as well, that was very important. No more so than when I wore the Meath jersey and the O'Mahonys jersey, it isn't about me or any of us, it is about the people that support you, will you on and wish you the very, very best.

That night in Galway was an incredibly proud moment for me.

I got to know a good few of the players over the years after ending up playing in four Rules Series and winning eight caps – it was great to play with them. Graham Canty was another man I looked up to as a full-back, and it was brilliant to get to play with him.

Tadhg Kennelly was one of those great players and I actually roomed with him briefly in 2006. After our first night in the room, I woke up in the middle of the night and Tadhg wasn't there. I didn't know where he had gone or what was after happening.

When I went down for breakfast the next morning there was Tadhg sitting with a big sleepy head on him and I asked him where did he go, because I thought he was after going out partying in Galway following his long season in Australia. But in his thick Kerry accent he turned round and said, 'Jesus you bollocks, sure you kept me up all night!'

Apparently I had been snoring so loudly that he had to go and book himself another room in the middle of the night and, from then on, for every other Test Series I was selected for, I ended up getting a room on my own – that all goes back to the broken nose incident in 2005, so Tadhg can blame Sean for that because he delayed me getting it fixed!

There were a few incidents surrounding that series that drew very public headlines.

If you look at it from the Australian perspective, they were coming off the back of a long hard season and they saw the trip to Ireland as an opportunity to let their hair down – there was an incident with Brendan Fevola and a barman, but that was an unfortunate incident.

Fevola got sent home out of a squad of 35 or whatever it was, so it was an isolated incident. Ordinarily, everything is very professional, but when you are the touring team there has to be a little bit of steam let off, but that was an isolated incident.

I remember when we went down to Australia for a three-week tour. For two and a half weeks of that we were training like professionals twice a day; we were eating and sleeping like professionals… we got our gym work in as well.

We were doing stats, video analysis, getting physio… it was very full on. To suggest it was a jolly couldn't be further from the truth.

After the Test Series was over, there were a few days down-time to enjoy ourselves, but the series had great integrity and it was held in high regard by all the players. There was nothing more we wanted to do than to beat the Australians, home and away.

We were so committed.

In 2011 we trained for two or three months for the series. As teams exited the GAA championship the players that were earmarked for the International Rules got together, and between Mike McGurn providing strength and conditioning programmes – to follow with regular assessments each week, – and Kieran McGeeney bringing us to John Kavanagh's SBG, we were preparing properly.

The sessions in Kavanagh's gym were intense.

This was before Conor McGregor became the global phenomena in UFC that he is now, but the first night we walked into that gym there was a picture of McGregor on the wall and Kavanagh told us he would make it big, but at the time I didn't even know what UFC was… never mind who Conor McGregor was.

For two or three months, every Thursday night between 8pm and 10pm, we trained in Kavanagh's gym in grappling and wrestling, just to make sure we were ready for whatever came our way in the series. They were the standards set by McGeeney and Anthony Tohill, that was the level of commitment and effort that went into those series.

To say that the whole thing was just thrown together and wasn't taken seriously was absolutely untrue. We trained as hard, if not harder than we did for inter-county GAA.

In the Second Test in 2006 there was a lot of controversy in the lead up to the game because Graham Geraghty had been cited for a knee to the head, and they took him out of it early on – I remember after the game Seán's anger.

When you are out on the pitch you become oblivious to some of the stuff that goes on, but after the game Seán was absolutely furious, I have never seen him as angry. When he is in a dressing-room he is firm and assertive, but his reaction after that game was absolute anger and disbelief.

He was very hurt by the lack of protection Graham was given and also by the fact that a lot of the Australian players had said in the media beforehand that there would be reprisals for Graham and it was delivered… that disgusted Seán.

My first involvement that day was interesting.

I came on as an inter-change player at centre-back. There was a bit of a melee as I came on and the first thing I saw was Sean Marty Lockhart, another really inspirational guy that I looked up to and learned a lot off, with a blood spattered face – it wasn't his blood, he had that glazed over look on his face.

He is such a gentleman off the pitch, but when you crossed that white line he was one of those guys who just went to war – McGeeney was another. Those lads were phenomenal, the intensity at which they played the game and the standards they set for themselves and others were huge. And by God, we had to live up to those standards.

JOE SHERIDAN

SENESCHALSTOWN 2-8 WOLFE TONES 1-8
Meath SFC Final
Páirc Tailteann
NOVEMBER 5 2009

A night under lights in Navan in 2009 (above), surrounded by his family and friends in Seneschalstown, was the centre-point of Joe Sheridan's action-packed football life.

★ **SENESCHALSTOWN:** D Lyons; P Carey, A Collins, G Sheridan; M Carey (0-1), J Cowley, S Sheridan; **J Sheridan (1-2)**, D Sheridan; G Conlon (0-1), C Macken, S Finnegan; S Clarke (0-1), R Ruddy (0-1), B Sheridan (1-2). Subs|: T Ledwidge for S Clarke, C Duffy for S Sheridan, B Clarke for Ruddy.

★ **WOLFE TONES:** D Nolan; R Brady, C McLoughlin, C Martin; B McGinn, E Harrington, G Beggy; S Corrigan (0-1), S Sheppard; D McGrath (0-1), N McLoughlin, M Coleman; A Fox, C Ward (1-6), P Byrne. Subs: S Power for McGrath, A McKeown for McLoughlin, A Callaghan for Byrne, J McKeown for Coleman.

THE ACTION

THERE WERE MANY who believed that Seneschalstown's SFC victory over the kings of Meath football, Navan O'Mahonys, in 2007 was a mere flash in the pan and their failure to follow up that success in '08 only served to underline the Yellow Furze side's good fortune.

In fact, in 2008 Seneschalstown were fortunate to escape being dragged into a relegation tussle with their sole win of the campaign, a two-point victory over Rathkenny, saving them from the play-off for the drop.

So, it was with a sense of determination and a hunger to prove people wrong that Seneschalstown embarked on their 2009 campaign, a championship that started slowly, but one that gathered momentum quickly and established Seneschalstown as one of the great sides in the later years of the first decade of the new Millennium.

While the group stages were a test of Seneschalstown's character, they emerged from the dogfight and embarked on a journey that saw them ride a roller-coaster of performances ranging from the fortunate to the ferocious.

Reaching the final against a strong Wolfe Tones team, Seneschalstown were fortunate to escape with a 1-13 each draw, as Brian Sheridan's free late in extra-time gave them a second bite at the cherry.

A bite they savoured like no other.

★★★★★

66

I'VE BEEN LUCKY TO have been involved in many great games, but the Meath senior final replay of 2009 stands brightest for me.

A Thursday night, a replay, under lights for the first time ever in Meath... the type of game it was, it just really stands out.

Even with the 2007 final and anything I did with Meath, it's the 2009 senior final replay that is extra special.

We had a couple of very good days with Meath, but there was something about that senior final replay that really stood out. Even the crowd that night was brilliant. I think it was one of the biggest crowds at a championship final... on a Thursday night!!

Even the way the game went, it was up and down. They started well, then we came back... just the whole game was something special. I wouldn't say that club is more important than county, but you do have more of an attachment with your club, that's for sure.

I could never say anything bad about playing for Meath, it's the biggest honour I've ever had... playing with Meath for so many years was amazing. I feel we should have done more in the time I was there, that is why I haven't picked one of the Meath games as the *Game of my Life*.

We probably should have been more successful in my time with Meath because we had a very good squad with a lot of really high-quality players. When you think about the best games you played, you automatically think about successes, but with Meath I feel we could have done more.

Obviously, we got to a couple of All-Ireland semi-finals in 2007 and '09, and we won the Leinster in 2010, but were they the biggest achievements of my career?

I know some of the best teams you play on might not be the most successful ones, but the 2009 Meath final replay is the one game that forever sticks out for me. The magnitude of the game, how it went and then to win the game was very important as well.

In 2007 we came from nowhere to beat Navan O'Mahonys and win the title. As a team we played very well, certain lads did great jobs in their roles and that is why we were successful at that time. After 2007, '08 was a bit of a disappointment because a lot of our top players got injured. We struggled in '08 to get to the levels we found in '07, though we did manage to win the Feis Cup that year. Going into '09 we were still confident we could do something and be successful.

With my dad (Damien) as manager, he always expected us to win the championship every year, so in 2009 we were a couple of years older, we had the experience of winning the championship before and we believed we could do it again, so that all stood to us.

Going into that year we were pretty confident and as the year went on that confidence grew, but we were lucky to get out of the group on score difference ahead of Simonstown.

After the group stages, we didn't take anything for granted and from then on we were fairly unstoppable and played some brilliant football. We had been so lucky to qualify that we just let the shackles off and we played some really good stuff.

We beat Navan O'Mahonys in the opening round and that was already an improvement on the previous year, but then we slumped to a disappointing loss to St Patrick's. We were held to a 1-15 each draw by Simonstown in round three and that sent us into the break for the inter-county season in a perilous position.

When we came back three months later we lost out by a point to Donaghmore/ Ashbourne and our place in the championship was hanging by a thread; we needed other results to go our way.

We won by eight points against Duleek/Bellewstown which gave us a scoring difference of plus seven and that gave us the edge over Simonstown. Duleek/ Bellewstown were a very good side, but we were determined not to be beaten. I remember standing on the pitch in Páirc Tailteann after that game waiting to hear other results, so when they came in and we were through there were plenty of celebrations… because we knew we had managed to qualify by the skin of our teeth.

Because of how we had qualified from the group we realised we had been let off the hook, so we cut loose a bit against Skryne in the quarter-finals. We started to focus on what we had to do and work on doing it properly. We played with a bit of relief and wanted to show what we were made of.

We were known for putting up decent scores and scoring goals – against Skryne the game was effectively over by half-time and that was down to us wanting to prove to people that we were the best team in Meath. Some people questioned if we were good enough or even if we deserved the championship in 2007, so we were determined to prove people wrong and we also believed we were a better team in '09.

We were very lucky in the semi-final against Summerhill.

They are always a team that give you a very good game and we have had some great battles with them down through the years.

With almost the exact same team, they had beaten us in an under-21 final with a goal in the last minute. I don't know if that was in the back of our heads going into that semi-final, but it certainly affected us. It was the same against Navan O'Mahonys in 2007. They had beaten us by 21 points in a minor final, and the following year they beat us by 11 points in an under-21 final, the year after that they beat us by four points in an under-21 final... we were getting closer and closer to them without beating them, so to turn that full circle and win a senior final against them gave us great confidence.

That knowledge helped us against Summerhill in the 2009 semi-final and we managed to scrape through.

Even in the drawn final against Wolfe Tones, we needed a late free from my brother Brian to secure the draw in extra-time and force the replay, but we knew we were the better team on the day. A couple of decisions went strongly against us, but we kept going and we got the draw.

We only had four days to recover for the replay because the Leinster Club game against Portlaoise was due to be played the following Sunday, so to turn around four days after a championship final which went to extra-time and have to do it all again was tough on both sides, but it was an incredible game.

The intensity of the game was huge throughout.

Our early goals were crucial and I happened to play a part in both of them which was great.

We actually didn't start too well, but Wolfe Tones missed a lot, including a penalty which Cian Ward kicked over the bar, and Cian also missed a couple of frees which certainly wasn't like him. Usually, he's lethal from anywhere within 45 metres.

We probably got a little bit lucky early on, but after 15 minutes a ball rolled over the sideline in the bottom corner down at the scoreboard end in Páirc Tailteann, under the stand. I remember dad roaring down the sideline, 'Don't rush it… take your time!'

But I just picked up the ball. Shane Clarke came jogging over to take the sideline because being a left footer he probably fancied his chances, but I caught my brother Brian running in towards the goals out of the corner of my eye and I hit one of the sweetest passes I ever hit in my life. He just ran straight onto the pass and met it with his fists, and it flew into the top right hand corner.

It was an amazing goal and if we tried it another 100 times, we'd never manage it again.

There was a lot of area to get the ball into and I knew if I could get it into that area then Brian would have a chance to get on the end of it… and I hit it so well.

Brian could have caught it and taken on his man, but he had a couple of inches on the guy who was marking him and he literally ran straight into it with his fists – it flew to the net and gave the goalkeeper no chance.

I have never seen a goal like that before; on reflection you would wonder how it even happened.

It was just one of those things that clicked and it really set us up and got our confidence going. Up to that stage we were a bit all over the place with our play; we were rushing everything and were playing too hectic, and we weren't concentrating on our basic skills or our game plan. But the goal settled us and we were the better team up until the last 10 minutes of the game.

We still have conversations about which was the best goal of the day, because I got a goal a few minutes later that wasn't too bad either. Brian maintains his goal was better, but I still think mine was. It is great to score any type of goal in a championship final because those opportunities don't come for everyone, so for both of us to score super goals was extra special.

I think my goal might have come from the next kickout.

It was another high ball, but I caught it well and I remember Ciaran McLoughlin hanging off my back. Referee Joey Curley wasn't going to give me a free, but I didn't mind that because myself and Ciaran have had some great battles down through the years; he's a brilliant defender, and a really nice fella who I still get on with very well.

We were always trying to outdo each other, almost in a show of strength.

I was very hyped up for the game and there was a bit of good-humoured jawing going on; no badness or nastiness, just the usual bit of jawing at each other. Obviously everyone wanted to win the game so when I won that ball and Ciaran was hanging off my back, I wanted to get everyone out of my way and lay down a marker… so I took the ball on and pulled clear.

Then there was another defender in front of me, but I was clear and I put the head down and lucky enough I caught it very sweet, and it ended up in the back of the net.

It was a goal that I am very proud of.

During lockdown, Declan Byrne posted the game on YouTube and then had a vote on which was the better of the two goals… mine or Brian's?

I think the vote finished level. It was great craic, but they were two great goals. They were special goals and any time you win a championship is incredibly special.

I had an assist, a goal and there was also another incident I ended up involved in that might have had a big part to play in the game.

As I said, there was a bit of jawing going on from the outset, nothing bad, but it was going on and Wolfe Tones goalkeeper David Nolan was giving a bit out from the goals before we even got the goals. Then we got the two goals and he was still roaring and shouting, and I just shouted back in at him to look up at the scoreboard.

I don't know if that was the reason – maybe it was a bit of frustration with how the game was going – but as I was walking in under the stand at half-time, I felt this punch in the back of the head from behind. The umpires caught what happened and told the referee and he gave David Nolan a straight red when he came back out after half-time.

I don't like to see anyone getting sent-off in a championship final; we've all taken a few bangs in games, but the officials saw what happened and the ref had to send him off.

I've obviously seen and spoken to David a few times since and we would still be close enough, so there is no hard feelings at all.

It was hard for them trying to get back into the game, but when you look back at the second-half, they probably drove on a bit and it's funny when a team goes down to 14 men how they pick up and play better with their backs against the wall.

Their intensity picked up after the break and because we were six or seven points up, we probably took our foot off the gas a bit and played like a side that was trying to hold them off rather than trying to kick on and win the game by a bit more. We invited pressure back on ourselves.

We missed a good bit in the second-half. I kicked a few wides myself and took the wrong option a couple of times. A couple of refereeing decisions brought them back into it; it wasn't about where the frees were given, it was all about momentum. Those frees got their momentum going and we had to hold them off in the end with some fantastic defending, with seven or eight lads throwing their bodies on the line.

We also have to hand it to our goalkeeper David Lyons, who made a save in the last two minutes. I was back in our full-back line in the closing stages and the ball broke out to Gordon Beggy just inside the 13-metre line.

I was standing right in front of him, and as he shot, I turned and the ball was right in my eyeline flying into the top corner. But as I was thinking... *Oh no... please don't go in*, Davy Lyons made one of the greatest saves I've ever seen.

That saved us. He also made another great save in the first-half, and even though Cian Ward's 14th minute penalty went over the bar, he was off his line quickly and probably would have saved that too if it was on target.

His kick-outs were brilliant too. There was no short kickouts back then; he would just launch his kickouts 70 or 80 yards down the pitch, and that gave us a great platform to attack and that was another major factor in us winning the game.

I scored 1-2, Brian scored 1-2, Davy made a few great saves and yet it was my other brother Damien who won the Man of the Match.

There have been jokes and arguments about that ever since.

We had a reunion of that team in 2019 and went over to Trim to play golf and then went to Lenihan's to have a few drinks where they showed the game again. And the amount of lads that were saying, 'How did Damien get the Man of the Match?'

It was all in good fun because in fairness to Damien, his work-rate was non-stop. You will never out-work Damien, he put so much unheralded work in for that team, up and down the pitch; he deserved that award as much as anyone else, not that I'll say that to his face!

Davy Lyons reckons he should have got it, I said I should have got it... Brian believes he should have got it and a few other lads think they should have got it too, but it was all good banter. Damien did deserve it.

We also won that replay without Bryan Clarke, who was injured in the drawn game. He did come on with about five minutes to go and was one-on-one and went to chip the keeper, but kicked it wide.

It would have been the icing on the cake if he had buried that.

We still laugh at that miss to this day, but it was nice that he got on the pitch because what he has done for Seneschalstown is fantastic. His free-taking is immense and he also won Man of the Match in 2007 kicking nine points. He's still playing too, he's a great player... I was delighted to see him get on the pitch.

When you look at the lads who were playing!

We had three or four sets of brothers, it was literally like a family. Wolfe Tones were the same, we would have played each other a lot at under-21 and minor, so we had massive respect for each other, so when you look back at the game there was no holding back and, at the same time, there was huge respect between both sets of players.

Both sets of players garnered respect from everyone. We were two teams going at each other fairly hard and that was the important thing for ourselves, to hold ourselves in a high standing; when you are in those situations you want to play the game in the right manner and in the right style.

To win the championship in 2009 was huge for the club.

To win was compensation for a lot of difficult times for the club.

In 2007, one of our selectors Tommy McDonnell passed away and we were still carrying that in '09. Every time we went on to the pitch, we remembered Tommy and we would use that to garner the inner strength to drive things on.

After the 2007 win we had a lot of younger people in the club who looked up to us. We wanted to put pride into the young lads, to help them to drive things on in the club. The impact of winning in 2009 has been huge for the club and we are starting to see that now.

The strength that is coming through our underage is fantastic and we have had some great people involved, like Tommy Finnegan, who is through and through 'Seneschalstown', Ian Maguire, Mickey Dillon and, of course, the late Tommy McDonnell. Massive club men, who have done so much for Seneschalstown; we were very lucky to have them involved with us.

Obviously, having dad as the manager was special too. He put a lot of work and emphasis on believing we were good enough. If it wasn't for him, a lot of lads wouldn't have believed we were good enough to do what we did over those couple of years.

As my father he always has my respect, but the respect he has from all the players and from everyone in the club is massive.

Some people might say we were lucky to win the first one, but winning the second one confirms that we are a great club and that was a massive achievement; for the club and for that group of players who nearly all moved together through the age groups. To be able to compete with the likes of Summerhill and O'Mahonys, teams who have been extremely successful… for us to compete with them and put our name amongst those great teams was fantastic.

We went on and got to a final in 2010, which we probably should have won… that still sticks out and we are still kicking ourselves because that would really have cemented our legacy.

For us, as the Sheridan family, it is a source of great pride too.

It is a fantastic achievement to have the three brothers on the team. Two of us scored 1-2 and the other picked up the Man of the Match award, and then we had dad as the manager. We also had my sister Mary as a physio, along with my mother and my cousin Gerry Sheridan was also playing that day.

We had Aunties and Uncles involved too; Liz was the chairperson at the time… it's great to have your family involved with you.

We sit down nearly every night talking about football. That is the way we have been bred and brought up; since we were able to walk, we have been kicking footballs.

Even though myself, Brian, Damien and dad have achieved so much, we are not even the most successful when we do sit down at our table – not when you look at the 14 or 15 ladies championships Mary and Mena have won. We haven't a leg to stand on compared to them to be honest.

We are all very grateful to have had successful careers over the years and to be able to look back now at it is great. When you take time to reflect on the great days, you can see the relationships you have developed with friends and families; those bonds are unbreakable and that is what we have gained over the years, friends for life, and life experiences that we'll never get again.

They are the most important things.

MICKEY BURKE

MEATH 2-14 LAOIS 0-10
Leinster SFC Quarter-Final
O'Connor Park, Tullamore
JUNE 19 2010

The most unforgettable day of Mickey Burke's footballing life with Meath ended in agony.

★ **MEATH:** P O'Rourke; C O'Connor, K Reilly, E Harrington; A Moyles, **M Burke,** C King (0-1); B Meade (0-1), M Ward; S Bray, G Reilly (0-4), S Kenny; J Sheridan (2-2), C Ward (0-3), S O'Rourke (0-3). Subs; C Gillespie for M Ward, O Lewis for Burke, G O'Brien for Moyles, B Murphy for Bray, C McGuinness for Kenny.

★ **LAOIS:** M Nolan; P O'Leary (0-1), M Timmons, P McMahon (0-1); C Healy (0-1), C Ryan, C Begley; B Quigley, K Meaney; J O'Loughlin, D Strong (0-1), C Rogers; MJ Tierney (0-4), D Kingston (0-2), R Munnelly. Subs|: D Booth for Begley, B Sheehan for Ryan, P Clancy for Strong, P Lawlor for Rogers, D Rooney for Quigley.

THE ACTION

MEATH OVERCAME THE 54th minute dismissal of goalkeeper Paddy O'Rourke to claim a 10-point replay win in Tullamore in the Leinster Championship.

Joe Sheridan (2-2) and Graham Reilly (0-4) were Laois' tormentors-in-chief, as the Royals advanced to a mouth-watering Leinster SFC semi-final against Dublin.

Meath led by 2-5 to 0-6 at half-time, thanks to Sheridan's goals, with MJ Tierney and Donal Kingston keeping Laois in touch.

However, Laois failed to score from play on the restart, allowing Meath to coast home.

12,659 spectators watched a game which Laois failed to get to grips with, as Sheridan's two-goal salvo in the first-half provided the catalyst for Meath to pull through.

O'Rourke's dismissal, following a straight red card, was referee Maurice Condon's only sending-off, but he issued nine yellow cards, including five for the Royals, in what was a hard-fought contest.

In the second-half, Laois were punished on four occasions inside a five-minute spell, as Meath raced into a 2-9 to 0-6 lead. Half-back Caoimhin King was on the end of a move involving Cian Ward and Gary O'Brien, edging the Royals six points clear.

Graham Reilly followed up with two more points and a well-taken Sheridan score opened up a double-score lead by the 40th minute. A second Kingston free was the lone score for Laois in the third quarter as Meath continued to show the greater cutting edge in midfield and up front.

Paddy O'Rourke was then handed his marching orders after lashing out at Laois captain Padraig McMahon, but despite the absence of their net minder, Meath had a relatively untroubled finish.

★★★★★

"

I MADE MY breakthrough onto the Meath panel in 2004 and I can't really recall how it happened or the phone call that must have come to ask me to go in.

I had just won a Junior B championship with Longwood and we had won the under-21 B as well that winter. I was a Meath minor in 2003 and then played under-21 in '04, '05 and '06, but I don't remember how I ended up getting the call to go into the seniors.

My first memory is of going in training under Seán Boylan in Beaufort College in Navan, that's where we did our running and gym work under Seán, where he had kitted out a full gym. I played O'Byrne Cup in the winter of 2004 and made my debut in the league in '05 and my championship debut later that year.

We got to All-Ireland semi-finals in 2007 and '09 and, when I look back at the group of lads we had between 2007 and '12, I really feel that we under-achieved because we had some really great players.

In 2009 we should have beaten Kerry in the All-Ireland semi-final. I believe they were there for the taking that day; it was an awful wet day, but we could have beaten them. Kerry struggled through the qualifiers that year. Sligo nearly beat them, but David Kelly missed a penalty and Antrim also pushed them all the way, so we felt we could take them, but we didn't.

They went on and turned it on in the All-Ireland final because they were playing Cork, but the following year Down blew them out of the water. Down did what we should have done because Kerry were certainly there for the taking.

We had so many good footballers, a great mix of big, mobile men and really talented players. We also only lost to Dublin by three points in 2012 – I know Jamie Queeney got a late goal to put a better look on it, but we could have won that year too. Dublin were All-Ireland champions at that time, but they weren't the machine that they are now. The gap grew wider after that, as we lost lads like Caoimhin King, Anthony Moyles and Nigel Crawford. We had a great team and we should have won more medals than we did.

The only medal of real significance that we did win in that time was the Leinster in 2010 and what a year that turned out to be for me on a personal level. The mood going into that 2010 championship was good. We had been in Portugal on a hot weather training camp for a week and we were in good shape.

Everyone thinks that when you go on these camps you could be out there drinking or sitting by a pool, but that week was absolutely horrendous because you were being pushed to your limits all the time in the heat.

Eamonn O'Brien was the manager and Bob O'Malley was a selector, and Bob was real old school. We used to train two or three times a day, not flat out in every session, but pushing hard all the time and you'd be very sore and tired because you didn't have much down-time.

On the first day of the camp Brian Sheridan pulled his hamstring, but he didn't get to rest. Bob had him crawling the length of the field. His forearms and his thighs were on fire. The sun was splitting the stones and we were looking over at Bob, urging Brian to keep going and keep going, it was relentless and so tough.

All you could hear was Bob shouting. 'COME ON... COME ON'... he was like a drill sergeant.

So, when we came home we went into the 2010 campaign full of confidence.

People forget that we hammered Offaly before we went on to play Laois on a very wet day in Croke Park. That ended as a draw and it was a mistake by Graham Brody that gifted us the draw. I felt massive pressure that day.

It was a very, very, very wet day and we were lucky.

We beat Laois well in the replay, and we put five goals by Dublin and then what happened in the Leinster final *happened* and probably over shadows our other performances before that day.

That Leinster final still upsets me in a way.

People say to me, 'You have a Leinster medal, don't you?'

I say, 'I do', but there is a bit of a tinge to it, it's hard to put my finger on it. Some people don't want to give us that medal, for whatever reason.

I look back on that final and while Louth were the better team for a lot of it, they didn't put us away. We hung in there and gave ourselves a chance. The general public all wanted Louth to win, but we clung on and, in the end, we all know what happened with Joe's goal.

I had broken my leg in the replay against Laois and missed the game, but I still count the medal and I'm proud to have one.

Of all the games that year and all the different things that happened, I reflect on the replay against Laois as being the game that sticks in my mind most of all. There are bizarre memories and bitter memories from that day, it's one that will live with me forever.

A footballer's nightmare injuries are cruciate, an Achilles tendon snap or a leg break… and, unfortunately, I did serious damage to myself in that replay against Laois.

It was an unbelievably warm day, in total contrast to the drawn game which was played in a downpour. We met in the Johnstown House before the game… I had my baseball hat on backwards thinking I was cool and all was well.

Bob O'Malley is someone I really looked up to.

He made me as a footballer and he did a lot of great things for me to become a man. He was a real guiding light for me and I'd love for him to know that and what he meant to me.

One of the things I always remember about Bob is that he told me to wear studs… to always wear studs. People ask me if I have any superstitions and I suppose I always have to wear studs all year round. Whether the ground is rock hard or quicksand, I wear the studs for every game and that is something Bob got me into.

The heat in Tullamore that day was savage. During the warm up I was thinking the ground was very hard and I was wearing my studs as normal, as Bob told me too… his advice was 'Don't slip when you are in corner-back!'

I don't remember much about the game. I started centre-back and then there was a bit of a collision early on.

It's hard to explain to someone the pain, if you haven't broken your leg. Some people think it's only a little injury like a hamstring or something, but no way. It's only when you break your leg that you realise the severity of it.

Dave Mackay was a Spurs footballer and he broke his leg two or three times and he always came back, so people used to reference him to me.

I remember the pain very vividly. People often think you go into shock and you don't feel anything, but that certainly didn't happen me. I felt a crunch after big John O'Loughlin fell on top of me after an awkward tackle.

I could hear Bob O'Malley and my father in my head screaming at me to get up and I tried to get up and run again, but I just collapsed.

Without trying to sound hardy, I had that old Meath spirit of never lying down and not allowing anybody to see you might be hurt. That was in my head and I said to myself… *F**k it, you have to get* up.

I tried to run, but I collapsed.

Frank Foley ran on to check on me and the team doctor Alison was with him. I squeezed her thigh with my hand and was screaming for pain killers. She gave me a few and I remember swallowing them as quickly as I could, but I got no relief whatsoever… none.

They gave me oxygen out on the field before carting me down to Tullamore hospital. I knew straight away it was serious. This was the most outrageous pain, I have never felt pain like it before or since.

It was excruciating, I was roaring and screaming and crying.

It turned out I had broken both my fibula and tibia, and I also tore the medial ligaments in my knee and the ligaments in my ankle as well.

That all led to more rehab.

The first man into the hospital after me was Seán Boylan. There I was, sitting in my No 6 jersey, roaring with pain and in came Seán. I was delighted to see him to be honest.

I was so disorientated.

All I wanted was a drink, but they wouldn't give me one.

I think it must have been Junior cert results night that night and there was a girl in the hospital who was so drunk she was uncontrollable. She was screaming the place down as the nurses and doctors were trying to get her to calm down so they could pump her stomach. The screaming out of her was driving me mad and my head was all over the place.

When Seán Boylan came in he said, 'You know there's one saving grace in all this. You will get seen by the best man for a leg break in all of Ireland… David Cogley'. It turned out my surgeon was Fred Cogley's son… Fred, the well-known RTE rugby commentator. And I was so thankful to him.

My father and mother obviously must have stayed on to watch the rest of the match and then word got to them that I was after having a bad injury, so they came down to me.

Dad came in and told me that Thomas Maguire was after being killed in a car accident. I was totally stunned. I started to feel guilty about my pain then. Here was me crying and roaring because of a broken leg while one of my mate's mother and father were going through unimaginable devastation after losing their son in a rallying accident up in Donegal.

It certainly put a lot of things into perspective.

Myself and Thomas would have been close at under-age level. He was Rory Maguire's first cousin and Rory and me are very good friends. Thomas would have been our underage goalkeeper the whole way up.

He was a year older than me, and he was a good goalkeeper.

He then went on to take on a different sport and he was very good at it. He was a co-pilot in rallying, the navigator, and by all accounts he was very good at it. He also played badminton with my father. He was a good Longwood man from Moneymore.

People always associate the day I broke my leg with the day Thomas Maguire was killed. I felt guilt for a long time after because any time I saw his father Tom after that he'd breakdown crying, because I obviously brought memories flooding back to him.

It was a sad few days, very sad times in the village.

In the hospital, I was still in my Meath gear when mam and dad came in.

I was so disorientated. The whole night is a bit of a blur and then I had the operation the next day. I have a plate in my leg for life and almost immediately after the operation my mind turned to, *Am I ever going to get back from this?*

Am I ever going to play again?

Will I ever get to play for Meath again?

I could hear the murmurs in the background of people doubting that I'd ever get back again or if I'd ever have the stomach for that again.

I got a text message off Bob O'Malley the next morning telling me I was going to have dark days during my rehab, but that if I put my mind to it I could come back and I certainly did that. While I was still wearing my jersey in the hospital I made a promise to myself to do everything I could to get back playing in that jersey – and I did.

I played against Kildare in the following year's qualifiers.

The dark days were tough. The rehab was lonely work and the questions kept popping up. *Was it going to be worth it?*

Was I going to be able to get back to where I was?

There were times when I did doubt myself. *Would I have the same mobility? Would I have the same energy? Would the leg ever be fully healed?*

I worked hard and I'm convinced that that injury made me a better footballer, a better trainer and gave me a better attitude. Sometimes when things are taken away from you, you realise how much they mean to you. I was in a privileged position playing for Meath and I wanted to get back there so badly. That drove me on to do everything I could to not just get back there, but to stay there.

I worked my socks off.

I worked unbelievably hard. To be honest, I ended up getting too big from the gym work. I was determined to make myself unbreakable, but I let myself get too big from weights.

I did a massive amount of pool work; it was all hard work, but worth it in the end. My ankle still needs mobility work to loosen it out and keep it free.

I was in the hospital for two or three days and immediately after I came home, I was straight on the berries and my mother was making me tuna salads. My bed was up on stilts to keep the blood flowing. I wore skins at night to help with the compression which would speed up the healing process.

I became fanatical about it.

I worked so hard to get back and when I was ready I was back playing in the internal games within 10 months. I was all set to come on in the qualifier game against Galway in Navan in 2011, but something happened and I didn't get on.

I kept working hard and I played really well in an internal game and I ended up starting the next game against Kildare, where I was asked to man-mark Eamonn O'Callaghan. I was out for a full 10 months so it was some journey.

I'm sure I've played better games and had more impact in outings, but that was such a standout day because of the tragic loss of Thomas Maguire for the village of Longwood and for me personally with the injury.

I went on and had a long proud career with Meath.

I won the Player of the Year in 2018 and that was a very proud moment. I also got two Supporters Player of the Year awards.

I don't know what the supporters thought of me. I'm a bit like marmite. Some people gravitate towards certain players and I'm the same. I have that old school Meath mentality of never giving up and I always tried to do my best and hopefully that's what people will remember from the number of years I played.

GRAHAM REILLY

MEATH 1-12 LOUTH 1-10
Leinster SFC Final
Croke Park
JULY 11 2010

There was only one controversial Leinster title in Graham Reilly's Meath career, but his four points haul against Louth, allied to Joe Sheridan's late goal, saw the county triumph.

★ **MEATH:** B Murphy; E Harrington, K Reilly, C O'Connor; C King, A Moyles (0-1), G O'Brien; N Crawford (0-1), B Meade; S Kenny, S Bray (0-2), **G Reilly (0-4)**; C Ward (0-4 frees), J Sheridan (1-0), S O'Rourke. Subs: C McGuinness for Moyles, P Byrne for O'Rourke.

★ **LOUTH:** N Gallagher; E McAuley, D Finnegan, J O'Brien; R Finnegan, M Fanning, R Greene; P Keenan (0-1), B White (0-4); A Reid (0-1), A McDonnell (0-1), M Brennan; C Judge (0-2), S Lennon, JP Rooney (1-1). Subs: S Fitzpatrick for Greene, A Hoey for Fanning, P Smith for Lennon, D Byrne for Reid.

THE ACTION

THE FINGER OF blame for the controversy that surrounded the Leinster SFC final of 2010 pointed in many directions.

Tyrone referee Martin Sludden shouldered the blame for allowing Joe Sheridan's late goal stand, despite the fact that the Meath man had clearly dropped the ball out of his hands and over the line as he attempted to boot it to the net.

Others held the umpires culpable for allowing the referee apparently overrule their initial decision not to go for the green flag.

Some even suggested Seamus Kenny could have avoided all controversy if he had scored from point-blank range, instead of having his shot blocked down by Paddy Keenan.

However, one man who rarely gets a mention in all the hullabaloo is Graham Reilly.

It was Graham Reilly's ball into the square that dropped short and led to the commotion.

If the St Colmcille's man's shot had landed over the bar, as he appeared to have intended, the game would most certainly have gone to a replay and surely there would have been no such debates the second time around.

From a Louth perspective, Reilly was one of the many Meath villains of the peace; from a Royal point of view he was one of many heroes and while his late, short distribution often gets lost in the translation of that most dramatic of football matches, his outstanding four-point return should also indicate one of his finest displays in the green and gold.

There was a 0-8 to 0-5 interval lead for Eamonn O'Brien's side.

When play resumed it was all Louth as Keenan (two), Judge and Adrian Reid boosted them into a 0-9 to 0-8 lead, and when JP Rooney blasted a brilliant goal to the net it looked all set for Louth to end their 53-year wait for a Leinster crown.

But Meath's miraculous powers of recovery kicked in. Two Ward frees, one from over 50 metres, closed the deficit to the minimum and the rest is history as Joe Sheridan's controversial 74th minute goal snatched victory from the jaws of defeat and sparked years of controversy ever since.

★★★★★

"

I CAME ONTO the Meath senior panel in 2007 when we got to the All-Ireland semi-final and were beaten by Cork. I was only a fringe player at that stage, No 30 on the panel every day.

It was 2008 when I made my debut against Carlow in Croke Park and I kicked a point – that was the year we were cruising against Wexford in the next round and then ended up getting beaten.

In 2009 I got a bad injury and was out for five or six months, so I wasn't in the frame at all. When it came towards the end of the year I stepped away because I wasn't going to make the squad, so 2010 was my first really big year.

I remember Sean Kelly ringing me and telling me they wanted me back on the panel, so I was delighted to get back. I started a lot of the league games that year at wing-back because Bob O'Malley, who was a selector at the time, was telling me that was where I was going to learn my trade as a wing forward. He insisted I would become a better wing forward by starting as a wing back and learning what it would be like when I wouldn't have the ball and that worked out well.

We can't really look at the 2010 Leinster final without reflecting on the semi-final win over Dublin. We beat Offaly on a scorching day in Portlaoise; that was my first championship start for Meath and I'll never forget it because I never felt heat like it. We then played Laois twice, drawing with them in Croke Park before beating them in Tullamore to set up the semi-final against Dublin.

From the outside, the perception was that we weren't a good Meath team and a lot of the Dubs who live around me in Bettystown were thinking we were no great shapes at all; they were thinking Dublin would win easily.

Going into that game we knew we had to go for it. We knew we needed goals and we would need plenty of them. We had a system that we wanted to play – we needed to nullify their better players and we managed that.

Stephen Bray's two goals were brilliant.

We had so many brilliant individual displays that day, the lads really stood up to the mark. I only managed a point that day… my performance wasn't up to much, I was more in awe looking around me at the huge crowd, but I always remember that Stephen and Joe Sheridan were absolutely brilliant and a lot of the lads really stood up to the plate. Any time you beat Dublin is really special.

As I've said, we made a conscious decision that day to go for goals if we had half a chance. Stephen's first goal was brilliant. He collected the ball near the sideline and he could have checked back and kicked the ball over the bar, but he didn't. He took on his man, put the head down and buried it.

That set the tone for the game, that really inspired us.

Joe's goal, Cian Ward's goal and Stephen's goals were brilliant.

We knew Dublin would step up to us because there was a perception that we had a slow forward line, but with lads like myself, Stephen Bray, Seamus Kenny... we had plenty of pace, so we exploited the space. When you talk to Dublin players now they will tell you they learned a hell of a lot from the day we hit them for five goals.

We stayed on after that Dublin game to watch Louth beat Kildare and they put up 1-22 with very free-flowing football. They dominated Kildare that day and they could have beaten them by more, and that was a very decent Kildare team.

We knew we would have a huge challenge in the Leinster final.

We knew the media would make us massive favourites because of our win over Dublin, but we also knew there were very few occasions between Meath and Louth where one team won easily or ran up a cricket score. I knew that the Louth lads wouldn't fear us and they certainly started full of confidence that day.

In the first-half they had two or three goal chances that we got away with, but at half-time we were three points up yet we hadn't really got going. I felt at half-time that Louth had thrown everything at us, but we were still ahead and that might cause them to drop their heads, but obviously I was very wrong because they had more to give.

Everything worked out well for me in the first-half.

I always seemed to find myself in the right position at the right time. For one of my scores the ball was played into Cian Ward. It was a poor enough ball, but it just flicked up off him and landed in my palm, and with no one near me so I kicked it over... everything went for me in that opening half.

It was scores like that that boosted my confidence.

Ray Finnegan was marking me that day, but for some reason he left me in a lot of space. I couldn't understand why he stood off me so much, maybe they thought I was the weakest forward at the time and that I was no danger.

I remember Gary O'Brien picked up a ball at one stage at wing back and Ray Finnegan just ran away from me towards Gary… all Gary had to do was flick the ball over his head and I was away in 30 yards of space.

I kicked the ball over the bar.

I know that sounds very simple, but that was the way it was, he just didn't pay that much attention to me in the opening half.

A couple of the scores I got were simple scores, I have no idea where my marker was… I couldn't believe how much room they afforded me. Maybe they were conscious of Stephen Bray, who was flying that year and they doubled up on him and didn't look at me.

That was the way our forward line worked that year.

If I didn't have a good day or if Stephen didn't play well, then you could be sure Joe Sheridan, Cian Ward or Brian Farrell would all step up too and it worked well like that; we all supported each other very well.

We had a very balanced forward line. Shane O'Rourke was a tall, strong young lad who could kick off both feet. Stephen Bray could use both feet and he was quick and strong. Seamus Kenny got up and down the pitch and got on a lot of ball… he was a nightmare to mark.

We all knew what Joe was capable of, and Cian Ward was lethal from frees and deadly from play too… then you had me, so I felt we had a very balanced forward line with different types of players. It was a brilliant team to play in.

Even though we had played poorly in the first-half, we knew we were in a good position with a three-point lead. The pressure on our forwards wasn't great, but our defence was very loose and Louth were getting a lot of easy scores and they were getting a lot of kick passes into their full-forward line and that caused us damage.

We needed to put more pressure on the ball out the field.

Bob O'Malley pulled me aside at the break and told me that despite having scored four points he didn't think I had played that well… that's typical Bob.

He thought my defensive game was poor; he said I wasn't tracking my man as well as I should have been and he said I should be getting on more breaking ball.

It was his way of reminding me why they had played me at wing-back during the league, to know the value of having to work harder in a defensive situation.

They came back at us well at the start of the second-half, but I never panicked until JP Rooney got that screamer of a goal. Then I remember looking to my right where there was a massive contingent of Louth fans in the stand and they were all I could hear... I couldn't hear the Meath supporters any more.

I was only a young lad at the time; I wasn't used to that environment.

I started thinking this is it... *We're doomed here!*

Louth were only getting going, they weren't giving the ball away and they came at us in droves and droves.

In fairness, Anthony Moyles then stepped up and kicked a brilliant point. Cian Ward kicked a free from over 50 yards out which brought the game back to a one-point game. I thought that was incredible considering the pressure we were under at the time. Those lads just stepped up; that is what they were there for and they kept us in the game.

Stephen Bray won the free from 50 yards out and Wardy just pushed everyone out of the way and took control of the situation to give us a chance – a real leader.

Then three minutes into injury-time, we were a point down and I think it might have been Chris O'Connor who played a ball across the field to me.

I'm not sure if the pass was meant for me, but it ended up in my hands.

For some reason, I thought I was a lot closer to the posts than I was, so I went for what I thought would be the equaliser, but as I kicked it I glanced to my right and I could see the 45-metre line, so I knew I was too far out... it was going to drop short.

Then all hell broke loose.

I didn't even see what happened.

All I saw was the ball hitting the net and I jumped for joy.

I quickly ran to pick up my man, but then all of a sudden there was a load of stuff going on with the referee. The referee then gave goal and when the ball was kicked out, that was it.

After the game I went to shake hands with Ray Finnegan and with Andy McDonnell, a lad who I would have known quite well because he is the same age as me and he's from Drogheda, but the two boys were having none of it.

I didn't know what was going on. It was only when they wouldn't shake hands with me that I thought something bad must have happened.

I thought Seamus Kenny had caught my short point attempt, had dummied a fella and got blocked by Paddy Keenan, but that his blocked shot had deflected into the net. I didn't know why the Louth lads were going mad.

I didn't realise what had happened until I got back onto the bus to go home.

There was so much emotion in the dressing-room after the game that nobody was really explaining what had happened. There was next to no celebrations going on at all. Eamonn O'Brien made sure that none of us were celebrating, but I was sitting there wondering... *Why can't we celebrate?*

Nobody really knew what was going on.

Joe was outside doing an interview on RTE so he wasn't in the dressing-room explaining anything to anybody, Seamus Kenny said he didn't see what happened after he was blocked down.

Peadar Byrne was close enough to it, and he said that he thought the ball had hit off Joe's knee and gone in, but there was nobody in the dressing-room who knew what all the commotion was really about.

We didn't really know until we got on the bus and we saw the highlights.

When I did get to see it we were having a few bottles of beer on the bus, so there was a bit more craic and atmosphere. We were looking at it from different angles. Gary O'Brien, who was sitting beside me, said, 'Well Joe should have got a penalty anyway, so justice was done!'

We went back to the County Club in Dunshaughlin and all the Meath fans were in great form. They couldn't care how we won, they were probably only wishing it was Dublin we had beaten like that.

We met up the next day in Gormanston and decided to leave all the fallout to the County Board to deal with. A few of the players said that the game was over and we had to focus on the All-Ireland quarter-final; they were telling us to forget about it and let the County Board deal with it.

My personal opinion is that we should have given them a replay.

We had played very poorly on the day; for the whole game, we didn't get into gear at all. We had a couple of spells of five minutes here and two minutes there where we had moments of individual brilliance, but outside of those moments it was a poor display from us.

I never said it to any of the other players at the time because I was still only a young lad, but I felt we should have given them a replay – we would have performed like we should have performed and we would have won the replay.

I didn't like the way it was left.

Obviously, I was a lot closer to the Louth border than a lot of Meath lads. My grandparents are from Drogheda and are Louth people, my aunties and uncles are all Louth, but it wasn't because of them that I felt we should have offered a replay. I felt if we were going to do it right, we could give them a replay and beat them the next day, but it was taken out of our hands by the GAA.

I'm sure if it had gone to a players' vote, there would have been a replay.

Maybe I'm wrong, but I'd be nearly one hundred percent sure that if the GAA had asked us would we give a replay, and if the County Board had backed us, I believe we'd have voted for a replay because we felt our performance on the day was so poor that we couldn't possibly be so poor again.

You can imagine what the atmosphere would have been like and the craic in the build-up to a replay. I'm sure Croke Park would have been sold out.

Some of the older players might have been asked their opinion, I don't know. I just know that none of the management team or any County Board official ever asked me for my opinion. I was only 21 at the time, and all I wanted to do was play football and the opportunity to play in Croke Park in front of 60,000 or 70,000 people again would have been great.

That was my view on it.

When I reflect on the game, I had a great first-half and everything I touched worked out well, but in the second-half Ray Finnegan marked me tighter, he didn't give me as much room. Louth dominated the first 20 minutes of the second-half. I don't think we even got the ball inside their '45' in any sort of meaningful attack in that spell.

Louth dominated the kick-outs, they won every break, they really pinned us down. If they had been clinical enough they could have been six or seven points up after that 20-minute spell, but they let us stay in the game.

It was a lot more difficult to get on the ball in that second-half.

I think I only touched the ball three times in the second-half. In the opening period nearly every time I touched it, I kicked it over the bar, so the second-half was a lot tougher.

It is hard to know if the fallout from that Leinster final had an effect on our preparations for the All-Ireland quarter-final against Kildare.

We had a really good two weeks between the games.

We went away to Enfield for two nights the weekend before the Kildare game and did a lot of prep work and we played an in-house game. The lads looked to have moved on from the Leinster final game and we looked to be moving well.

We did our homework on Kildare and we were ready for them.

We also had a bit of a point to prove after the Leinster final, so maybe that was there in the first 15 to 20 minutes when we were flying and went 1-3 to 0-0 up, but then we faded badly and that is disappointing.

We felt we left so much behind us that year.

If you told any Meath fan or Meath player that after winning the Leinster title you would have to beat Kildare and Down to get to an All-Ireland final, where you would play Cork, then you would have really fancied our chances.

Obviously, those three teams were strong that year. I'm not saying we would have won the All-Ireland, but with Dublin, Kerry, Mayo and Tyrone out of the equation, it was a very open All-Ireland and one I feel we could have won.

We didn't look beyond the Kildare game at the time because they had some really good players, but the goal before half-time and the one near the end put a nail in our coffin. Our second-half against Kildare was so disappointing.

I've always wondered since did we peak too soon to beat Dublin, because we never really got going again after that. Maybe beating Dublin was the main focus for a lot of lads, but for me we had a great chance of reaching an All-Ireland final that year and to be beaten by Kildare after all we achieved was devastating.

Printed in Poland
by Amazon Fulfillment
Poland Sp. z o.o., Wrocław

80785342R00137